ENDO

"This extraordinary collection of essays summarizes the most recent conclusions derived from near-death experience research. The strength of such work is enhanced by integrating a fresh analysis of experiences such as terminal and paradoxical lucidity, alternate lives during medically-induced coma, end-of-life dreams and visions from the hospice/palliative care community, shared death experiences (similar to near-death, but in healthy bystanders), and observations on related phenomena witnessed in animals. This treasure trove is a major contribution to the emerging science of consciousness. Highly recommended!"

Eben Alexander, M.D.,
former Harvard Neurosurgeon and author of *Proof of Heaven,*
The Map of Heaven, and *Living in a Mindful Universe*

"Near-death phenomena constitute one of the major anomalies threatening the status quo: If consciousness survives, materialism dies. This volume contributes to such a vital research program with a much-needed balance between boldness and humility."

Alex Gomez-Marin, Ph.D.
in theoretical physics, professor of neuroscience
at the Spanish Research Council, and director of the Pari Center

"Academic discussions of near-death phenomena date back to the 19th century, but took until the end of the 20th century until they received the interest of researchers they deserve. The new and expanding frontiers are reported in this remarkable book. Not only will readers learn about the varieties of NDEs, but also about the lucidity that sometimes occurs just before death, post-mortem survival, and the related experiences on non-human animals. Each chapter is reader friendly and engaging, making these findings available for a wide audience as well as essential reading for consciousness researchers and other investigators of mind and psyche."

Stanley Krippner, Ph.D.,
author of *A Chaotic Life*

"This welcome contribution brings together research and theory involving an unusual variety of phenomena occurring in proximity to death, such as paradoxical terminal lucidity, unusual and sometimes shared dreams, shared-death experiences, near-death experiences occurring under extreme physiological conditions such as deep general anesthesia and/or cardiac arrest, and apparent after-death communications from deceased persons to their grieving loved ones. Collectively, these phenomena have important implications both for our science-based picture of the world and for the care of critically ill and dying persons, and it's great to find them all treated authoritatively in one place. Highly recommended!"

Edward F. Kelly, Ph.D.,
Professor in the Division of Perceptual Studies, Department of Psychiatry and Neurobehavioral Sciences, University of Virginia School of Medicine, and lead author of *Irreducible Mind* (2007), *Beyond Physicalism* (2015) and *Consciousness Unbound* (2021)

"This book advances the study of near-death phenomena to a new level. World-leading authors provide a comprehensive overview of the evidence regarding the main types of near-death phenomena, pointing to many of the necessary theoretical, clinical, and research developments."

Alexander Moreira-Almeida, Ph.D.,
Professor of Psychiatry and Director of the Research Center in Spirituality and Health (NUPES), School of Medicine, Federal University of Juiz de Fora (UFJF), Brazil. 2025 Oskar Pfister Award, American Psychiatric Association. Former chair of the Section on Religion, Spirituality and Psychiatry of the World Psychiatric Association

"Post-materialist consciousness research has long needed a deeply-sourced volume on near-death phenomena—I'm so grateful to see that some of the most qualified and thoughtful scientists in the field have teamed up to provide this volume, edited by an international group of editors who are also experiencers themselves. I believe this volume will be considered de rigeur reading in the field for decades to come."

Julia Mossbridge, Ph.D.,
Center for the Future Mind, Florida Atlantic University

"This important anthology boldly wades into metaphysical shallows where neuroscience fears to tread—on the very banks of the river Styx. With empirical rigor and a clear-eyed gaze, the authors investigate near-death and end-of-life phenomena that challenge the prevailing dogma of brain-bound consciousness. For those open to the possibility that the mind is more than the brain, this volume is both a scientific provocation and a surprisingly comforting companion."

Dean Radin, Ph.D.,
Chief Scientist, Institute of Noetic Sciences,
and author of *The Science of Magic* and other books

"This amazing book will expand what you know about dying and consciousness during clinical death and coma. An innovative and ground-breaking key work that paves the way for future research."

Pim van Lommel, Ph.D.,
cardiologist, NDE-researcher, author of *Consciousness Beyond Life*

"'At the Banks of the River Styx' is a landmark volume that beautifully synthesizes the extensive and often-overlooked evidence—from clinical observations to compelling case reports—demonstrating the non-local nature of consciousness at the threshold of death. In bringing together leading voices and new research on terminal lucidity and related phenomena, the editors masterfully collate the wealth of clinical, anecdotal, and scientific records that challenge current assumptions about consciousness. The breadth and depth of these accounts offer compelling evidence that our consciousness may extend far beyond the brain and body."

Helané Wahbeh, Ph.D.,
Director of Research, Institute of Noetic Sciences, Novato, California.

On the Banks of the River Styx

New Perspectives on Terminal Lucidity and Other Near-Death Phenomena

Volume VI
Postmaterialist Sciences Series

Edited by
Michael Nahm
Marjorie Woollacott
Natasha Tassell-Matamua

PRESS

© copyright 2025
by The Academy for the Advancement of Postmaterialist Sciences
(AAPS)

AAPS Headquarters, Tucson, AZ.
AAPS Press and Information on AAPS,
P.O. Box 156,
Battle Ground, WA 98604

All rights reserved. No part of this book may be reproduced or utilized in any form of by any means, electronic or mechanical, including photocopying, recording, or by any information storage and retrieval system, without permission in writing from the publisher.

L.C. Cat. No.: 1-14973013921

ISBN-13: 978-1-7354491-9-7 print edition
ISBN-13: 978-8-9997716-0-6 e-book edition

This book was typeset in Adobe Source Sans/Serif.
Layout: Jana Rogge
Cover design: Michael Nahm. The photograph on the front cover was made by Olaf Nahm (©).

To send correspondence: aapsglobal@gmail.com

To the well-organized mind, death is but the next great adventure.

Albus Dumbledore

TABLE OF CONTENTS

Introduction to Occurrences on the Banks of the River Styx 1
    Michael Nahm, Marjorie Woollacott & Natasha Tassell-Matamua

Part 1
New Perspectives on Terminal Lucidity

1. Terminal Lucidity. An Introduction, Some Case Examples in Children, and Questions They Raise 6
    Natasha Tassell-Matamua & Karalee Kothe

2. Terminal Lucidity in Adults: A New Case Collection 19
    Chris A. Roe

3. A Look at Terminal Lucidity Through the Prism of Witnesses 35
    Maryne Mutis

4. Implications of Terminal Lucidity for Consciousness Studies and Health Care 47
    Marjorie Woollacott

Part 2
New Perspectives on Other Near-Death Phenomena

5. Clear Minds in Dysfunctional Brains: An Introduction to "Paradoxical Awareness" 62
    Michael Nahm

6. Near-Death Experiences: A Glance Beyond the River Styx 77
    Marieta Pehlivanova & Bruce Greyson

7. Alternate Lives During Medically Induced Comas 95
    Alan Pearce

8. Implications of Medically Induced Comas in Intensive Care Units . . 106
    Kali Dayton

9. The Paradox of Dying: Spiritually and Emotionally Alive
   at the End-of-Life 119
   Hannah Maciejewski & Christopher Kerr

10. The Shared Death Experience: Expanding the Scientific
    and Philosophical Understanding of Consciousness and Death 133
    William J. Peters, Monica Williams & Nancy Philpott

11. End-of-Life Experiences in Animals 147
    Michael Nahm, Pam Smart & Rupert Sheldrake

12. (Crisis) After-Death Communications: A Universal and
    Comforting Experience Suggestive of Survival 162
    Evelyn Elsaesser

13. The Coherence Enigma: Detecting Non-Local Consciousness
    Correlates via Random Events Generators (REGs)
    at Life's Final Edge....................................... 174
    Vasileios Basios

Epilogue 184
   Michael Nahm, Marjorie Woollacott & Natasha Tassell-Matamua

Author Biographies 186

Academy for the Advancement of Postmaterialist Sciences........... 192

Scientific Medical Network / Galileo Commission 193

Index 195

Introduction to Occurrences on the Banks of the River Styx

In Greek mythology, the river Styx represents the boundary between the land of the living and the land of the dead. Dying and critically ill people approach this boundary. Many of them, but also bystanders at their beds, report what has been called "end-of-life experiences" and other death-related phenomena. These experiences metaphorically concern occurrences on the banks of the river Styx. They include terminal lucidity (an unexpected surge of mental clarity shortly before death in mentally confused, demented or nonresponsive people), unusual dreams and visions at the end of life, and shared death experiences (people seem to participate in the dying process of others). But critically ill people sometimes also return from this boundary between life and death, having taken glimpses of the river bank on the other side, as in near-death experiences (NDEs). In yet other cases, bereaved are sure they have been contacted by those who already crossed the river, as in after-death communications.

These phenomena have been described for centuries and they represent stable elements in the literature on death and dying. In the past decades, however, they have become increasingly studied by academic researchers as well. This research demonstrates that these phenomena occur universally and on a regular basis. They are indeed a frequent part of the dying process of human beings. Moreover, these phenomena sometimes question the supposition that consciousness is a mere product of brain chemistry—supposition that is maintained in particular by many Western scientists. Although it is obvious that under normal circumstances, states of the mind are tightly correlated to states of the brain, this doesn't always seem to be the case in near-death states.

For example, numerous people have reported intense personal experiences and out-of-body experiences in the context of life-threatening "critical NDEs", such as after cardiac arrest. In such situations, the oxygen deprivation is so severe that veridical perceptions of the surroundings, coherent consciousness, much less states of heightened awareness, should not be occurring according to standard brain physiological models—but they do (Rivas et al., 2023). Similarly, terminal lucidity sometimes occurs in people with severe neurodegenerative brain conditions, which is why such instances can be called "paradoxical" terminal lucidity (Nahm, 2022). Extrasensory perception may also be involved when dying people have visions of deceased people of whom they didn't know they had already died (Greyson, 2010). This can likewise be the case in after-death communications.

Such phenomena are at odds with the supposition that consciousness is produced by the brain's chemistry alone, thus providing added evidence for fostering a post-materialist perspective regarding the foundations of consciousness and the world at large. The present book provides an overview and update on research concerning the mentioned phenomena, focusing on research into terminal lucidity performed by members of our own research group in the first four chapters in Part 1. The contributors not only describe research into the phenomenon itself, such as terminal lucidity in children (Chapter 1 by Natasha Tassell-Matamua and Karalee Kothe) and in adults (Chapter 2 by Chris A. Roe), but also discuss practical implications of terminal lucidity for witnesses of such episodes and for health care (Chapters 3 and 4 by Maryne Mutis and Marjorie Woollacott).

This practice-oriented aspect of raising the awareness regarding the occurrence of unusual phenomena on the banks of the river Styx is also present in Part 2 of this book. It contains perspectives on a variety of other near-death phenomena and includes important topics that have not received much attention among researchers and the public until very recently: Coma experiences. Part 2 begins with an overview of unusual states of awareness in nonresponsive people, in particular "locked-in experiences" in seemingly comatose people (Chapter 5 by Michael Nahm). This is followed by an overview and update on research into NDEs (Chapter 6 by Marieta Pehlivanova and Bruce Greyson) and a chapter on certain kinds of experiences that are reported from medically induced comas. They are typically described as extremely terrifying and clearly need to be researched in much more depth (Chapter 7 by Alan Pearce). The greatly negative effects of medically induced comas on the psyche and the body of patients are detailed in the subsequent Chapter 8 by Kali Dayton, who also provides recommendations about how the practices of health care in Intensive Care Units can be improved significantly.

Chapter 9 by Hannah Maciejewski and Christopher Kerr provides an overview on their studies into end-of-life dreams and visions, and closes with describing implications for practice. In Chapter 10, William J. Peters, Monica Williams, and Nancy Philpott present an overview on the phenomenon of shared death experiences, again based on their own research projects. This is followed by an overview of reports signifying that end-of-life experiences are not only occurring in human beings but also in non-human animals (Chapter 11 by Michael Nahm, Pam Smart, and Rupert Sheldrake). Thereafter, Evelyn Elsaesser offers an overview of research on phenomena suggestive of the survival of bodily death, after-death communications (Chapter 12). Part 2 concludes with a study according to which the dying process might even cause measurable aberrations of quantum processes in the vicinity of the dying, thus offering novel avenues for research aiming at objectifying potential anomalies during the last phase of life (Chapter 13 by Vasileios Basios).[1]

All contributors of this volume agree that it is vitally important to advance research into the spectrum of near-death phenomena. Sooner or later, all of us will be confronted with death—be it in the communities of our loved ones or in the face of our own mortality. Gaining increased knowledge about what happens in near-death states and at death is highly relevant for all of us, both regarding theoretical questions of a philosophical and spiritual nature, and regarding practice-related questions about how to best treat critically ill and moribund patients. We hope that the contents of this volume contribute to raising the awareness regarding the occurrence of near-death phenomena such as terminal lucidity, locked-in experiences, coma experiences, end-of-life dreams and visions, NDEs, shared death experiences, and also after-death communications—and this not only concerning human beings but also non-human animals. This book is the first to cover all these different phenomena in a single volume. We also hope it will stimulate further systematic research into the covered variety of near-death phenomena. As the contributors of our book have demonstrated already, such studies can increasingly shed more light on what happens on the banks of the river Styx and on how to best deal with its ferryman.

Michael Nahm, Marjorie Woollacott, Natasha Tassell-Matamua

---

[1] Note: We have retained the chapter authors' own writing styles in British and American English.

References

Greyson, B. (2010). Seeing dead people not known to have died: "Peak in Darien" experiences. *Anthropology and Humanism, 35,* 159–171.

Nahm, M. (2022). The importance of the exceptional in tackling riddles of consciousness and unusual episodes of lucidity. *Journal of Anomalous Experience and Cognition, 2,* 264–296.

Rivas, T., Dirven, A., & Smit, R. H. (2023). *The self does not die: Verified paranormal phenomena from near-death experiences* (2nd ed.). International Association for Near-Death Studies.

PART 1

New Perspectives on Terminal Lucidity

Chapter One

Terminal Lucidity. An Introduction, Some Case Examples in Children, and Questions They Raise

NATASHA TASSELL-MATAMUA
& KARALEE KOTHE

Abstract

Terminal lucidity (TL) is a phenomenon that forms part of a spectrum of experiences that occur during the physical dying process. Characterised by spontaneous and unanticipated changes to cognitive state and abilities, much about TL remains unknown, including how it might be defined, how it occurs, why it occurs, and what it contributes to understandings about the range of human experiences transpiring in association with death. Although recent investigations have explored TL in adult populations, few studies have systematically documented or studied TL in children. A small group of researchers from around the globe have been collecting accounts of TL in children for the past several years. In this chapter, several of those case reports are provided and discussed. Beginning with a general overview of TL and some of the contentions related to defining the phenomenon, we argue why investigating TL in children is important, before presenting and summarising the five case studies. We end by posing several questions that instances of TL in children raise.

An Introduction to Terminal Lucidity

Exceptional experiences that occur on the precipice of death have been reported across cultures around the globe and throughout recorded history. Broadly categorised in Western scholarship as end-of-life experiences (ELEs), the phenomena that constitute ELEs are known by a range of names, thus suggestive of the idea they are distinct syndromes, despite their apparent phenomenological similarity. These profound occurrences typically transpire in the final minutes, hours, or days before and sometimes even after physical death, and suggest the dying person or deceased person (in the case of experiences occurring after death) has a shift in conscious experience that transcends current materialist understandings of spatiotemporal possibilities.

Central to this chapter are a type of ELE that has come to be known as "terminal lucidity" (TL) (Nahm & Greyson, 2009). Due to the limited research investigating TL to date, the pool of literature about the phenomenon is sparse, yet current understandings suggest the duration and intensity of TL can fluctuate amongst experiencers and there are some common characteristics. Specific to TL is an unexpected surge of mental clarity that is marked by changes to cognitive state and abilities just prior to physical death, which are spontaneous, unanticipated, contravening of medical expectations, and can be accompanied (although not always) by alterations to physical capabilities and verbal communication.

These cognitive, verbal and physical changes typically manifest as any of the following: particularly meaningful communication with family, friends, and/or caregivers, which can include providing reassurance that the dying person and their significant others will be "OK"; verbally reporting or inferring through physical actions or eye movement the presence of non-visible entities, such as deceased significant others; acknowledgment and/or acceptance of impending death; stating they have been journeying back and forth between different realities or dimensions; indicating they are about to go on a journey; and, positive affect and gestures, including happiness, excitement, joy and peace, as well as smiling and singing. Sometimes affective responses including reluctance, fear, and sadness, may also be expressed by the dying person.

Interest in such lucidity episodes has increased in recent decades, perhaps on account of the perplexing questions they raise about the relationship between brain health and cognitive function due to their juxtaposition to the dying person's prognosis. Much of this interest has been directed to aging populations, especially older adults who have neurodegenerative conditions, such as Alzheimer's disease. In some of these cases, the term "paradoxical lucidity" has been applied, which defines episodes of enhanced mental clarity in those with conditions of severe neurocognitive decline, but who do not necessarily die immediately after such episodes (Mashour et al., 2019). Unlike paradoxical lucidity, instances of TL have, without fail, a propinquity to death (Nahm, 2022a). Indeed, the timing of lucid episodes and in particular whether they occur in immediate proximity to death, has inevitably generated debates about how they can and should be defined (e.g., Nahm, 2022a, 2022b; Peterson et al., 2022). Similar definitional concerns are also reflected in the field of end-of-life studies in general and notably revolve around developing sufficient criteria for identifying and categorising the full range of exceptional experiences associated with death (e.g., Parnia et al., 2022; Peters et al. in Chapter 10 of this volume).

Adding to these definitional concerns, at least in cases of TL, is the fact that many if not all, published accounts of TL are based on the eye-witness testimony of those who were with the dying person as their TL episode occurred, or are based on reports of people who were not present at the death but who had the TL episode relayed to them by someone else who was with the dying person (e.g., where a nurse was present and family members were absent, and the nurse later recounted the experiences to the family). Although some who have TL may speak to aspects of the experience as they are having it (e.g., indicating that they are seeing deceased others), the phenomenological spectrum of TL features can currently only be inferred from the perspective of those who witness it or have it relayed to them, as opposed to those who experience it. Consequently, definitions of TL remain challenging to develop consensus on due to, among other things, the potential inaccuracy, social conditioning, and unconscious bias that can colour eye-witness testimony (Mickes et al., 2025) and the interpretations that are drawn from it.

These definitional debates and ongoing concerns may, in part, be responsible for the lack of systematic and extensive research into TL to date. Despite the limited scholarship about TL, given its historical and apparent cross-cultural occurrence, it is a phenomenon that may occur with relative frequency, at least in adults. Anecdotal accounts of family members attest to occurrences prior to the death of loved ones that seem to reflect the same common features of published TL experiences. Nurses who work with dying adult patients in hospice settings anecdotally report TL is a well-known phenomenon among such health professionals. The few studies that have addressed TL suggest an estimated 2–6% of all dying adults, irrespective of medical condition at death, experience TL (Batthyány & Greyson, 2021; Fenwick & Brayne, 2011; Nahm & Greyson, 2009; Nahm et al., 2012).

Terminal Lucidity in Children

Published reports of TL in children are not prominent in Western scholarship. Indeed, only a handful of cases (e.g., Doka, 2020; Hyslop, 1918; Nahm et al.

2012; Morse & Perry, 1990) and some recent clinical examples (e.g., Roehrs et al., 2024) are available. This limited number of children's cases may be due to several factors, such as the ethical sensitivity associated with any research conducted with or about children, the fact children's mortality is proportionately lower than older adults thus presenting less comparative opportunity for TL to happen, as well as the very real possibility that perhaps TL simply does not occur as often in children as it does with adults. Even in light of these possibilities, greater understanding of TL in children remains essential for a number of reasons.

Firstly, it cannot be assumed that the phenomenology of TL in children and adults is synonymous. As previously discussed, all TL reports are based on the testimony of witnesses, who are often adults; thus, TL in children has, as far as we know, only ever been interpreted through the lens of adults, which will inevitably be layered with various levels of social conditioning that children may not necessarily possess. In that regard, how adults interpret the TL they witness may not necessarily correspond with the phenomenology of TL as experienced by the child. Moving forward, TL researchers must remain cognisant of their positionality and how this might influence their interpretation of TL in children.

Secondly, because the causal mechanisms underlying TL have not been studied, it is not yet known whether TL arises as a result of the same neurological functions in children as in adults; that is assuming such experiences causally arise from the brain. According to this dominant materialist perspective (that conscious experience is a result of healthy brain function) the developing brain of a terminally ill child should not be capable of some of the same functions as the developed brain of adults, and therefore some of the characteristics seen in adult TL accounts should not necessarily be mirrored in children's TL account. And yet such characteristics do indeed occur in children as in adults.

Equally, established convention suggests children psychologically and emotionally process the world in different ways to adults, and this is particularly notable in terms of their conceptualisations of death (Longbottom & Slaughter, 2018). Yet, reports of TL in children suggest their understandings of death are more sophisticated than expected, raising questions about whether current understandings of children's psychological, cognitive, emotional, and spiritual development are being accurately captured by current methodologies and epistemologies.

Finally, and perhaps most importantly, TL may indeed be a natural part of the dying process. If so, then it has necessary and pertinent implications regarding the wellbeing and care of the terminally-ill children. Improved understandings of TL in children will enable caregivers and family members to make more informed decisions about what kinds of treatment may or may not be useful around the time children display episodes of TL.

It is for these reasons and many more that the phenomenon of TL in children needs further exploration as part of a wider agenda to advance understandings about the full range of human experiences near death that occur across all ages. Yet, the phenomenology, manifestation, and antecedents of children's experiences of TL have not been systematically studied, and consequently, very little is known about TL in children.

Responding to this dearth of information, a small group of researchers from around the globe have been soliciting eyewitness accounts of apparent TL in children since 2023. To date, our team[1] has collected a total of 14 contemporary cases of children that appear to exhibit characteristics of TL, from the United States, Spain, Mexico, and Aotearoa New Zealand. While we have disseminated several of the 14 cases in full or in part in other works (see Roehrs et al., 2024; Woollacott & Tassell-Matamua, 2025), here we present five cases of young boys. We use pseudonyms and provide brief summaries about how each case is characteristic of what is known about TL.

Some Case Examples

'James'

A 67-year-old social worker from the United States recounted details of the following experience of young James. In her career as a social worker, she had cared for at least 20 terminally ill children who had substantial cognitive impairment as a result of their illness, but who had all unexpectedly experi-

---

[1] The current team of researchers includes Natasha Tassell-Matamua PhD, Massey University, Aotearoa, New Zealand; Karalee Kothe MS, University of Colorado; Marjorie Woollacott PhD, University of Oregon; Michael Nahm PhD, Institute for Frontier Areas of Psychology and Mental Health, Freiburg, Germany; Bruce Greyson MD, University of Virginia; Chris A. Roe PhD, University of Northampton, UK; Allan Kellehear PhD, Northumbria University, UK; Maryne Mutis PhD, University of Lorraine, France; Evrard Renaud PhD, University of Lorraine, France; Alex Gomez-Marin PhD, Institute of Neuroscience, Alicante, Spain. Philip Roehrs MD, from the University of Virginia previously worked with the team. Peter Fenwick MD, was also part of the team until his death in November 2024.

enced a lucid episode towards the end of life. The following case recounts the very first time she witnessed TL in a child.

> "James had been ill for a very long time, and was very, very sick. He had suffered chronic kidney failure from birth, but towards the end of his life had lapsed into a semi-comatose state. His mental awareness had declined substantially. Prior to his TL episode, James had been mumbling, as if he was talking to somebody. His parents had been at his bedside for days and were exhausted. The nursing staff suggested they go home, shower, get a meal, and then come back. Once the parents left, James regained awareness. He wanted to say goodbye to his parents, but because they weren't there he instead spoke to the nurses. He asked them to 'Tell my Mom and Dad that I will be ok. So-and-so is going to help me cross over. So-and-so is going to be with me.' James died shortly after communicating this message to the nurses."

Characteristics of TL in James' case include a decline in mental awareness as indicated by his semi-comatose state, followed by a spontaneous surge of lucidity immediately prior to his death. James clearly had some recognition of his imminent death, and also implied (through his mumbling and direct communication that someone was going to be with him) the presence of unseen others. Although it is not possible to know who James indicated would help him cross over, the fact he provided a name suggests the person was known to him and his parents. His statement that he was going to be helped to cross over also implies recognition of a journey of some kind, although exactly where he thought he was going remains subject to speculation.

'Joe'

The same social worker who recounted the TL episode of James, also described the occurrence of TL she witnessed in another young boy.

> "Joe was a 9-year-old boy who had relapsed with leukaemia. In the days before he died, Joe told me about seeing a white light and talking with Jesus. One morning, he talked with me while he was in his room, and I was in the hallway. He wanted me to come in and yelled back verbal responses to my thoughts. When Joe lapsed into the semi-comatose state that nurses had described in other dying children, I worked with staff and volunteers to keep the family at the bedside, tend to their needs and support them when Joe came to alertness just before dying. He told his

> parents not to worry about him as grandma was going to be with him. He remained alert and seemed peaceful and not in pain for less than an hour, before dying in his mom's arms."

Joe's case reflects several TL characteristics, including verbally reporting the presence of non-visible entities (i.e., Jesus, grandma), and exceptional cognitive abilities (i.e., apparent telepathic knowledge acquisition). His lapse into a semi-comatose state indicates he experienced a decline in mental awareness before a spontaneous surge in lucidity immediately prior to death. Stating his deceased grandmother was going to be with him suggests Joe was aware of his imminent death, but also aware of his parent's emotions in relation to that and the need to provide them with reassurance to not worry. He also demonstrated positive affect (i.e., peace) prior to dying.

'John'

This case was recounted by a 63-year-old hospice nurse from Aotearoa New Zealand, who often worked with terminally ill children. The mother of the child who experienced TL was present during the episode and later retold what she had witnessed to the hospice nurse.

> "John was a 12-year-old boy from New Zealand who had a brain tumour and lost the use of his legs as a consequence. He was near the end of this life and he and those around him knew he was dying. People used to tell him he would be able to run and play again after he died. John was not comfortable with this thought and wanted to work in a library helping the librarian to get books. Prior to his death, John became unconscious for many hours, but roughly 24 hours before he did die, he woke again and told his mum that he had met a funny, happy man during the period he was apparently unconscious, and that the man was going to be taking care of him. The man he went on to describe was in fact his mother's younger brother who had died in her teenage years. She had never spoken to John about her deceased brother, and she was very emotional as she recounted the story to the hospice nurse. John also told his mother that there was a big library in the place that he was going to and the lady there wanted him to help her with the other children."

TL characteristics in this case include unconsciousness followed by a spontaneous surge of lucidity just prior to death. John also indicated the presence of a deceased significant other, who was later identified by the mother as her deceased brother. The fact John had no prior knowledge of his deceased uncle is also indicative of apparent exceptional cognitive abilities. The identification of a big library where he was going to, implies John believed he would be undertaking a journey to another place.

'Juan'

While most of the accounts we have collected have been recalled by health professionals who were part of a team caring for the child, the following case was described by a 47-year-old parent from Spain. The parent cared for her child, Juan, who was seven years old when he passed as a result of a brain tumour. Just prior to death Juan had lapsed into a semi-comatose state, but during this time he also had several lucid episodes.

> "There were several episodes. The day before, Juan began predicting his imminent death. He also told me that he would take care of his siblings and that the Lord Jesus would take care of him as much as, if not more than, I would. It was a long conversation... It was a calm, peaceful conversation. He only got nervous when he told me they were already touching him. He knew they were coming to greet him. But, as he told me, 'I didn't want to die.' He didn't want to go. The next day, among other things, he told me that 'it was his turn.' After a few hours of napping, he set off on his journey."

TL characteristics common to this case include Juan's recognition of his imminent death through his predictions the day before he died as well as his statement just prior to his death that it was "his turn." His references to the Lord Jesus and that he was being touched implies the presence of unseen others. Although he reportedly maintained a positive affective state, he also indicated a reluctance to die, and anxiety related to whoever/whatever he thought was touching him. Although Jose lapsed into a semi-comatose state prior to death, because he had several lucid episodes during this time, it is not possible to know whether his mental state had declined sufficiently enough for his final lucid episode to be considered an unanticipated surge of lucidity that contravened medical expectations. The case of Juan highlights some of the challenges involved in specifying definitional criteria for TL, as Juan has many of the cognitive changes characterising TL, but not necessarily the spontaneous and unexpected surge in mental clarity just prior to death.

'Jack'

A healthcare provider in the United States recounted this experience when she was 76 years old, although she had worked with children with serious illnesses for a long time. She indicated this case had been described to Elisabeth Kübler-Ross who subsequently met the child and spent time with him prior to his death. The child had leukemia since infancy, but by the time the healthcare provider met him, he was seven years old. She cared for him for a further two years before he died.

> "By the time he came into my workplace he was 7. We were trying for a bone marrow transplant. But things changed. He began to respond and be healthier. Jack was feeling better because he said he had been to a place called Summerland, over a rainbow bridge. There were other children there and they told him that he could not stay, so he came back and got better physically. He did okay under treatment until the age of eight and he died at nine. At eight, he was getting worse. Jack was now at the children's hospital and not doing well. He was on difficult medications. He was like a little old man. He began to visit Summerland in times when he was failing. He would come back and report to the caregivers that he had interacted with other children, by name, who had died at the children's hospital. A child would die, and then Jack would go to Summerland. This happened repeatedly. Jack then talked to his mom and said, 'I want to go to Summerland for good.' Mom called me and we went to Jack and explored that. Mom said, 'Okay, you can go.' They then stopped treatment. The staff agreed. This child had known nothing but cancer treatment, in bed, etc. He wanted to go to Summerland. I was there. He had gone in and out. He became unconscious. It was goodbye time. Before he became unconscious, he said, 'The bridge. The rainbow bridge. There they are!' "

Although it is not certain whether Jack had personally met any of the children who died at the hospital, that he indicated interacting with them in another place (i.e., Summerland) and he was able to name the children who had died, hints at the exceptional cognitive abilities (i.e., unexplained knowledge acquisition) that are characteristic of TL. Jack's plea to go to Summerland for good implies he was preparing for a journey of some kind. Although Jack did become unconscious, it appears that his lucid episode where he explained seeing the rainbow bridge may have not been a surge of mental clarity as is typically seen in TL, but rather a continuation of everyday conscious awareness, prior to moving into a state of unconsciousness. Jack's case again highlights the challenges of defining TL.

Interesting Questions Remain
Notable to the above cases is that they all display characteristics of TL that have been reported in adult cases. Yet as noted, at least two cases, Jack and Juan, displayed the exceptional cognitive feats as a continuation of their everyday conscious responsivity and not after a *surge* in lucidity after a decline in mental state. Although no consensually agreed definition of TL has been developed, current understandings suggest the surge of lucidity is an essential component of how TL should be conceptualised. However, in the absence of a *surge*, these cases still highlight some remarkable characteristics that contribute to the ELE literature, and we felt should not be overlooked for their lack of one key feature—at least not at this stage when understandings about TL in general are still in their infancy. So, we have included the two cases to highlight the challenges of identifying TL, but also the challenges associated with developing definitions for the spectrum of phenomenon that occur during the end-of-life, when there appear to be so many phenomenological similarities. To rule in cases or rule out cases on the basis of limited understanding and conceptualisation of a phenomenon, could not only do a disservice to the pool of developing knowledge about exceptional experiences at the end of life, but could also do a disservice to those who witness them and are seeking explanations about what they saw. And so, we encourage systematic investigations of TL across the lifespan as an essential activity moving forward.

Despite currently lacking a robust definition for TL, the above cases are still enigmatic and raise many interesting questions about the mind-brain relationship and its implications for physical, psychological, emotional and spiritual development.

For example, in each of the above cases, the children demonstrated through their verbal communication, awareness they were about to die, recognition of the permanency of that process (e.g., by indicating they wanted to say "goodbye" or that it was "their turn"), and concern for the impact of their death on their parents. Children apparently do not grasp the permanency, causation, or inevitability of death until they are eight years old or older, at least in Western cultures (Longbottom & Slaughter, 2018). Although children who experience TL have most often suffered a terminal illness and likely been exposed to death and dying discourses that may have elevated their understandings about the dying process, it still cannot be assumed that the way they understand death is the same as adults. In fact, the above cases suggest the children's ability to cognitively process the impact of their death on their parents *while they were in a moment of rapid cognitive revival,* is sophisticated and beyond what would be expected of young children according to established models of child development.

Another particularly intriguing question is how can children return to a state of *immediate* lucid awareness after being comatose or semi-comatose? During coma or semi-coma states, the expectation is that children will not have awareness, while established thinking suggests that a return from such states of unconsciousness to lucid cognitive functioning is a gradual process, that is if full functionality returns at all (e.g., Azouvi et al., 2009; Pandharipande et al., 2012). That children who experience TL seem to traverse the spectrum of unconsciousness to lucid consciousness *instantaneously,* contradicts this established thinking and medical expectations about what is possible in light of the dying child's prognosis. Notably, the medication regimes of the five children in the above cases were not always known by those who reported the experiences, so medication cannot be ruled out as a contributing factor to the enhanced mentation apparent in each of the children's TL episodes. But, given the rapid nature of the return to cognitive lucidity, it seems unlikely that medication could fully account for this in all five cases. What can account for it, remains subject to future confirmation.

Conclusion

Although we have presented just five cases above and all are of young boys, this should not detract from the fact lucidity episodes are, at least according to anecdotal reports, common phenomena occurring during the dying process of some children. While we have not attempted to explain in materialist or post-materialist terms, how or even why TL happens in children, we have no reason to doubt the veracity of these reports. Instead, we have focused on presenting the cases as they were reported to us. It appears that some of the typical elements characterising TL in adults are also commonly reported in cases of TL in children, although challenges remain with identifying children's TL cases in the absence of a consensually agreed definition. There is still so much more to be learnt about this phenomenon, including its antecedents, manifestation, and importantly its implications for enhancing understandings about cognitive, as well as emotional and spiritual functioning at the end of life. The small sample of cases we have collected to date are the initial contributions to what we hope will build into a more robust and comprehensive pool of knowledge about TL in children.

Acknowledgements

The authors wish to acknowledgement members of the Terminal Lucidity Research team, whose collective wisdom is implicitly embedded in this chapter. This work was supported by funding from the Bial Foundation (Application ID:129/2022).

References

Azouvi, P., Vallat-Azouvi, C., & Belmont, A. (2009). Cognitive deficits after traumatic coma. *Progress in Brain Research, 177,* 89–110.

Batthyány, A., & Greyson, B. (2021). Spontaneous remission of dementia before death: Results from a study on paradoxical lucidity. *Psychology of Consciousness: Theory, Research and Practice, 8,* 1–8.

Doka, K. (2020). *When we die. Extraordinary experiences at the end of life.* Llewellyn Publications.

Fenwick, P., & Brayne, S. (2011). End-of-life experiences: Reaching out for compassion, communication, and connection-meaning of deathbed visions and coincidences. *American Journal of Hospice and Palliative Care, 28,* 7–15.

Hyslop, J. H. (1918). Visions of the dying. *Journal of the American Society for Psychical Research, 12,* 585–645.

Longbottom, S., & Slaughter, V. (2018). Sources of children's knowledge about death and dying. *Philosophical Transactions of the Royal Society B, 373,* 20170267.

Mashour, G. A., Frank, L., Batthyany, A., Kolanowski, A. M., Nahm, M., Schulman-Green, D., Greyson, B., Pakhomov, S., Karlawish, J., & Shah, R. C. (2019). Paradoxical lucidity: a potential paradigm shift for the neurobiology and treatment of severe dementias. *Alzheimer's & Dementia, 15,* 1107–1114.

Mickes, L., Wilson, B. M., & Wixted, J. T. (2025). The cognitive science of eyewitness testimony. *Trends in Cognitive Sciences*, published online, https://doi.org/10.1016/j.tics.2025.01.008.

Morse, M., & Perry, P. (1990). *Closer to the light: Learning from the near-death experiences of children*. New York, NY: Villard.

Nahm, M. (2022a). The importance of the exceptional in tackling riddles of consciousness and unusual episodes of lucidity. *Journal of Anomalous Experience and Cognition, 2*, 264–296.

Nahm, M. (2022b). Terminal lucidity versus paradoxical lucidity: A terminological clarification. *Alzheimer's & Dementia, 18*, 538–539.

Nahm, M., & Greyson, B. (2009). Terminal lucidity in patients with chronic schizophrenia and dementia: A survey of the literature. *Journal of Nervous and Mental Diseases, 197*, 942–944.

Nahm, M., Greyson, B., Kelly, E. W., & Haraldsson, E. (2012). Terminal lucidity: A review and a case collection. *Archives of Gerontology and Geriatrics, 55*, 138–142.

Pandharipande, P. P., Girard, T. D., Jackson, J. C., Morandi, A., Thompson, A. L., Pun, Brummel, N. E., Hughes, C. G., Vasilevskis, E. E., Shintani, A. K., & Moons, K. G. (2013). Log-term cognitive impairment after critical illness. *New England Journal of Medicine, 369*, 1306–1316.

Parnia, S., Post, S. G., Lee, M. T., Lyubomirsky, S., Aufderheide, T. P., Deakin, C. D., Greyson, B., Long, J., Gonzales, A. M., Huppert, E. L. & Dickinson, A. (2022). Guidelines and standards for the study of death and recalled experiences of death—a multidisciplinary consensus statement and proposed future directions. *Annals of the New York Academy of Sciences, 1511*, 5–21.

Peterson, A., Clapp, J., Largent, E. A., Harkins, K., Stites, S. D., & Karlawish, J. (2022). What is paradoxical lucidity? The answer begins with its definition. *Alzheimer's & Dementia, 18*, 513–521.

Roehrs, P., Fenwick, P., Greyson, B., Kellehear, A., Kothe, K., Nahm, M., Roe, C., Tassell-Matamua, N., & Woollacott, M. (2024). Terminal lucidity in a pediatric oncology clinic. *Journal of Nervous and Mental Disease, 212*, 57–60.

Woollacott, M., & Tassell-Matamua, N. (2025). Lucidite terminale chez les enfants: Une etude enc cours [Terminal lucidity in children: An ongoing study]. In C. Fawer (Ed.), *Ces enfants qui dissent voir ou entendre des defunts [Children who say they see or hear the deceased]* (pp. 85–99). Editions Exergue.

Chapter Two

Terminal Lucidity in Adults: A New Case Collection

CHRIS A. ROE

Abstract
At the end of life, the dying person may have experiences that are difficult to explain in terms of the prognosis of their health condition. Some of these experiences have been termed "transpersonal" and may involve visions of deceased friends and relatives whose purpose seems to be to ease spiritual suffering and anxiety prompted by their imminent demise. Other end-of-life experiences (ELEs) have been termed "final meaning" and seem to enable the dying person to put their affairs in order and have closure with the people that have been important to them in life. Because ELEs are poorly understood, their occurrence can be confusing or even distressing for unprepared witnesses. Mapping the circumstances, phenomenology and impacts of ELEs could thus have important implications for how we care for people in their final days and weeks. In this chapter, I describe a project that focuses on better understanding terminal lucidity, a final meaning ELE. Terminal lucidity can be defined as unusual or unexpected periods of mental clarity occurring in confused, drowsy, or otherwise nonresponsive patients in the hours or days before death. I describe some of the characteristic features of such cases, and reflect on the degree to which they might be attributable to the underlying health condition or changes in treatment or medication. I present examples of transpersonal elements that can occur in terminal lucidity episodes, and note the preferred interpretations of witnesses tend to invoke spiritual or dualistic constructs.

Introduction
Death is as unavoidable as taxes—to paraphrase a quote attributed to Benjamin Franklin—but in the modern era contemplating and witnessing it tends to be avoided, and as a consequence people may be less prepared for death

as they become less exposed to it through witnessing the deaths of others. Uncertainty arising from unfamiliarity can lead to death anxiety (also called thanatophobia after Thanatos, the Greek God of Death) with respect to one's own annihilation, and also the dying process itself. The former is reduced in older people (reported to peak in one's 20s and disappear in the elderly; e.g. Russac et al., 2007) but fear of the process of dying may still be high. Religious faith has a mixed relationship with fear of death—positive in having a conviction in an afterlife, but negative in fearing the outcome of judgement and possible punishment (e.g. Rose & O'Sullivan, 2002). In his 1973 book, The Denial of Death, Ernest Becker introduced Terror Management Theory, which proposes that many human actions are undertaken primarily as a means to ignore or evade death: some individuals avoid thinking about it at all, while others devote their energy to leaving a legacy that could make them "immortal". Terror management theory was developed further in subsequent years (e.g., Solomon et al., 2015).

Health professionals and psychologists who work in palliative care have provided lots of guidance on how to support people at the end of life (e.g., Breitbart & Alici, 2014; Faull & Blankley, 2015). While these typically include material on religious and existential questions that patients and their loved ones might have, particularly around honouring doctrinal beliefs and traditions, they do not usually acknowledge that people might have experiences at end of life that are difficult to make sense of in conventional materialist terms. Such experiences can therefore be surprising and unexpected, and so become a source of distress or confusion, particularly for the dying person's family members and loved ones (Roe, 2020).

An exception to this general neglect of spiritually-interpreted experiences are guides produced by palliative care nurse Sue Brayne in conjunction with psychiatrist Peter Fenwick (Brayne & Fenwick, 2008a, 2008b). These were intended for practitioners and family members respectively, and draw a clear distinction between what they call "genuine" end of life experiences (ELEs) and drug-induced hallucinations, with which they may be confused by the uninformed. Brayne and Fenwick also differentiate between final meaning and transpersonal ELEs, as illustrated in Table 1. The former includes efforts towards closure and reconciliation, such as putting one's affairs in order, affirming bonds with family and close friends, and preparing oneself for the end of life. Transpersonal ELEs involve experiences that seem to possess an other-worldly quality which not only seems to predict approaching death, but can often calm and soothe the manner of dying. Transpersonal ELEs are typically interpreted by witnesses in religious or spiritual terms. Of course, in practice these two types of ELE are not mutually exclusive and witnesses can report features of both.

While ELEs are quite unfamiliar to many people, they are not particularly rare (Fenwick et al., 2007). Silva et al.'s (2024) review found that the prevalence of ELEs ranged from 50% to 90% in studies that focused on patients, and 28% to 95% in studies that focused on healthcare professionals. Osis and Haraldsson (1977/2012) conducted extensive questionnaire and interview research with doctors and nursing staff in the US and India, and found that these phenomena cannot easily be linked to the pathological process of dying, for example as resulting from organic disease or as side effects of medical treatment. Indeed, the tendency for ELEs to ease spiritual suffering and distress was in marked contrast to the anxiety and anguish that can be caused by drug-induced hallucinations (Fenwick & Fenwick, 2008; Fenwick et al., 2010).

Table 1. ELE types outlined by Brayne and Fenwick (2008a).

Final meaning ELEs
* A sudden desire to become reconciled with estranged family members or to put personal and family affairs in order.
* Unconscious or dying people may appear to possess the capacity to wait for the arrival—or departure—of relatives before they die.
* Unconscious or dying people may appear to possess the capacity to wait for the arrival—or departure—of relatives before they die.
* Profound waking or sleeping dreams which help the individual to come to terms with what may have happened during their life, perhaps in part to prepare them for their death.
* Previously confused, semi-conscious or unconscious individuals might experience unexpected lucid moments that enable them to rally enough to say farewell to those around them.

Transpersonal ELEs

* Visions or dreams involving deceased family members or religious figures who come to help the dying through their transition.

* Reports of travelling to and from other realities, often involving love and light.

* People with the dying person may witness vapours, mists and shapes around the body. These can be accompanied by feelings of love, light and reassurance.

* Carers may feel a "presence" in the room for a short period after death.

* Domestic animals can behave strangely.

* Other "strange" phenomena occurring at or around the time of death, such as a change in room temperature, or clocks stopping synchronistically.

ELEs can act as predictors for impending death, even when it's not thought by caregivers to be imminent. The following examples are taken from Osis and Haraldsson (1977/2012):

> A 68-year-old Polish housewife was afflicted with cancer. Her mind was clear. She was settling some financial matters and asked for her purse. She had not thought of dying. Then she saw her husband who had died twenty years before. She was happy, with a sort of religious feeling and, according to her doctor, she lost all fear of death. ... She died within five or ten minutes.

> A ten-year-old girl in a hospital in Pennsylvania recovering from pneumonia. Her temperature had subsided, and she seemed to be past the crisis. The mother saw that her child seemed to be sinking and called us [nurses]. She said the child had just told her she had seen an angel who had taken her by the hand—and she was gone, died immediately. That just astounded us because there was no sign of imminent death. She was so calm and serene—and so close to death!

One feature of ELEs that has received less scientific attention until recently is the sudden and unexpected change in condition that enables previously confused, semi-conscious or unconscious individuals to be sufficiently lucid and aware of their surroundings to be able to say farewell to those around them. Nahm and Greyson (2009) termed this terminal lucidity and presented examples from the published record. They focused on patients with chronic schizophrenia and dementia, although other organic brain conditions such as tumors and meningitis also caused the reported mental disorders. The majority of these records were over 150 years old and most of the cases were not described in much detail. Nahm et al. (2012) subsequently reported on additional and more recent cases involving brain abscesses, tumors, meningitis, strokes, and affective disorders. These publications are important in drawing attention to the unexpected occurrence of terminal lucidity, and have helped stimulate research interest in the phenomenon and a consideration of their implications for our understanding of psychopathology and neuropathology of people close to death. However, a weakness of cases collected in this way is that they represent incomplete accounts that may be missing key pieces of information that might reveal patterns in the circumstances, phenomenology, and impacts of terminal lucidity that shed light on their putative mechanisms. This provided the impetus for the current project.

The Current Project

A coalition of researchers interested in the phenomenon of terminal lucidity worked together to produce an online survey tool that would more systematically capture a range of details about terminal lucidity episodes.[1] Accounts secured in this way would be more comprehensive and could be compared against one another to identify necessary conditions for terminal lucidity to occur, or associations between patient circumstances and phenomenology. The questionnaire asked about the person who was believed to have experienced a terminal lucidity episode (referred to here as the subject), their underlying medical condition, treatment regimen (including recent changes), and their physical and mental capacities immediately prior to the terminal lucidity episode, as well as a detailed description of changes that occurred during the episode itself. Finally, the survey gathered information about

---

1   The team comprised (in alphabetical order): Peter Fenwick, Bruce Greyson, Allan Kellehear, Karalee Kothe, Michael Nahm, Chris A. Roe, Philip Roehrs, Natasha Tassell-Matamua, and Marjorie Woollacott.

how witnessing such an episode has affected caregivers and family members (here referred to as the survey respondent).

The survey was constructed using JISC online surveys (https://online-surveys.jisc.ac.uk), which is the preferred platform for UK survey research because data management complies with GDPR and ethical requirements. It also allows the survey to tailor questions to the respondent; for example, if they reported that the patient regained physical abilities that they had lost due to their health condition then the survey would ask additional questions about the nature of that physical recovery (e.g. to be able to move their head, to sit up, to be able to speak, etc.).

The survey is still open.[2] In this chapter I will report on the data from the first 24 respondents, comprising 20 females and four males (Mean age = 67.2). Only eight described themselves as a religious person (14 said no, 1 unsure, 1 declined to answer), but all identified as spiritual. Respondents were primarily from the USA, with additional cases from the UK, Australia, Austria, Belgium and Latvia. In terms of professional background, the sample is quite heterogenous. The largest group are nurses (N = 7) followed by physicians (N = 3), hospice workers (N = 3), with the remainder describing themselves as physical therapists, social workers, volunteers, and one chaplain/counsellor. Witnessing a terminal lucidity episode is not necessarily a rare experience for respondents, with a majority reporting multiple experiences, as shown in Figure 1.

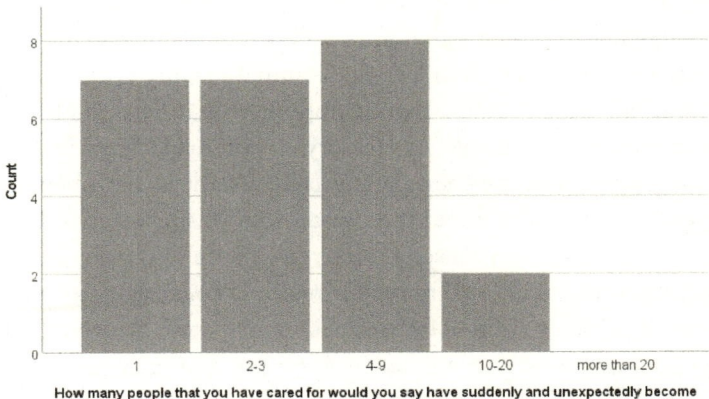

Figure 1. Frequency of witnessing terminal lucidity.

---

2   See https://app.onlinesurveys.jisc.ac.uk/s/northampton/terminal-lucidity-adult-survey.

The terminal lucidity subjects were more equally distributed, with 10 males and 14 females. Their mean age was rather higher, at 70.8 years, reflecting the fact that they were near death, but the age range was from 28 to 100 years. A majority of subjects (N = 14) were described by respondents as being religious or spiritual, but for many of the remainder (N = 6) this information was not known. Underlying ailments varied, with cancer being most frequent (N = 8), followed by forms of dementia and Alzheimer's disease (which were listed separately here; N = 3 for each). Other patients had significant infections, including pneumonia (N = 3) with the remainder presenting with cardiovascular disease, congestive heart failure, end-stage renal failure, and stroke. Treatments primarily involved antibiotics and pain management.

We asked the respondent to describe the subject's degree of mental impairment prior to their period of terminal lucidity and also during that period. There is a characteristic improvement from moderate to severe impairment beforehand to no or mild impairment during the episode. This is illustrated in Figure 2. There is a surprising number of cases where the subject's mental state is described not as severely impaired, but further investigation of cases described as "other" reveals that many of these subjects were actually unconscious or unresponsive so that the respondent felt unable to evaluate their mental state. Of course, sudden and unexpected recovery from a period of unconsciousness or unresponsivity could qualify as an instance of terminal lucidity.

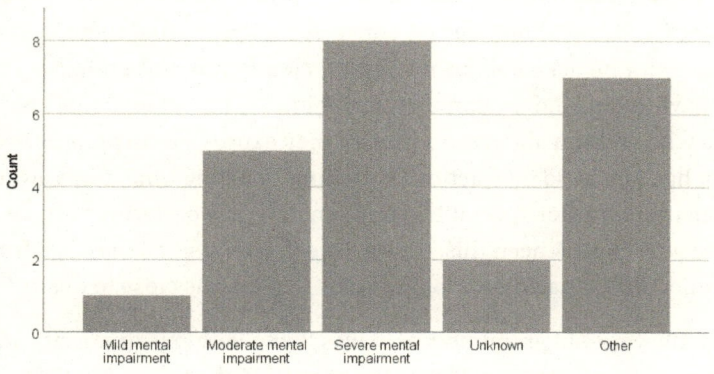

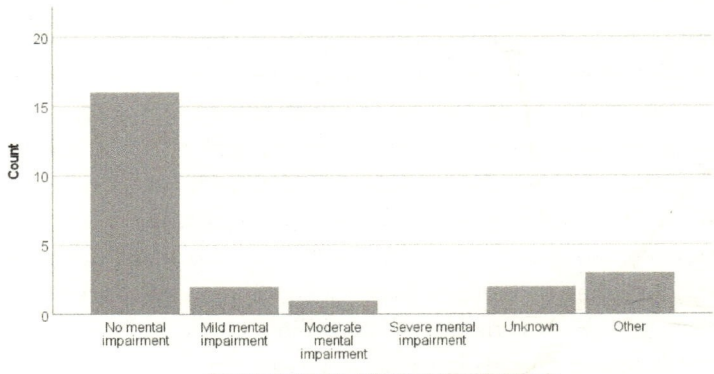

Figures 2a and 2b. Level of mental impairment before and during the terminal lucidity episode.

Respondents were asked to describe the terminal lucidity episode in their own words. The following examples illustrate the spontaneous and surprising nature of the recovery:

> "I went to visit my ex father-in-law while vacationing in Florida. I had not seen him for several years, but knew that he was now in skilled nursing care due to dementia. His wife and son reported that he usually did not know who they were, and had warned me to be prepared. As I came into his room, I said 'hi' and told him who I was, and he greeted me with obvious understanding that he knew who I was. I don't recall exactly what we talked about, but we conversed about shared memories and at one point he asked about my father, clearly remembering his relationship with him and my connection to him. We had a very lucid visit. I told his wife and son about our visit and they expressed surprise as they had not had any lucid interactions with him for a long time. I was aware that something rather special had happened, and wondering why I was the one who experienced this. About a week later, I got a message from the family that Al had died. No one knew that he was close to death." [008]

> "My 108-year-old grandmother ... was living with my aunt Betty and had been doing ok. Around 2020 at the age of 106 she fell and sustained a hip fracture at home. She had surgical repair but had a prolonged recovery with physical therapy. Over the next two years her mental capacity declined as her body became more fragile and reconditioned. By April

2022 she would only answer simple questions every so often and only seldomly have situational awareness. Most normally, she would go through the day in silence from a chair to bed and only really get up to eat small portions of food. On April 26, at around 10:26am, on a visit from my cousin, Abuela suddenly starts talking and clearly states that on May 1st, the men will come at 10am and [she will] go then. This is captured on a video recording made on April 26th. Abuelita died on May 1st around 10am while sitting at home and having just had a bite to eat." [009]

The change in lucidity occurred across a number of modalities, as shown in Table 2 (the figures refer to any notable change compared with before the terminal lucidity episode), including being more aware of their general surroundings, recognising significant others, communicating appropriately with them, being more physically able, and being more positive and energetic in mood.

Table 2. Type of change in lucidity during the terminal lucidity episode.

	Yes	No	Unsure
To be aware of or interact with their surroundings	12	4	7
To recognize or interact appropriately with other people	13	7	4
To understand spoken language	7	9	8
To understand written language	1	10	13
Changes in their appetite or capacity to eat or drink	2	17	4
Physical abilities (e.g. ability to talk, sit up, move extremities, or even walk)	11	8	5
Mood or emotions	11	7	6

When asked for further information about the recovery of capacities that had been lost prior to the terminal lucidity episode, respondent comments included:

"The lady who I remember most vividly had been unresponsive for days and was considered to be in the terminal phase of her life. I came in one morning expecting to read that she had died overnight only to find her sitting up in bed eating her breakfast—she was happily chatting to her family who were a bit stunned to say the least. As I was aware that this may be a case of terminal lucidity I explained to the family that her bright condition may not last—she died that night." [013]

"I had been called by a GP to advise on the end-of-life care of a lady dying at home from metastatic bowel cancer. On my visit she was drowsy and unable to swallow fluids or take oral medication. A subcutaneous infusion of morphine and a sedative (Midazolam) was commenced, and on follow up 24 hours later she was unresponsive and seemingly pain free. I handed the care back to the GP but, knowing she was close to death, I phoned the family each morning to check on her progress. On the following day the family reported that their mother was 'unconscious' and seemed comfortable. The same was said on day 2. She had not stirred in the previous 24 hours even when an indwelling catheter was inserted during this time. On day three the daughter reported that her mother was 'out of bed and sipping champagne.' She then went on to say that it's her mother's birthday and when the family had informed her of that she opened her eyes and upon hearing that family had gathered at her home she asked to be helped to the kitchen where she sat with them and celebrated her birthday. She returned to bed shortly after. Went to sleep and did not regain consciousness. She died within 24 hours of the experience." [011]

Experiences tend to be brief, typically lasting minutes rather than hours (see Figure 3), and occurred as a single continuous event rather than an intermittent transition to and from lucidity. Of course, asking for cases of terminal lucidity may have led to a self-fulfilling bias, but it is interesting to note the close proximity of the terminal lucidity episode to death. In 16 of the 24 cases the subject died within 24 hours of the terminal lucidity episode, despite the phenomenon suggesting a recovery of function and an improvement in their condition.

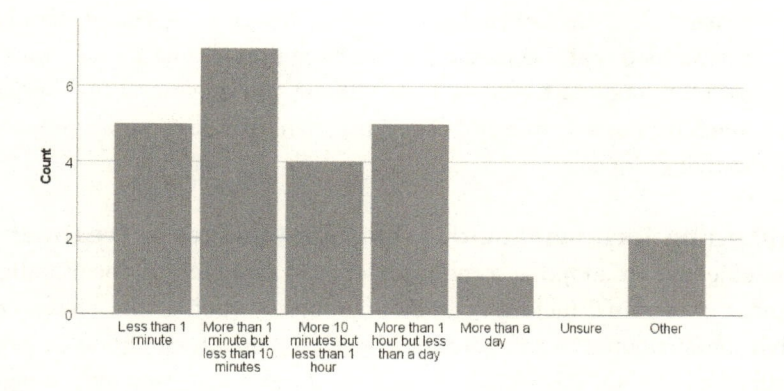

Figure 3. Duration of the terminal lucidity episode.

In the introduction I described how ELEs can provide an opportunity for closure for the dying person. Many of the terminal lucidity episodes in the current collection seemed to satisfy this need to say goodbye to loved ones.

> "Patient had been in and out of hospital and rehab facilities for several days or weeks. [In the] days before the patient passed away, while two family members were sitting with the patient, the patient suddenly became very clear and adamantly started to ask by name for every family member to come to the bedside, all five children, their spouses and grandchildren. All but two family members were able to make it to the bedside that evening. Patient was somewhat disappointed that those two members did not show up. The next few days the patient slipped in and out of consciousness, often calling out to deceased relatives and becoming increasingly more somnolent. The patient passed away three days later." [007]

The goodbye messages could also be intended for caregivers as an expression of gratitude for all they did for them in their final weeks or months:

> "A 63-year-old patient with an advanced brain tumor was unable to communicate adequately for about two weeks and was neither oriented in time, place nor person. His condition deteriorated visibly and his death seemed to be already near. At night he was restless, his breathing was irregular. I sat down at his bedside and held his hand, which he refused to let go of. His breathing became shallower and he seemed more

relaxed now. Unexpectedly, he opened his eyes, looked at me and he maintained that eye contact. Then he addressed me by my name and said 'I thank you for being here. I thank you in general for everything you have done for me and especially thank you for your accompanying in dying.' " [003]

Explaining Terminal Lucidity: Links to Changes in Treatment

One objective in adopting a more systematic approach to documenting instances of terminal lucidity is to be able to test whether the phenomenon might be attributed to the person's underlying health condition or to their medical treatment. We asked respondents if there had been any changes in the person's condition, including fever, and treatment prior to the terminal lucidity episode that might suggest some causal connection. Respondents did note some such changes, though these often referred to a progressive deterioration in their condition, and none felt that fever or changes to treatment could have been responsible for the phenomenon (see Table 3).

Table 3. Changes in health condition and treatment and their connection to the terminal lucidity episode.

	Yes	No	Unsure
Had there been any marked change in the person's condition (improvement or deterioration) prior to their terminal lucidity episode?	11	11	2
Did the person have a fever just prior to their lucid episode?	3	15	5
Had there been any marked change in the person's medication or treatment prior to their terminal lucidity episode?	2	14	6
Do you think changes in their condition, or their medication/treatment prior to their terminal lucidity episode could have been responsible for their experience?	0	18	5

Transpersonal Experiences

In a small number of cases, respondents referred to elements of the experience that align with what Fenwick and Brayne described as transpersonal ELEs. These often involved an encounter between the subject and a deceased person, seemingly intended to greet the person and help with their transition, as illustrated in the following examples (NB in these descriptions, I am reflecting the ways in which experiencers describe their experience, rather than necessarily endorsing a particular interpretation):

> "A. was a 42-year-old single mother of a 9-year-old daughter. The patient suffered from terminal end-stage renal failure, for which she came for dialysis three times a week. She had been waiting for a kidney transplant for more than four years. Already twice a suitable kidney was available, but the transplantation could never take place because A. had an infection each time. One of the other dialysis patients, Mr. K. an older man, comforted her and the two became friends. When Mr. K. passed away, A. was very sad and she explained that now she had lost her only friend. After months again a suitable kidney became available for A. Again, she came to the hospital full of hope. She said that this time it had to work. Unfortunately, the transplant had to be postponed again because A. was suffering from a previously undetected fungal infection of the lungs. The patient's disappointment was huge and that same night she developed a high fever. She started having seizures and she lost consciousness. Dialysis was performed, but the patient's condition deteriorated rapidly. A. was obviously dying and we had to stop dialysis. Then quite unexpectedly, A. suddenly opened her eyes and she straightened her upper body. She looked around the room and she seemed confused. Then her eyes widened, she pointed to the left corner of the room and smiling she greeted a person invisible to us. When I asked who she had just greeted, A. replied with a smile, 'Mr. K., of course!' And with a happy expression on her face, she explained that Mr. K. had come to pick her up. ... Then she fell back into her pillows, her breathing seemed very deep and after a few minutes A passed away." [004]

> "I was a hospice volunteer working with an 89-year-old woman who was dying. She was living in a care facility, was somewhat disoriented and was nonverbal. I had been coming to see her 2x a week for four weeks. In the previous visits she did not reference her mother, but in my last

visit with her, she showed me a picture of her deceased mother. She told me her mother was in the room with her. We talked about our mothers, and she repeatedly looked into the corner of the room and told me her mother was here with her. Shortly after my visit with her, she lapsed into a coma and died." [017]

In this context, it is perhaps not surprising that respondents were inclined to interpret the experience in spiritual terms rather than as a by-product of the subject's health condition or its treatment (see Table 4).

Table 4. How best to explain the lucidity events the respondent witnessed.

	Frequency
It was simply a biological event caused by changes in the brain	1
It was probably brought about by medication or the illness	0
It was probably due to imagination in a situation with heightened emotion	0
It was a sign that the person's life was coming to an end	13
It was an indication that our consciousness is independent of brain activity	11
It was a religious experience	2
It was a spiritual experience	11
Other	6

Summary and Conclusion

We set out to collect new cases of terminal lucidity using a survey tool that would ask about the circumstances, phenomenology and impacts in a more systematic manner than has been done previously. This would enable us to analyse cases collectively, looking for points of similarity and difference. In this chapter I have summarised 24 new cases that were collected by this method. They illustrate the characteristic sudden and surprising shift in state from being relatively unaware of and unresponsive to one's surroundings to actively interacting with friends, family and caregivers in ways that facilitate closure. As with previous case collections, witnesses are sceptical that the transformation can be explained in terms of the natural progression of the patient's illness or as a result of changes to their medication. Indeed, terminal lucidity seems to be associated with quite a wide range of end-of-life conditions. Many cases also include what Brayne and Fenwick (2008a, 2008b) described as transpersonal elements, especially encounters with deceased persons who are interpreted as a "welcoming committee" to accompany them to wherever death might take them. Witnesses very commonly prefer a spiritual or dualistic interpretation of their experiences that allows for consciousness to continue even where brain functioning is severely impaired.

Of course, the current database is very small and it would be premature to draw any strong conclusions from the cases presented. The survey is still open (see above, footnote 2) and we encourage readers who have experience of terminal lucidity to consider contributing to it. Many more cases are needed if we are to produce a more refined analysis of features and covariates. For now, perhaps it is sufficient to follow Nahm and Greyson in raising the profile of this intriguing phenomenon in the hope that it encourages more interest among the scientific and medical community both to conduct original research and to consider the implications of this phenomenon for our understanding of what it is to be a conscious being.

References

Becker, E. (1973). *The denial of death.* Free Press.
Brayne, S., & Fenwick, P. (2008a). *End of life experiences: A guide for carers of the dying.* Available at: https://newcosmicparadigm.org/wp-content/uploads/2019/05/ENDOFLIFEPROF.pdf
Brayne, S., & Fenwick, P. (2008b). *Nearing the end of life: A guide for relatives and friends of the dying.* Available at: https://www.rcpsych.ac.uk/docs/default-source/members/sigs/spirituality-spsig/resources/spirituality-special-interest-group-publications-fenwick-nearing-the-end-of-life-guide.pdf

Breitbart, W. S., & Alici, Y. (2014). *Psychosocial palliative care.* Oxford University Press.

Faull, C., & Blankley, K. (2015). *Palliative care (2nd ed).* Oxford University Press.

Fenwick, P., & Fenwick, E. (2008). *The art of dying.* Continuum.

Fenwick, P., Lovelace, H., & Brayne, S. (2007). End of life experiences and their implications for palliative care. *International Journal of Environmental Studies, 64,* 315–323.

Fenwick, P., Lovelace, H., & Brayne, S. (2010). Comfort for the dying: Five-year retrospective and one-year prospective studies of end of life experiences. *Archives of Gerontology and Geriatrics, 51,* 173–179.

Osis, K., & Haraldsson, E. (1977/2012). *At the hour of death: A new look at evidence for life after death.* White Crow Productions Ltd.

Nahm, M., & Greyson, B. (2009). Terminal lucidity in patients with chronic schizophrenia and dementia: A survey of the literature. *Journal of Nervous & Mental Disease, 197,* 942–944.

Nahm, M., Greyson, B., Kelly, E. W., & Haraldsson, E. (2012). Terminal lucidity: A review and a case collection. *Archives of Gerontology and Geriatrics, 55,* 138–142.

Roe, C. A. (2020). Clinical parapsychology: The interface between anomalous experiences and psychological wellbeing. In J. Leonardi & B. Schmidt (Eds.) *Spirituality and wellbeing: Interdisciplinary approaches to the study of religious experience and health* (pp. 44–63). Equinox.

Rose, B. M., & O'Sullivan, M. J. (2002). Afterlife beliefs and death anxiety: An exploration of the relationship between afterlife expectations and fear of death in an undergraduate population. *Omega, 45,* 229–243.

Russac, R. J., Gatliff, C., Reece, M., & Spottswood, D. (2007). Death anxiety across the adult years: An examination of age and gender effects. *Death Studies, 31,* 549–61.

Silva, T. O., Ribeiro, H. G., & Moreira-Almeida, A. (2024). End-of-life experiences in the dying process: Scoping and mixed-methods systematic review. *BMJ Supportive & Palliative Care, 13,* e624–e640.

Solomon, S., Greenberg, J., & Pyszczynski, T. (2015). *The worm at the core: On the role of death in life.* Random House.

Chapter Three

A Look at Terminal Lucidity Through the Prism of Witnesses

MARYNE MUTIS

Abstract

This document explores the phenomenon of terminal lucidity, which refers to an unexpected surge of cognitive functions in patients near death. Despite being a clinical reality observed by healthcare professionals, terminal lucidity remains poorly understood and unpredictable. A research project in France aimed to collect testimonies from two groups—family members and healthcare teams—who had witnessed terminal lucidity. Semi-directive interviews explored various facets of the experience, such as its impact on grieving and the understanding of the phenomenon. The data were analyzed using interpretative phenomenological analysis (IPA).

The results reveal that terminal lucidity is perceived as an unforeseen event in the end-of-life trajectory, disrupting the expected progression toward death. Notably, it could introduce a level of uncertainty that challenges both families and professionals. This phenomenon has indeed significant implications on the grieving process. For some, it offers a final moment of connection, which can be deeply comforting and a cherished memory. However, this unexpected revival can also create false hope, making the subsequent passing even more challenging to accept. Concerning professionals, this phenomenon often leaves caregivers feeling powerless, struggling to manage the situation effectively and meet the needs and expectations of the families. When professionals are prepared or informed about, terminal lucidity can offer valuable insights into patient care and enhance their understanding of end-of-life experiences. Discussing terminal lucidity is then crucial as it helps both families and healthcare professionals better understand and be prepared, ultimately enhancing the quality of care and support provided.

Introduction

Whispers are spreading in the corridors of palliative care units and retirement homes that a "miracle" may be happening on the threshold of death. People who have lost their motor and/or cognitive faculties, who are suffering from neurodegenerative disorders or cancer, or who are worn down by age, come back from the (almost) dead just before they pass on. Speech returns to them, as do memory and locomotion. From then on, they take advantage of this period of remission to reunite with their families. An unhoped-for but short-lived revival, occurring just before they take their last breath.

You may have recognized the phenomenon now internationally known as terminal lucidity. First introduced in 2009 by Michael Nahm and Bruce Greyson, this term refers to situations of unpredictable partial or total ante-mortem reversibility of cognitive dysfunctions associated with renewed alertness (Mutis et al., 2024). This definition remains provisional, however, pending further research. Especially as, in view of the various forms of lucidity that can be observed, it would seem interesting to look at terminal lucidity as a potential continuum.

And yet, despite this scattered and still scarce information, terminal lucidity is a clinical reality, observed for a long time by modern healthcare professionals, whose effects have not waited for research to make themselves felt and create confusion in the hallways of hospitals or retirement homes. Indeed, how does one react to the unexpected revival of one's loved one or patient when, on the contrary, medicine predicted a more or less rapid deterioration before the end? With the aim of exploring these implications, we have launched an innovative research project in France in the form of a four-year thesis under the supervision of Renaud Évrard and Marie-Frédérique Bacqué.

Our aim was to collect the retrospective testimonies of people who had witnessed a case of terminal lucidity. Our data were collected during a semi-directive interview exploring for example the unfolding of the experience, the understanding of the experience, the influence of the experience or the grieving process. To this end, we decided to gather testimonies from two distinct groups of people: on the one hand, the family and friends of patients who have experienced terminal lucidity, and on the other, the healthcare teams who have been confronted with the phenomenon. It seemed to us that, faced with an identical phenomenon, these two groups could bring complementary experiences and perspectives to enable us to apprehend different facets of terminal lucidity.

Paramedic for 11 years, Cédric is a 37-year-old who witnessed his mother's decline from cancer. After several days in a coma when Cedric thought the end had come, his mother woke up one morning to find him at her side in hospital. She confessed to him that she had heard their words when she was in a coma, and that she wanted to fight to see her grandson grow up, before asking him for something to eat. Delighted to be reunited with his mother in this way, Cédric hopes for a lasting improvement in her condition, encouraged by a nurse calling out to him in the corridor to tell him about the "miracle" his mother is going through. The next day, they talk again about their future together. At the end of the day, she finally encourages him to go home and enjoy New Year's Eve, despite the circumstances. Her death will be announced to the family at five o'clock the following morning.

A Final Moment of Shared Experience

Beyond these initial movements, our research has demonstrated that terminal lucidity often provides an opportunity to reconnect with the individual and share valuable moments. Observations indicate that, during this period, individuals frequently express specific needs or communicate messages verbally. The literature corroborates these findings, with numerous authors associating this phenomenon with a chance for patients and loved ones to express themselves, engage in one last meaningful conversation, or undertake a final action (Chiriboga-Oleszcak, 2017; Kheirbek, 2019; Schreiber & Bennett, 2014).

During episodes of terminal lucidity, families typically observe that their loved one seemed conscious of their imminent passing, which was conveyed directly or indirectly through behavior or words. Many accounts describe how this awareness resulted in individuals expressing their final wishes through various requests or communications directed at family members or friends.

> Étienne experienced this personally with his wife, whom he accompanied for several years in her battle against breast cancer, which had progressively spread. Étienne is a 55-year-old research engineer and father of two. In the last months of her life, Étienne's wife was no longer able to communicate, being in a state of minimal consciousness. However, one Friday in July, Étienne was at his wife's bedside with friends and noticed that she was opening her eyes and beginning to join in the discussions.

> At the end of the day, she asks him to bring back her blue dress when he returns from dinner at their home with their friends. A few days later, on a Sunday, his wife asks him for her make-up bag, then asks the nursing staff to help her get ready. When Étienne returned to the room, he found his wife looking radiant and smiling. She made herself comfortable, closed her eyes and said she was ready to leave. Astonished by this, Étienne waited at her bedside for several hours until, death not appearing, his wife finally asked to call various people, friends and colleagues, on the telephone, to discuss her impending death and say her goodbyes.

Regarding the way in which patients themselves may interpret the episode of terminal lucidity, many professionals point out that it may have been an opportunity for them to express their last wishes, whether in the form of desires to eat, to accomplish something, to see certain people or to confide certain words. Some professionals describe that the episode of terminal lucidity could also be a privileged moment for patients to enter a deeper dimension of their being, with the initiation of a life review and different interests than before.

> At the age of 65, Claire describes herself as a doctor who has travelled widely and touched many things in her forty years of practice. She explains that she experienced only one case of terminal lucidity during her medical studies, when she was an extern in an intensive care unit. She describes the case of a patient suffering from an internal health problem, who had been in a coma for several weeks and was considered to be on his way out. One day, his wife came into the unit, dressed all in black, looking like a widow, according to Claire. She remains at the foot of her husband's bed for a while, without speaking to him, and then leaves. At the end of the day, the patient wakes up, setting off a wave of activity on the department, with the team working hard to look after him. He then asks to go outside, to see nature, mobilizing the team once again to respond to his request. Claire accompanies this patient in an armchair, wrapped in blankets, infusions hanging from a support, to the hospital parking lot. It's early summer, the temperature is pleasant, and the trees are covered with green leaves. As evening falls, the professionals want to take the patient back to his room, but he asks to stay a little longer to watch the stars. Claire stays with him, wandering around the parking lot in silence, enjoying the moment. Eventually, they return

and settle the patient back into his room, where he dies later that night. Claire adds that it was nice of him not to die in the parking lot, as it would have been difficult to justify his escapade.

Many families reported that these moments were calming, allowing them to see their loved ones serene and smiling despite the approach of death, in peaceful acceptance. For some, this provided an unexpected opportunity to spend more time with the person and see them outside the illness context, as they had known them before. Families often use these moments as the last chance to communicate with the person and share something meaningful before their departure, or at least to reconnect.

This generally positive experience of terminal lucidity is documented in modern literature (Schreiber & Bennett, 2014), describing it as a final opportunity to connect with close individuals (Fenwick & Brayne, 2010) or as a period for families to prepare for the impending death through these last interactions. Predicting the occurrence of terminal lucidity could be beneficial for ensuring the presence of loved ones when it happens (Macleod, 2009).

Telma is a 77-year-old woman who has been widowed for years and more recently shared her life with a companion for seven years. She describes accompanying him as he faced the end of his life with prostate cancer, adding that at the end, he was like a living dead man who was difficult to get up. One Monday, however, he had a moment of increased awareness, during which he verbalized that it was time for him to go. He and Telma then exchange a few hours about having fought enough, and pass on words of love for the last time.

Terminal Lucidity, and Afterwards?

When faced with terminal lucidity, some families report that the subsequent deterioration after a brief period of renewed energy can be particularly challenging. Terminal lucidity temporarily alleviates the imminent threat of death, but it can lead to cruel disappointment for loved ones when death ultimately occurs. In these circumstances, death is perceived as much more abrupt by families due to the often rapid sequence of events, such as the episode or the time between the episode and death. The suddenness of death may be exacerbated by confusion and lack of understanding of the event, which followed an improvement grounded in hopes of remission rather than being seen as an expected stage at the end of life. This sentiment is echoed by Milo, who describes a more complex and prolonged grieving process following the event, perceiving it as a shock. Without recognizing the temporary nature of terminal lucidity, there is a risk of fostering false hopes or regrets about end-of-life decisions, potentially complicating the grieving process.

For others, terminal lucidity serves to find solace in the temporality of life's end, particularly through moments of exchange and sharing, and the opportunity to rediscover the person and observe their serenity. For Telma, this experience is integral to the preparation for loss, specifically through the ability to reconnect with the individual and bid farewell during this period. The chance to reunite with the person and create more positive and pleasant memories amidst the challenging times at life's end provides comfort for many, alleviating the sadness associated with grief. This comfort is described as beneficial in the grieving process, rendering it less painful and more soothed by these shared moments of lucidity. It is therefore essential to recognize terminal lucidity as an opportunity to say farewell, aiding in the preparation for these phenomena, as supported by Kinsella et al. (2022) in their work on the comfort provided by end-of-life experiences.

As for them, most professionals note that explaining things to families can be challenging, particularly when discussing the possibility of death or addressing uncertainties from loved ones seeking answers about the phenomenon, prognosis, or the need to resume care. Despite these initial challenges, with experience and support from other team members, terminal lucidity has become a useful tool for many in detecting the imminent end of life and is increasingly integrated into clinical practice. Consequently, clinical practice has evolved, reducing the risk of misinterpretation and enabling the use of this experience in family explanations.

Addressing terminal lucidity in care practices appears to lead to improved professional practices, with a shared sense of providing better care by recognizing the phenomenon and incorporating it according to different conceptions of care. For instance, terminal lucidity encourages vigilance during an episode, allowing caregivers to assist the person nearing death, and making this experience a valuable tool with potential benefits for management and quality of care. Several caregivers also indicated that being able to accompany and respond to requests during episodes of terminal lucidity provided a sense of professional satisfaction and the impression of delivering high-quality care.

A Key to Understanding and Acceptance

Given the various risks and benefits associated with terminal lucidity, both families and professionals emphasize the necessity for a deeper understanding of this phenomenon. Such comprehension is crucial to optimally manage experiences and mitigate potential difficulties. Participants expressed a desire for increased knowledge about terminal lucidity to better anticipate its occurrence, align their expectations regarding end-of-life care, and enhance their practices. This knowledge would allow them to utilize these moments to create lasting memories or improve care provision.

These findings underscore the importance of awareness and recognition of terminal lucidity by healthcare teams, as noted in existing literature. Proper preparation for such experiences offers opportunities for improved management (Nahm et al., 2012). Caregivers who are well-informed can educate families to minimize surprise and confusion, thereby helping them maintain realistic expectations and encouraging meaningful engagement during the remaining time with their loved ones (Wholihan, 2016). Many authors have highlighted the significance of disseminating information on recommendations and the phenomenon itself to avoid false hopes while promoting positive outcomes (Ney et al., 2021; Schreiber & Bennett, 2014).

To gradually integrate terminal lucidity as a recognized stage in the dying process, we have compiled several recommendations from professionals for their colleagues and other interested parties. For all caregivers, the initial step in managing terminal lucidity involves providing a warning, a name, or an explanation for this experience to offer families a preliminary framework for understanding, thereby legitimizing and normalizing their experience. Furthermore, it is crucial for professionals to exercise caution in their communication and interpretation of the phenomenon, avoiding the endorsement of any hypothesis amidst uncertainties, especially regarding remission. Transparency and clarity about the possibilities of terminal lucidity are essential, emphasizing that no prognosis can be confirmed with certainty, despite the often-unfavorable implications.

Professionals have reported sharing their own limitations in knowledge with families to maintain honesty and transparency, without compromising patient care. Many have also encouraged families to utilize any additional time to converse one last time, when not initiated by the families themselves. This highlights the importance of addressing the risk of imminent death with families and the urgency of prompting them to take final actions and prepare for the eventuality of death.

Conclusion

First and foremost, we observe that the experience of terminal lucidity provides benefits and a platform for discussing end-of-life issues, offering families an opportunity to prepare for loss. Our research indicates that terminal lucidity serves as a period for sharing final, intimate moments and expressing last wishes. This phase can also enable families to attribute meaning to their end-of-life experiences through the acknowledgment of death as a natural transition, the possibility of saying farewells, or the exchange of personal achievements—key elements for loss preparation.

Conversely, terminal lucidity may induce significant uncertainty regarding its origin, progression, or outcome, which the literature suggests can exacerbate difficulties for families, leading to confusion, stress, anxiety, and even depressive states (Hebert et al., 2006). Numerous participants reported feelings of surprise and challenges associated with the inability to comprehend this situation, which often contradicts their expectations or medical perspectives. In such a scenario, terminal lucidity may hinder the process of preparing for the loss of a loved one by subjecting families to uncertainties due to its unpredictable, incomprehensible, and inexplicable nature.

It is also relevant to examine how this unexpected phenomenon challenges clinicians in their ability to deal with the unknown and uncertainty, which professionals recommend as part of preparation for such phenomena. How should one cope with terminal lucidity? Ultimately, it is important to acknowledge that complete preparedness may never be achieved. Terminal lucidity emphasizes the importance of understanding rather than simply performing tasks, aligning with the ability to appreciate the clinic's most surprising manifestations, tolerate doubt and uncertainty, and remain present with the patient, despite feeling powerless to do anything else.

Moreover, being present and alleviating a person's suffering, regardless of its nature, is a key aspect of the caregiver's role. Caregivers often experience frustration, powerlessness, and exhaustion when they are unable to relieve such suffering (Dobrina et al., 2020). Many have noted the professional satisfaction that terminal lucidity can bring, allowing caregivers to address essential aspects of care, enhancing their professional support by making it more vigilant, adaptive, and individualized.

Although long recognized but not fully understood, terminal lucidity is now considered a significant element of the end-of-life process in both scientific literature and clinical practice. This aspect of dying bears important implications for those left behind, whether they are loved ones or medical professionals. Whether perceived as a poisoned surprise or unexpected help, it leaves no one indifferent.

Ongoing dialogue and communication about terminal lucidity and the end-of-life process remain essential to maximize the understanding and application of this phenomenon's various aspects. Knowledge of terminal lucidity and its ramifications, including the eventual death of the individual, appear crucial in shaping the experience of those who witness it. Consequently, we emphasize the urgent need to disseminate information to the public and provide comprehensive training for healthcare professionals, who play a core role in supporting patients and their families through this unique and profound end-of-life process.

References

Chiriboga-Oleszczak, B. A. (2017). Terminal lucidity. *Current Problems of Psychiatry, 18,* 34–46.

Dobrina, R., Chialchia, S., & Palese, A. (2020). "Difficult patients" in the advanced stages of cancer as experienced by nursing staff: A descriptive qualitative study. *European Journal of Oncology Nursing, 46,* 101766.

Fenwick, P., & Brayne, S. (2010). End-of-life experiences: Reaching out for compassion, communication, and connection – Meaning of deathbed visions and coincidences. *American Journal of Hospice and Palliative Medicine, 28,* 7–15.

Hebert, R. S., Prigerson, H. G., Schulz, R., & Arnold, R. M. (2006). Preparing caregivers for the death of a loved one: A theoretical framework and suggestions for future research. *Journal of Palliative Medicine, 9,* 1164–1171.

Kheirbek, R. E. (2019). Terminal lucidity. *Journal of Palliative Medicine, 22,* 1023.

Shared Crossing Research Initiative (2024). The spectrum of end-of-life experiences: A tool for advancing death education. *Omega, 88,* 1314–1334.

Lim, C.-Y., Park, J. Y., Kim, D. Y., Yoo, K. D., Kim, H. J., Kim, Y., & Shin, S. J. (2020). Terminal lucidity in the teaching hospital setting. *Death Studies, 44,* 285–291.

Macleod, A. D. (2009). Lightening up before death. *Palliative and Supportive Care, 7,* 513–516.

Mutis, M., Bacqué, M.-F., Gulliford, L., & Evrard, R. (2024). Grief in the face of terminal lucidity: An illustration with a contrastive case study. *Mortality,* 1–14.

Nahm, M., & Greyson, B. (2009). Terminal lucidity in patients with chronic schizophrenia and dementia: A survey of the literature. *Journal of Nervous and Mental Disease, 197,* 942–944.

Nahm, M., Greyson, B., Kelly, E. W., & Haraldsson, E. (2012). Terminal lucidity: A review and a case collection. *Archives of Gerontology and Geriatrics, 55,* 138–142.

Ney, D. B., Peterson, A., & Karlawish, J. (2021). The ethical implications of paradoxical lucidity in persons with dementia. *Journal of the American Geriatrics Society, 69,* 3617–3622.

Schreiber, T. P., & Bennett, M. J. (2014). Identification and validation of premortem surge. *Journal of Hospice and Palliative Nursing, 16,* 430–437.

Smith, J. A. (2004). Reflecting on the development of interpretative phenomenological analysis and its contribution to qualitative research in psychology. *Qualitative Research in Psychology, 1,* 39–54.

Wholihan, D. (2016). Seeing the light: End-of-life experiences – Visions, energy surges, and other death bed phenomena. *Nursing Clinics of North America, 51,* 489–500.

Chapter Four

Implications of Terminal Lucidity for Consciousness Studies and Health Care

MARJORIE WOOLLACOTT

Abstract

Research on terminal lucidity shows that clear consciousness can continue in people, despite disease processes such as severely impaired brain function from advanced dementia, severe stroke, or coma. A model of consciousness positing that conscious awareness is fundamental to human existence, and that brains only filter this more fundamental conscious awareness, is supported by the data. Evidence suggests that at the end stages of life, activity in brain filters such as the default-mode network and left-brain language centers, which normally limit awareness to mundane levels of processing, diminish so much that individuals gain momentary access to vaster consciousness, and return to mental clarity. Another key insight from research on caregivers of individuals who experience terminal lucidity before passing, is that death can and should be transformative. It is therefore critical that terminal lucidity experiences become more fully understood and reframed as a natural part of the dying process.

Introduction

The previous chapters covered research on the nature of terminal lucidity in both adults and children. They have provided data indicating that when the brain and associated physiological systems have been compromised by disease at the end stage of life, these patients often experience confusion and loss of the ability to communicate and move. These changes are often associated with documented damage to sensory, cognitive, and motor areas of the brain. Nevertheless, in a small but significant subpopulation, varying degrees of lucidity return to the individual in the period just before death. This phenomenon can be as simple as a wife who had been unable to move or speak due to dementia or coma, opening her eyes and saying her deceased husband's name with a smile on her face, just before she dies. The phenomena can also include more animated and extended interactions with family, during which an individual eats a last meal and converses lovingly and with gratitude, before the person lapses back into coma and passes away.

What are the implications for consciousness studies, if we accept with curiosity the credibility of the data from these studies on terminal lucidity? This research does not support the commonly held hypothesis that consciousness solely emerges from neural activity. This is because in instances of terminal lucidity, despite the absence of normal neural function in key brain cortical areas in for example advanced dementia, severe stroke or coma, clear consciousness is present.

In this chapter we will examine specific examples of documented end-of-life loss of brain and associated physiological function in which, despite this, individuals return to clarity in their last moments of life. We will then discuss aspects of a model of consciousness that accommodates this phenomenon of terminal lucidity. We will also explore implications of the research findings for end-of-life care, including giving family members more opportunity to be with loved ones at the time of death. In fact, it may be valuable to alert families to the possibility of a last caring communication with their loved one, if family members are able to be present with the dying person in the last days or hours of life.

As a neuroscientist, and a professor in the Institute of Neuroscience and the Department of Human Physiology at the University of Oregon, I trained in the materialist theory of consciousness in which activities in specific areas of the brain are considered the sole producer of awareness. Because of this training, I struggled for years to accept the validity of the data on terminal lucidity presented in the previous chapters.

Here are the data that are challenging from the materialist lens. Individuals with Alzheimer's disease at the end of life have been documented to have severe damage to or loss of nerve cells, and those cells' connections in the brain. This is associated with loss of memory, confusion and the inability to recognize family members. Forms of dementia such as Alzheimer's, Lewy Body Dementia, and Fronto-parietal dementia, are considered irreversible (Schneider, 2022). An example of this irreversible brain atrophy is shown in Figure 1.

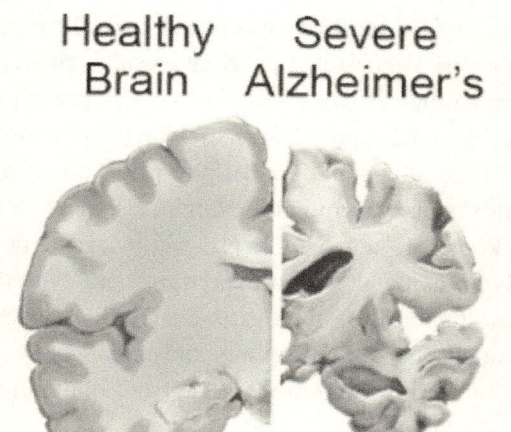

Figure 1. Diagram of the cross-section of a healthy brain vs. one of an individual with Alzheimer's disease. (National Institute on Aging: https://www.nia.nih.gov/health/alzheimers-and-dementia/alzheimers-disease-fact-sheet)

As this brain degeneration is defined as irreversibly damaging the function of the brain, lucidity returning at the end of life should be impossible, according to the materialist hypothesis in which lucid awareness is solely produced by the brain. Thus, the data presented in numerous scientific studies and in the previous chapters are fascinating, but puzzling and controversial. The data imply that mind or consciousness can continue in some way that is uncoupled from the brain.

In an interview on the topic of the occurrence of unusual lucid episodes in dementia diseases and their implications, Dr. Basil Eldadah, the chief supervisory medical officer at the Division of Geriatrics and Clinical Gerontology at the U.S. National Institute on Aging (NIA) said, "The opportunities are immense. It gives us some pause with regard to our current theories and understanding about the nature of dementia. We've seen enough examples of this to be reassured that dementia can be reversed—albeit temporarily, very transiently—nevertheless, it does reverse. And so the question then is how." He also said, "Based on the preliminary data that we heard from our [six NIH] grantees, I think it's safe to say that this phenomenon exists, and it likely exists more often than we expect, or than we would have believed" (Godfrey, 2021).

Possible Models of Consciousness that Could Support the Phenomenology of Terminal Lucidity Experiences

With data accumulating on the phenomenon of terminal lucidity, and increasing acceptance of the validity of research on the phenomenon, are there other models than the current materialist/physicalist model of consciousness, which could better explain terminal lucidity's existence? In fact, there is an alternative view known as "idealism" in philosophical traditions. It posits that consciousness is fundamental to human beings and everything that exists. It is therefore also the basis of our awareness (Farris & Göcke, 2022; Planck, 1931). In this context, many philosophers and scientists posit that the brain functions as a filter to this more fundamental and non-materialist aspect of reality (Grosso, 2015; James, 1903).

Described as the filter theory, this model proposes that the brain serves a permissive or transmissive function, controlling access to expanded awareness or consciousness. William James and others proposed that the brain is not the generator of conscious awareness, but is instead the organ that adapts or channels wider awareness into the needs of everyday living. The brain is then normally seen as functioning as an interface, which selects, focuses, and constrains the processes of a wider mind and consciousness (Woollacott & Weiler, 2025).

These theories that postulate the fundamental nature of consciousness (Hoffman, 2014; Kastrup, 2017, Kelly et al., 2015) are often described as theories of non-local consciousness (Nahm, 2023). These researchers question the view that conscious awareness can be completely understood as based on neuronal activity, within what they consider a causally closed system of solely physical processes.

According to this theory of non-local consciousness, certain perceptual or cognitive phenomena take place outside the constraints of brain-based neural processing and the five senses. Therefore, under certain circumstances—such as altered states, deep meditation, or end-of-life experiences like terminal lucidity—conscious awareness and associated behaviors may exist beyond the physicality of an individual organism. This would allow the organism to interact with a wider cognitive domain or information field, in a way that is not yet understood within dominant neuroscientific frameworks (Herce, 2016; Kuhn, 2024; van Lommel, 2013; Wahbeh et al., 2022; Woollacott & Weiler, 2025).

With this model of conscious awareness in mind, the disease process of the dementias, for example, could be hypothesized to cause the deterioration and death of cells within normal neural pathways underlying brain-based memory, such as the hippocampus, and also underlying cognitive orientation, such as the frontal lobes. This brain deterioration would lead to the documented symptoms of these diseases, including memory loss, disorientation and confusion, as these physical pathways would be either compromised, or no longer functional (Schneider, 2022).

However, it is possible that at the end-stages of life, activity in the filters such as the default-mode network, left-brain language and conceptual filters, which normally limit awareness to more mundane levels of processing, is also substantially diminished (Woollacott & Weiler, 2025). Because of this reduction, the individual now has access to wider non-local consciousness, allowing their lucidity to return briefly before the physiological systems shut down entirely, and death of the physical body occurs.

An interesting paradox regarding these cases of dementia, is that traditional medical perspective assumes the lucid self is extinguished by the diminished and altered states of awareness associated with neural loss. However, when the original self returns despite this physical degradation of the brain, this phenomenon suggests the existence of a more permanent selfhood, or personal identity, apart from the brain. This return of lucidity implies that for one's original self to return it must have remained during the physical conditions of dementia and other brain disorders, although hidden (Batthyány, 2023; Nahm, 2012).

Research supported by the U.S. National Institute on Aging is currently exploring the physiological activity in the brain during these end stages of life in patients with dementia. Answers to these questions may be further elucidated in the coming years (Gilmore-Bykovskyi et al., 2022).

Implications of the Results of the Current Research on Terminal Lucidity for Patient Care

To emphasize the power of research on terminal lucidity for transforming patient care, I share one nurse's response after witnessing terminal lucidity in a patient with dementia. Like the examples discussed in chapter 4, this shows terminal lucidity through the eyes of a witness, emphasizing the effect of these experiences on the family and on care givers. The nurse said:

> "Before this happened, I had become fairly cynical about the 'human vegetables' I cared for. Now I understand that I am caring for nurslings of immortality. Had you seen what I saw, you would understand that dementia can affect the soul but it will not destroy it. I only wish I would have known this earlier." (Batthyány, 2014)

In terms of how witnessing a terminal lucidity experience can transform the spiritual beliefs of the caregiver, I wanted to share this particular response, as it is very profound. The life of a young woman whose fiancé was dying from a brain tumor was transformed into a deep interest in things beyond the material, as a result of witnessing his terminal lucidity. She wrote:

> "In the summer of 1975 my lover was diagnosed with a brain tumor. It was located in the left brain hemisphere near the speech center and too deeply embedded to be operated out. Not long after, he lost his power of speech. From one day to the next he was struck dumb. He was 42 at the prime of life and fully engaged in building a career. He was transferred to the palliative care unit and over the following six months I would visit him daily to comfort and support him on his downhill journey. At first during my daily visits, I would talk to him about what was going on in the world. But this didn't hold his interest for very long. Soon he would sink back into himself in a deep place inside, where he was engulfed with grief. And so I witnessed the phases of his deterioration from human to animal to vegetable first hand.
>
> Then three days before he passed, when I entered the familiar room, I was surprised at the brightness there. It was like summer sunshine. It came from his face which was glowing and his eyes were very bright and sparkling They spoke to me of joy, hope and wonder. His soul had returned to give me a message of life eternal and oneness. I was 36 at the time and my life totally changed. I had to find out. I had been like most of my generation, not open to anything beyond the material. I was with a political group and it was all about changing the outer world. But then I was so thrown by it that I spent several years learning meditation..., because I had to find some answers. So that is how I found my life path, that lasted to the age I am now. My main purpose is to experience rather than think. And to become more aware through meditation, which I have been doing since then, to have a deeper experience while I am living, and not on the level of words."

These two examples among many, give a sense of the profound transformation that is possible in the worldview of a caregiver, upon seeing the return of clarity and the light to an individual whose body and mind have been ravaged by dementia, cancer, or stroke.

The implications of this information regarding states of awareness of individuals with dementia, debilitating stroke, end-stage cancer and/or coma (as discussed especially in Chapter 5) are enormous.

First, as documented in Chapter 5, it might be possible that an individual diagnosed with conditions including dementia or end-stage cancer, is fully aware, even though they are seemingly minimally conscious or unconscious. In one 1820 case of terminal lucidity, a nun went "raving mad" after contracting scarlet fever, and was admitted to an asylum. The nun's madness continued for three years until three weeks before her death, when unexpectedly all traces of her madness disappeared.

When the nun's sister visited her, the nun remembered all details of the three years of insanity and said she felt regretful for her behavior. She soon died lucidly and in peace, in the arms of her brother-in-law. However, when an autopsy was performed after the nun's death her brain was clearly pathological, including the tissue being swollen and soft (Nahm et al., 2012).

While many healthcare workers already are aware of terminal lucidity, the implication of these cases is that it is important to speak personally and lovingly to patients with these conditions of severe mental confusion, apparent minimal awareness, or coma. All caregivers need to cultivate the understanding that there is a sacred human being inside that body, who may be hearing all that you say and all that you do, and that this is a person who deserves being respected and cared for. And in order to encourage family members to be open to this understanding, it is especially important for the health provider to role-model this perspective and behavior.

Implications for End-of-Life Care in Children and Adults

The terminal lucidity experiences described in the previous chapters were very meaningful for families, their dying loved ones, and also witnessing healthcare workers. Learning from these experiences, we believe it is important to create care environments for adults and children in their last stages of life, which support emergence of periods of terminal lucidity.

End of Life Care in Adults

In recent years an important addition to end-of-life health care in most countries has been increased availability of hospice care, and the option to die at home, surrounded by family and friends. However, though at-home hospice care is often available, a recent review noted that very many patients still die in acute and long-term care facilities. In Western countries, 45% of dementia deaths occur in skilled nursing facilities, and 17 percent in acute care hospitals. These hospital settings reduce the opportunities for close interactions with family members, friends, health care providers, and spiritual mentors, all of which nurture patients spiritually, and can encourage terminal lucidity (Clyne et al., 2022; Edwards et al., 2010).

In a recent review covering the need for medical professionals to understand patients' perceptions of their own spiritual needs when approaching the end of life, the authors concluded that this understanding is essential in supporting the delivery of patient-centered care. They noted that spiritual care is internationally considered to be an essential arena of palliative care. Spiritual care does not simply refer to having access to a counselor from a religious community, but includes spirituality more broadly, defined as "the aspect of humanity that refers to the way individuals seek and express meaning and purpose, and the way they experience their connectedness to the moment, to self, to others, to nature and to the significant or sacred" (Clyne et al., 2022, p. e550).

With this in mind, it is notable that spiritual care is typically not provided by healthcare professionals, with the barriers to this care being lack of time; personal, cultural or institutional factors; and professional educational needs (Clyne et al., 2022). One reason noted for this was insufficient spiritual training for palliative care professionals.

Thus, one of the recommendations from this study was to acknowledge that relationship itself is an intrinsic component of spirituality. The study recommended the cultivation of relationship as a central focus of spiritual care, for patients at the end of life. This would involve emphasizing the development of palliative care training focused on how to engage patients on topics of spirituality. This includes listening openly and attentively to patients, being guided by patients, and allowing them to express what is important to them.

The authors also noted the importance of facilitating the family in providing spiritual care, making sure that family has access to patients in inpatient facilities, and that the environment includes comfortable visitation rooms (Clyne et al., 2022).

The application of these suggestions seems highly relevant to the topic of terminal lucidity. It is possible that healthcare professionals increasingly educated in this area of spirituality and end-of-life care, will be more attentive to these moments of lucidity at the end of life, call attention to them in communicating with family members, and also be transformed themselves by witnessing these events. In relation to the above comments, I recently had the following interchange with a physician from the Netherlands on this topic.

A few months ago, I shared in a podcast interview our team's research on healthcare workers and family members witnessing dying patients' terminal lucidity. After the interview I was contacted by a physician in the Netherlands who works with patients with dementia, and who expressed interest in our work. When I asked if he had witnessed terminal lucidity, he told me he had not.

He said, "It is true that I am often not present in the hours before death or only for a short time to assess whether someone is comfortable." However, he followed by saying, "It makes me more aware now to specifically ask about those moments of clarity in the phase just before dying... Recently, I participated in an ayahuasca ceremony with my sister, and it has greatly changed my perspective on life and death. I do not believe it is a coincidence that what is happening now is coming my way."

Clearly personal experience, which enhanced his own interest in spirituality, has significantly increased his curiosity about these end-of-life experiences, contributing to his becoming more aware as a physician. This shows us that awareness of end-of-life phenomena, including terminal lucidity, is very limited among physicians who treat patients with dementia and other similar illnesses. This may be one reason there are not more reported incidences of terminal lucidity among individuals, at the ends of their lives on earth.

This story also suggests that if a physician undergoes a spiritual experience, their curiosity about terminal lucidity, and thus awareness of it, increase dramatically. I believe their sensitivity to the presence of these phenomena in their patients also significantly increases. This physician mentioned he will question other health care workers about their own experiences of terminal lucidity, to better appreciate its prevalence as an end-of-life experience.

About research on terminal lucidity, he said, "It is a beautiful perspective that aligns with my new experiences."

End of Life Care in Children

As noted in Chapter 1, terminal lucidity also has been reported in children who have had severe mental impairment, during the final stages of diseases, such as cancer. During their lucid episode, the children may report an awareness of their coming death and reassure parents that they will be okay (Roehrs et al., 2024). Are there ways we can increase awareness of the possibility of terminal lucidity during end-of-life care in children? This awareness is growing in pediatric care in America, and in other countries as well.

An American healthcare worker who has been an advocate of the creation of nurturing end-of-life care environments for children is Dr. Kathy Hull, a psychologist in pediatric oncology. Dr. Hull founded George Mark Children's House, in a rural area of California, to offer medical care and management related to end-of-life experiences for children (Novak, 2004). Hull remarks that there are currently only two possibilities in the U.S. for families to find care for their children who are terminally ill. One possibility is, with the aid of hospice care, to die at home, though these services are not easily available. Alternatively, children may die in a hospital, with this often occurring in an intensive care unit (Woollacott & Tassell-Matamua, 2025).

In response, she and her clinical team have created a residential medical care environment, which offers a beautiful setting giving quality of life for these children during this time of their life. This setting, with kind and loving healthcare, then promotes the natural emergence of end-of-life experiences as part of the dying process. These environments also help families and their children have meaningful and intimate moments of communication, during this important phase of life.

In Europe and New Zealand end-of-life care for children is also becoming a priority in the healthcare system. The European Association for Palliative Care has published an atlas of children's palliative care in the countries of Europe (Fraser et al., 2020). New Zealand leaders have developed Rainbow Place, a specialist hospice service for children which focusses on supporting families to enhance their time together, acknowledging that parents and caregivers know their children best.

While these advancements are heartening, the majority of children still die in ICUs. Therefore, an important need is to educate hospital medical personnel in the advantages of the compassionate and nurturing care that is required, so that children and families can be more consistently together—physically, emotionally, psychologically, spiritually—at this critical time in life (Woollacott & Tassell-Matamua, 2025).

Summary and Conclusions

Research on terminal lucidity does not support the commonly held belief that consciousness solely emerges from neural activity. Instead, research shows that clear consciousness is present in each individual, despite situations such as severely impaired brain function from advanced dementia, severe stroke or coma. This alternative model, which posits that conscious awareness is fundamental to human existence, and that the brain functions as a filter to this more fundamental aspect of reality, is supported by the data.

It is thus possible that at the end stages of life, activity in the brain filters such as default-mode network and left-brain language centers, which normally limit awareness to more mundane levels of processing, are so diminished that the individual now has access to wider non-local consciousness. This access in turn allows their clarity to return briefly in instances of terminal lucidity, before the physiological systems shut down entirely and death of the physical body occurs.

Another key insight from our research on the narratives of caregivers and family members of adults and children who experience terminal lucidity before passing, is that death can and should be transformative. This is the case for the dying individual, whether a child or an adult, and for their families.

Terminal lucidity is physically, emotionally, psychologically, and spiritually nurturing, for the individual having the experience. At the same time, simply witnessing terminal lucidity transforms the worldview of the vast majority of family members and medical caregivers, increasing their sense of spirituality, decreasing their fear of death, and realigning the way they interact with others.

It is therefore critical that terminal lucidity experiences become more fully understood and reframed as a natural part of the dying process. It is also critical that a dying individual's environment is one that promotes the occurrence of terminal lucidity.

As terminal lucidity is recognized, the feelings of family, caregivers and friends regarding the passing of their loved ones, need no longer be solely feelings of sadness. Instead, those feelings can also include peace and joy, knowing that the final days, hours and moments of their loved ones included an unanticipated yet exceptional experience, which was powerfully transformative for all.

This experience of terminal lucidity suggests that the essential nature of their family member—their spirit or consciousness—did not die with the body. Instead, this essential nature simply separated from the diseased body at the time of death, and moved into another realm that the loved one considers "home" (Woollacott & Tassell-Matamua, 2025).

Acknowledgements

The authors wish to acknowledgement members of the Terminal Lucidity Research team, whose collective wisdom is implicitly embedded in this chapter. This work was supported by funding from the Bial Foundation (Application ID:129/2022).

References

Batthyány, A. (2014). Terminal lucidity: Preliminary data. Presentation held at the *International Association of Near-Death Studies Annual Conference.*

Batthyány, A. (2023). *Threshold: Terminal lucidity and the border of life and death.* St. Martin's Essentials.

Clyne, B., O'Neill, S. M., Nuzum, D., O'Neill, M., Larkin, J., Ryan, M., & Smith, S. M. (2022). Patients' spirituality perspectives at the end of life: A qualitative evidence synthesis. *British Medical Journal Supportive & Palliative Care, 12,* e550–e561.

Edwards, A., Pang, N., Shiu, V., & Chan, C. (2010). Review: The understanding of spirituality and the potential role of spiritual care in end-of-life and palliative care: A meta-study of qualitative research. *Palliative Medicine, 24,* 753–70.

Farris, J., & Göcke, B. P. (Eds.). (2022). *The Routledge handbook of idealism and immaterialism.* Routledge.

Gilmore-Bykovskyi, A., Griffin, J. M., Mueller, K. D., Parnia, S., & Kolanowski, A. (2023). Toward harmonization of strategies for investigating lucidity in AD/ADRD: A preliminary research framework. *Alzheimer's and Dementia, 19,* 343–352.

Godfrey, A. (2021). 'The clouds cleared': What terminal lucidity teaches us about life, death and dementia. Interview with B. Eldadah, quoted in *The Guardian.* Retrieved March 23, 2025. https://www.theguardian.com/society/2021/feb/23/the-clouds-cleared-what-terminal-lucidity-teaches-us-about-life-death-and-dementia

Grosso, M. (2015). The "transmission" model of mind and body. A brief history. In E. F. Kelly, A. Crabtree, & P. Marshall (Eds.), *Beyond physicalism: Toward reconciliation of science and spirituality* (pp. 79–113). Rowman & Littlefield.

Herce, R. (2016). Non-locality of the phenomenon of consciousness according to Roger Penrose. *Dialogo, 3,* 127–134.

Hoffman, D. D. (2014). The origin of time in conscious agents. *Cosmology, 18,* 494–520.

Kastrup, B. (2017). An ontological solution to the mind-body problem. *Philosophies, 2,* 10.

Kelly, E. F., Crabtree, A., & Marshall, P. (2015). *Beyond physicalism: Toward reconciliation of science and spirituality.* Rowman & Littlefield.

Kuhn, R. L. (2024). A landscape of consciousness: Toward a taxonomy of explanations and implications. *Progress in Biophysics and Molecular Biology, 190,* 28–69.

Nahm, M. (2012). *Wenn die Dunkelheit ein Ende findet: Terminale Geistesklarheit und andere Phänomene in Todesnähe.* Amerang.

Nahm, M. (2023). *The arcane nexus. Assessing the roots of non-local consciousness.* Available at: https://noetic.org/prize-2024/

Nahm, M., Greyson, B., Kelly, E.W., & Haraldsson, E. (2012). Terminal lucidity: A review and case collection. *Archives of Gerontology and Geriatrics, 55,* 138–142.

Novak, L. (2004). A home away from home for dying children. *New York Times,* accessed Feb. 8, 2024. https://www.nytimes.com/2004/02/10/health/a-home-away-from-home-for-dying-children.html

Planck, M. (25 January 1931), *The Observer,* interview; p. 17, column 3.

Roehrs, P., Fenwick, P., Greyson, B., Kellehear, A., Kothe, K., Nahm, M., Roe, C., Tassell-Matamua, N., & Woollacott, M. (2024). Terminal lucidity in a pediatric oncology clinic. *Journal of Nervous and Mental Disease, 212*, 57–60.

Schneider, J. (2022). Continuum: Lifelong learning in neurology. *Neurology of Dementia, 28*, 834–851.

van Lommel, P. (2013). Non-local consciousness a concept based on scientific research on near-death experiences during cardiac arrest. *Journal of Consciousness Studies, 20*, 7–48.

Wahbeh, H., Radin, D., Cannard, C., & Delorme, A. (2022). What if consciousness is not an emergent property of the brain? Observational and empirical challenges to materialistic models. *Frontiers in Psychology, 13*, 955594.

Woollacott, M, & Weiler, M. (2025). Neural filters to conscious awareness and the phenomena that reduce their impact. *International Review of Psychiatry,* published online ahead of print, https://doi.org/10.1080/09540261.2025.2478907

Woollacott, M., & Tassell-Matamua, N. (2025). Lucidite terminale chez les enfants: Une etude enc cours [Terminal lucidity in children: An ongoing study]. In C. Fawer (Ed.), *Ces enfants qui dissent voir ou entendre des defunts [Children who say they see or hear the deceased]* (pp. 85–99). Editions Exergue.

PART 2

*New Perspectives on Other
Near-Death Phenomena*

Chapter Five

Clear Minds in Dysfunctional Brains: An Introduction to "Paradoxical Awareness"

MICHAEL NAHM

Abstract

In this chapter, I present an introductory overview on phenomenon of "paradoxical awareness." It concerns the presence of lucid awareness, including the ability to think, in unresponsive people with brain conditions that are usually thought to render impossible the abilities to reason coherently and form memories. In the past, most examples of paradoxical awareness have been reported from the context of near-death experiences. During recent years, however, the presence of lucid awareness in seemingly unconscious comatose patients has gained increased interest as well. This chapter introduces such instances of "locked-in experiences." It puts them in relation to near-death experiences and the phenomenon of awareness during anesthesia, and provides terminological clarifications.

The presence of clear minds in nonresponsive patients whose brain functions are assumed to be severely compromised or even nonfunctional calls for systematic research into this phenomenon. Such investigations could advance our understanding of the circumstances and underpinnings of these paradoxical occurrences. They bear vitally important implications for practical health care and may open new lines of evidence challenging the supposition that consciousness is a mere result of brain physiological processes.

Introduction

Models of brain functioning and neuronal correlates of human consciousness are typically concerned with intact brains. This limitation is unfortunate. The history of scientific progress demonstrates that crucial advances are often made when investigating phenomena at the fringes of established knowledge and theoretical models. Studying the exceptional can lead to much greater advances than studying what lies inside the norm of a given field of research. The presence of lucid awareness under anomalous brain conditions offers such intriguing research possibilities. For more than two centuries, different kinds of such occurrences have been reported by physicians and lay persons. The literature of the early 19th century, for example, contains various accounts concerning people who had a clear mind when their brain functions were thought to be largely dysfunctional (for examples, see Nahm, 2012). Of these phenomena, experiences that have been termed "near-death experiences" (NDEs) have become increasingly known since the 1970s and have lately been recognized as a research topic that warrants serious academic investigations (see Chapter 7 of this book). The interest in several less known but related near-death phenomena has only gained traction among researchers in mainstream settings during recent years. This development is very welcome because it holds the potential to advance our knowledge about the dying process as well as the interplay of the mind and the brain, including the wide variety of brain conditions under which it is apparently possible to be consciously aware.

Nevertheless, attempts to classify these related near-death phenomena and to give them appropriate names are largely lacking or represent unconnected approaches that sometimes conflict with each other. In this chapter, I provide a preliminary typology of the presence of lucid awareness in different kinds of circumstances where lucid awareness should not be occurring according to current models of brain functioning. The aim of this typology is to facilitate communication and streamline future research about these anomalous phenomena. As an overarching concept and term for the presence of lucid awareness under brain conditions that should not allow its occurrence, I use the term "paradoxical consciousness."

The attribute "paradoxical" signifies the anomalous and extraordinary nature of these occurrences. I use it in the tradition of the work of neurosurgeons Keasley Welch and Wilder Penfield who performed brain surgeries in patients with severe epilepsy. When they studied the effects of the removal of brain areas to prevent epileptic seizures, they noticed that the removal of brain areas that were capable of causing movement in limbs when electrically stimulated did sometimes not result in increased paralysis of these limbs, as normally expected, but rather in an improvement of their usability. Welch and Penfield (1950) called this surprising finding "paradoxical improvement."

Similarly, a few years ago, a team of authors including myself have introduced the term of "paradoxical lucidity" into the literature to characterize lucid episodes in people with advanced neurodegenerative diseases (Mashour et al., 2019). The paradoxical nature of these lucid episodes is due to the supposition that the people concerned should not be able to display the reported degrees of lucidity because of their brain conditions. It can be defined as follows:

> An episode of unexpected, spontaneous, meaningful, and relevant communication or connectedness in a patient who is assumed to have permanently lost the capacity for coherent verbal or behavioral interaction due to an advanced neurodegenerative brain condition. (Nahm, 2024a)

Probably the most striking examples are unexpected lucid episodes that occur shortly before people die. Nonresponsive people suffering from a variety of brain conditions such as strokes, tumors, or neurodegenerative dementia diseases have been reported to become unexpectedly lucid again and then die—often, only seconds, minutes, or a few hours after this lucid episode (Batthyány & Greyson, 2021; Nahm, 2012; Nahm et al., 2012; Roehrs et al., 2024). Such cases represent instances of paradoxical terminal lucidity (Nahm, 2022a, 2022b).

In the light of these previous terms, introducing the umbrella term of paradoxical consciousness for an overarching concept referring to clear consciousness under brain conditions that render its occurrence highly improbable appears apt. In fact, there exist several different kinds of such conditions. A basic distinction between two categories of paradoxical consciousness concerns

1. cognitive feats that occur despite considerable anatomical brain deficiencies and
2. cognitive feats that occur despite dysfunctional brain physiology.

In a previous review publication, co-authors and I provided an overview of the first category of paradoxical consciousness, i.e. of grave anatomic deficiencies of the brain that are at odds with the corresponding high degree of cognitive functioning. Among other etiologies, such instances of "paradoxical cognitive functioning" include cases reported from the contexts of the hydrocephalus syndrome (maldeveloped brains due to excess of cerebrospinal fluid that cannot drain from the skull), hemihydranencephaly (people born with only one cerebral hemisphere), and hemispherectomy (operations in which one brain hemisphere is surgically removed or disconnected from the rest of the brain) (Nahm et al., 2017). In some situations, such as lucid episodes occurring in coma with physical brain damage, brain tumors, and in advanced neurodegenerative dementia diseases, anatomic brain damage can go hand in hand with impaired brain physiology. Then, these two categories overlap.

In this chapter, I focus on the presence of a clear mind under circumstances in which severe brain physiological dysfunction appears to play the decisive role for rendering a patient seemingly unconscious. I call this category of paradoxical consciousness "paradoxical awareness" and I define it as follows:

> Paradoxical awareness describes the phenomenon of lucid awareness, including the ability to think, in unresponsive people with brain conditions that are usually thought to render impossible the abilities to reason coherently and form memories. (Nahm, 2024a)

In the following sections, I introduce two subcategories of paradoxical awareness: Those occurring in NDEs and in comas. I describe examples of them and provide clarifications regarding the use of certain terms. Thereafter, I briefly discuss the phenomenon of "awareness during anesthesia" and its relation to paradoxical awareness. A schema of how these different phenomena are related is given in Figure 1 below.

Paradoxical Awareness in NDEs

The presence of clear consciousness in brain physiological states that deviate grossly from the normal condition is probably best known from NDEs, in particular from "critical NDEs" (Nahm & Weibel, 2020) that occur in life-threatening situations due to severe oxygen deprivation of the brain, e. g. after cardiac arrest (Rivas et al., 2023). Paradoxical awareness thus occurs in people who appear to be unconscious for external observers and who can only report having been conscious after they regained their usual waking consciousness.

Recently, however, a team of NDE-researchers assessing cognitive activity and awareness during cardiac arrest referred to the presence of clear minds during NDEs as instances of "paradoxical lucidity" (Parnia et al., 2023). It is understandable that mental feats during critical NDEs when brain physiological functions are severely compromised are depicted as "paradoxical," but it is unfortunate that an already-defined term that refers to a different phenomenon that exclusively occurs in people who are awake and able to communicate with others in real time (see above and Mashour et al., 2019) is transferred to the context of NDEs. Inappropriate usage of terms dilutes and distorts existing definitions and should be avoided. Given that even the name of this study ("AWAreness during REsuscitation", = AWARE) explicitly refers to researching awareness in seemingly unconscious patients, the term "paradoxical awareness" is much better suited for emphasizing the presence of remarkable cognitive feats after cardiac arrest.

Paradoxical Consciousness

Cognitive feats despite anatomical brain deficiencies
- Paradoxical cognitive functioning (hydrocephalus, hemihydranencephaly, hemispherectomy, severe brain lesions)
- Paradoxical (terminal) lucidity

Cognitive feats despite dysfunctional brain physiology
- Paradoxical awareness
  - Critical near-death experiences
  - Locked-in experiences in comas
  - Awareness during anesthesia

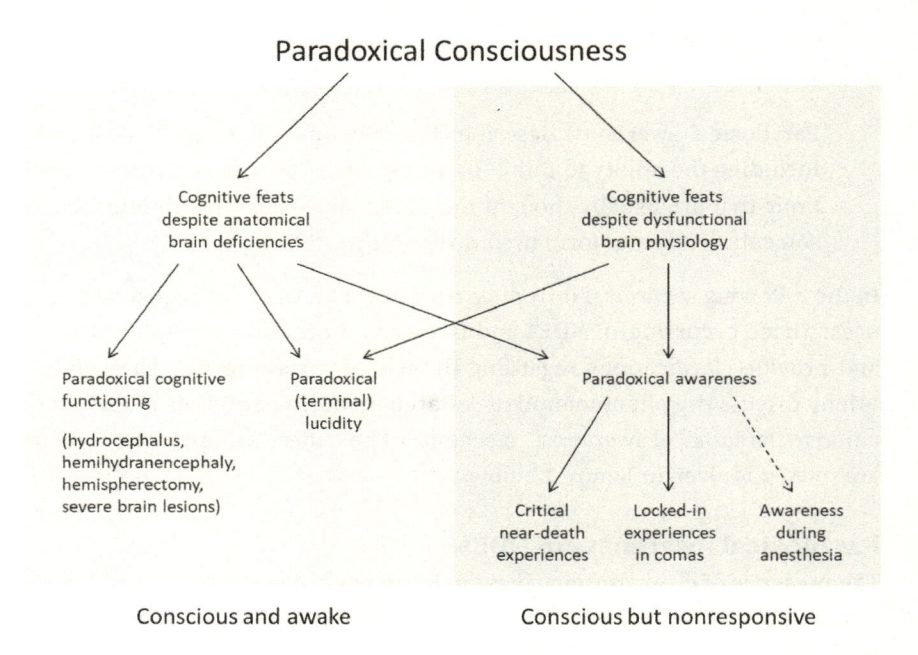

Conscious and awake | Conscious but nonresponsive

Figure 1. Overview of different pathological brain conditions under which it is still possible to have a clear mind. Because these discrepancies are at odds with current neuroscientific models of brain functioning, the presence of clear consciousness in these situations can be regarded as "paradoxical." In this chapter, I present a brief overview on the phenomena subsumed under the subcategory "paradoxical awareness" (see the right lower area of this Figure).

That these cognitive feats do really occur during the time of the severe physiological dysfunction but not during the recovery phase when the brain is slowly regaining its functions is evidenced in particular by out-of-body experiences (OBEs), in which seemingly unconscious people appear to perceive the events in their surroundings from an elevated position in space and in real time. In contrast to what is sometimes asserted by authors promoting neurophysiological models of NDEs, these OBEs can be used as a time marker for the occurrence of NDEs. The supposition that these OBEs are hallucinations reconstructed during the recovery phase is contradicted by empirical evidence and by standard explanatory models for OBEs that typically treat them as experiences made in real-time (Nahm & Weibel, 2020).

But not only OBEs and the probably best known variety of NDEs, pleasurable NDEs, can be regarded as instances of paradoxical awareness in life-threatening situations. The different varieties of distressing NDEs (Greyson, 2023; Melloul et al., 2024) and potential "hallucinations" should likewise not be possible in brains with severely dysfunctional neurophysiology. They can therefore be regarded as instances of paradoxical awareness as well.

In rare cases, paradoxical awareness and paradoxical lucidity can even occur in one and the same person, albeit at different times. This situation can be exemplified with a case of a largely nonresponsive patient in the terminal stage of Alzheimer's disease who was deemed to be barely conscious during the last two years of her disease. When awake, she only stared at the ceiling and didn't seem to follow anything that happened in her surroundings. The night before she died, however, she unexpectedly became lucid (= paradoxical terminal lucidity). She stated she had been fully aware throughout the time of her unresponsiveness (= paradoxical awareness) and thanked the nurses and family members for all they did for her during that time (Bruhn, 2009).

Paradoxical Awareness in Coma Experiences

Case reports of dementia patients who claim having been fully aware when they enter lucid episodes are very rare. But in the context of psychiatric disorders, similar accounts have been reported in the context of terminal lucidity as well. In these cases, people state that they had been present with their normal self during the time of their psychiatric disturbances, but felt forced to behave in this pathological manner and could not let others know that their true self was still present "behind the scenes" as well (Nahm, 2012).

Nevertheless, reports about people who have been comatose but who consciously perceived what happened in their surroundings using chiefly their acoustic sense, have been reported for a very long time. These kinds of paradoxical awareness can be called "locked-in experiences." The patients concerned are aware of the fact that their physical body is in a nonresponsive condition, and their center of awareness is located in this physical body. These people are fully conscious but are virtually trapped in their immobile body.

Such experiences are also known from the "locked-in syndrome." People with this condition are completely paralyzed because of neurological damage to their brain stem that can be caused by various injuries and diseases (Das et al., 2024). Sometimes, physicians and those who visit people suffering from the locked-in syndrome know that these patients are consciously aware inside a nonresponsive body because they previously monitored the trajectory of the disease leading to this final locked-in state, or the patients can still move their eyes in response to questions. In such cases, the cerebral cortex and its physiology are known to function normally, and they can therefore not be regarded as instances of paradoxical awareness.

Regarding coma patients, recent studies in which their brain activity was assessed via EEG and fMRI scans indicated that 25% of them showed signs of cognition (Bodien et al., 2024) and thus, of awareness. Similarly, 25 to 40% of patients who had seemingly been unconscious for some time but awoke from this state, reported that they had been able to hear and understand conversations in their surroundings during that time (Lawrence et al., 2023).

Again, such cases should not be regarded as instances of paradoxical awareness in case it has been established via EEG or fMRI scans that the cortical areas of the brains react in a similar manner to sensory stimuli as brains of healthy people do (Blundon et al., 2020). But neuropsychiatrist Adrian Owen also reported a case in which the brain of a comatose man, Juan, showed no reactions that are indicative of successful processing of stimuli during two scanning examinations. Consequently, he concluded that Juan must be entirely unconscious. Nevertheless, Juan woke up from his coma later. It turned out that he had been fully aware of his environment during all this time. During the scanning procedures, he had tried to show that he was perfectly awake but he could not let others know about his true state. But he remembered and recounted all details of his stay at Owen's hospital correctly. Given that the brain scans of Juan showed no signs of consciousness and cognition, Owen admitted he had no explanation for Juan's experiences in his coma (Owen, 2017).

Owen did not explicitly state whether Juan perceived his surroundings from an in-the-body or from an out-of-the-body perspective, but it seems the former was the case. Similarly, also Bruhn (2009) did not specify whether the mentioned Alzheimer's patient perceived her surroundings from an out-of-body perspective, as in a similar case that was reported to me (Nahm, 2022b), or from an in-the-body perspective. In fact, there are a number of cases in which comatose people with seemingly nonfunctional brains woke up again and reported having been consciously aware and having followed what happened around them from an in-the-body perspective.

One of these cases concerns Gil Avni from Israel. He was diagnosed with a cerebral edema and suffered severe anoxic brain damage that had already affected his brain stem, as evidenced by responses to specific tests of reflexes. As a result, Avni was put in a medically induced coma to minimize the brain's oxygen consumption. He was nevertheless expected to die within hours. However, he recovered again and as in the case of Juan, it turned out he had been consciously aware throughout the 44 hours he stayed in this coma. Avni was able to describe every occurrence and to repeat every conversation that had been held at his bedside. Although he also experienced occasional OBEs throughout his coma, he usually followed what happened around him from an in-the-body perspective via the sense of hearing (Nahm et al., 2025).

Similar locked-in experiences have been reported from a variety of contexts such as a severe infection (Levy, 2015), a severe stroke (Orange, 2014), an accident with a motor vehicle (Morales, 2008), or suffocation followed by cardiac arrest (another case briefly described in Nahm et al., 2025). Some of these patients have even been considered to be "brain dead" and heard the doctors advocate organ donation or the termination of life support at their bedsides (Levy, 2015; Morales, 2008; Orange, 2014).

Such locked-in experiences can be utterly traumatic for those who go through them. It is therefore vital that the occurrence of lucid awareness even in patients whose brain functions are assumed or known to be severely impaired or nonfunctional becomes much better known among medical professionals and the general public.

The presence of lucid awareness in patients whose brain functions are known to be severely compromised is truly paradoxical. But it does occur and the described instances of locked-in experiences demonstrate that it does not only manifest in the manners typically reported from (critical) NDEs. One can only speculate about how many comatose people who never regained consciousness but died in their coma had in fact been consciously aware of their situation and surroundings—even when their brain functions had been severely compromised and showed no sign of conscious cognition, as in the case of Juan—and therefore, perhaps even in the process of organ donation (Nahm et al., 2025; see also Morales, 2008; Rady & Verheijde, 2010).

Awareness during Anesthesia

Another phenomenon that is related to NDEs and coma experiences, and thus to paradoxical awareness, is awareness during anesthesia. It is defined as "postoperative recall of events occurring during the administration of general anesthesia" (Leslie, 2010, p. 75). The relationship between these phenomena is obvious because many NDEs occur under anesthesia, and medically induced comas can likewise be seen as a prolonged kind of anesthesia. Typically, however, the phenomenon of awareness during anesthesia refers to situations in which patients are anesthetized because they undergo surgical operations. But they are not unconscious. They are aware of what is going on. They may lapse in and out of consciousness only briefly, but can also be fully awake but unable to move for considerable time periods. In drastic cases, patients follow the operation while being fully awake inside and experiencing excruciating pain because of the surgical procedures. Needless to say, these experiences are deeply traumatizing as well.

Such cases of awareness during anesthesia are often attributed to inadequate sedation. The brain's usual physiology is not shut down as should be the case. Hence, although this kind of awareness during anesthesia also represents an experience in which people feel trapped inside a nonresponsive body, it cannot be considered an instance of paradoxical awareness.

But the situation is more complex because in fact, a variety of different experiences are lumped together under the umbrella of awareness during anesthesia. These experiences begin with the usual tactile, olfactory and auditory modes of perception mediated via the biological senses. In case the eyelids are not shut completely (Evans, 1987), they can also comprise visual perception. But these perceptions can also blend with hallucinatory elements and become distorted, thus resulting in dream-like experiences of frequently a distressing nature. Still, other kinds of experiences that are unrelated to intraoperative events and that are regarded as dreams during anesthesia have also been described (Leslie, 2010).

Moreover, in several studies on anesthesia awareness, OBEs were likewise reported from anesthetized patients. In some cases, they reported veridical perceptions of the environment from an elevated position, just as in typical NDEs (Mainzer, 1979; Sebel et al., 2004). These OBEs are interpreted as dissociative elements of anesthesia awareness (Osterman et al., 2001; Sebel et al., 2004).

But now, things become tricky! In case OBEs of this kind cannot be explained with the prevailing brain physiology under deep general anesthesia, but are nevertheless regarded as instances of awareness during anesthesia, it is obviously inappropriate and mere circular reasoning to invoke the phenomenon of anesthesia during awareness to explain these OBEs (and NDEs) on a physiological basis (e. g., regarding the NDE of Pamela Reynolds; see Woerlee, 2011, and the critique of Woerlee's approach by Rivas et al., 2023). Similarly, claiming that the occurrence of dreams during deep general anesthesia suffices already to explain all kinds of conscious experiences during anesthesia in neurophysiological terms (Augustine, 2015) is premature and factually presupposes what needs to be explained. We can even turn the tables around: If we assume that our habitual waking consciousness is not produced exclusively by the brain, this obviously also applies to dreams (Nahm, 2024b)—and therefore, also to OBEs and NDEs.

From a scientific and practice-orientate research perspective, the most important task is to systematically assess the correlations between states of mind and brain under conditions of anesthesia. And there is already very compelling evidence that sometimes, they can be decoupled, thus representing instances of paradoxical awareness. This might even apply to dreams and dream-like experiences under conditions of severe brain malfunction, such as deep general anesthesia, distressing critical NDEs, and certain kinds of coma experiences (Pearce & Pearce, 2024; see also Chapter 7 of this book).

In short, it might well be that some kinds of awareness during anesthesia do represent instances of paradoxical awareness. The term and concept of awareness during anesthesia is very general and only refers to the presence of awareness in anesthetized patients. But it says nothing about the reasons for this awareness, be it explicable in neurophysiological terms or not. It is therefore important to perform large-scale systematic studies investigating the incidence and phenomenology of different kinds of awareness that are reported from patients who woke up from anesthesia (and from medically induced comas). Only then can we hope to learn more about their conditions and underpinnings. Performing in-depth interviews and creating scales as a means to assess and describe the different types of awareness in seemingly unconscious patients would be very useful in this respect.

Outlook

The spectrum of cognitive feats despite dysfunctional brain physiology raises questions regarding the standard models of brain functioning. These models rely on the postulate that in order to experience a clear mind, the brain must be in a largely healthy condition and produce matching neuronal correlates to these cognitive feats. But notwithstanding the limited amount of research, researchers, and funding, evidence that undermines this postulate is constantly growing. For example, locked-in experiences under conditions of severe brain malfunction have so far not played a prominent role in these discussions, but I wouldn't be surprised if they are more common than currently assumed and many more remarkable cases could be found. This probably applies to the entire spectrum of coma experiences.

Similarly, more and more related findings regarding other phenomena discussed in this book are constantly being unearthed, and there are even additional areas of research that contribute to the overall picture but are not discussed in this book. I mention only shared dreams (Nahm, 2024b), transplant cases (Carter et al., 2024; Guzzi, 2024), unusual memories of young children (Nahm, 2011; Ohkado, 2014), and importantly, reincarnation cases (Matlock et al., 2024; Nahm, 2023). The manifold interrelations between all these phenomena show that they all are rooted in the same consciousness-related background of reality (Nahm, 2011, 2023).

Taken together, these phenomena provide solid evidence for the notion that mental feats are not always dependent on corresponding brain states. Therefore, they also provide a solid foundation for endorsing a post-materialist view. This view is not only relevant for philosophical and spiritual considerations. For example, accepting the possibility that unresponsive, comatose people can be consciously aware even when their brain functions are severely compromised has very important implications for practical health care. Nevertheless, it needs more research to flesh out phenomenological details and relationships of instances of paradoxical awareness and coma experiences. Different kinds of coma experiences might also require different post-coma coping strategies. I hope that this and other chapters of this book will contribute to the necessary shift in assigning these phenomena and experiences the outstanding significance they deserve, both from theoretical and practical perspectives.

References

Augustine, K. (2015). Near-death experiences are hallucinations. In M. Martin & K. Augustine (Eds.), *The myth of an afterlife: The case against life after death* (pp. 529–569). Rowman & Littlefield.

Batthyány, A., & Greyson, B. (2021). Spontaneous remission of dementia before death: Results from a study on paradoxical lucidity. *Psychology of Consciousness: Theory, Research, and Practice, 8,* 1–8.

Blundon, E. G., Gallagher, R. E., & Ward, L. M. (2020). Electrophysiological evidence of preserved hearing at the end of life. *Scientific Reports, 10,* 10336.

Bodien, Y. G., Allanson, J., Cardone, P., Bonhomme, A., Carmona, J., Chatelle, C., Chennu, S., Conte, M., Dehaene, S., Finoia, P., Heinonen, G., Hersh, J. E., Kamau, E., Lawrence, P. K., Lupson, V. C., Meydan, A., Rohaut, B., Sanders, W. R., Sitt, J. D., ... Schiff, N. D. (2024). Cognitive motor dissociation in disorders of consciousness. *New England Journal of Medicine, 391,* 598–608.

Bruhn, J. (2009). *Blicke hinter den Horizont. Nahtodeserlebnisse: Deutung, Bedeutung* (2. ed.). Alster-Verlag.

Carter, B., Khoshnaw, L., Simmons, M., Hines, L., Wolfe, B., & Liester, M. (2024). Personality changes associated with organ transplants. *Transplantology, 5,* 12–26.

Das, J. M., Anosike, K., & Asuncion, R. M. D. (2024). *Locked-in syndrome.* StatPearls [Internet]. http://www.ncbi.nlm.nih.gov/books/NBK559026/

Evans, J. M. (1987). Patients' experiences of awareness during general anaesthesia. In M. Rosen & J. N. Lunn (Eds.), *Consciousness, awareness and pain in general anaesthesia* (pp. 184–192). Butterworths.

Greyson, B. (2023). The darker side of near-death experiences. *Journal of Scientific Exploration, 37,* 683–698.

Guzzi, J. (2024). The phantom of the organ. *New England Journal of Medicine, 390,* 2236–2237.

Lawrence, M., Ramirez, R. P., & Bauer, P. J. (2023). Communicating with unconscious patients: An overview. *Dimensions of Critical Care Nursing, 42,* 3.

Leslie, K. (2010). Dreaming during anesthesia. In G. A. Mashour (Ed.), *Consciousness, awareness, and anesthesia* (pp. 74–89). Cambridge University Press.

Levy, A. (2015). Coma victim back from the dead after hearing doctors ask her husband permission to switch off her life support. *Daily Mail.*

https://www.dailymail.co.uk/news/article-2998990/Coma-victim-dead-hearing-doctors-ask-husband-permission-switch-life-support.html

Mainzer, J. (1979). Awareness, muscle relaxants and balanced anaesthesia. *Canadian Anaesthetists' Society Journal, 26,* 386–393.

Mashour, G. A., Frank, L., Batthyany, A., Kolanowski, A. M., Nahm, M., Schulman-Green, D., Greyson, B., Pakhomov, S., Karlawish, J., & Shah, R. C. (2019). Paradoxical lucidity: A potential paradigm shift for the neurobiology and treatment of severe dementias. *Alzheimer's & Dementia, 15,* 1107–1114.

Matlock, J. G., Weerasekera, A., & Nahm, M. (2024). The case of Gnanathilaka Baddevithana: An early independent investigation of one of Ian Stevenson's reincarnation cases. *Journal of Scientific Exploration, 38,* 614–635.

Melloul, A. A., Kinnunen, K., & Cardeña, E. (2024). The phenomenology of distressing near-death experiences and their aftereffects. *Journal of Anomalous Experience and Cognition, 4,* 192–224.

Morales, N. (2008). "Dead" man recovering after ATV accident. *nbcnews.* https://www.nbcnews.com/id/wbna23768436

Nahm, M. (2011). Reflections on the context of near-death experiences. *Journal of Scientific Exploration, 25,* 453–478.

Nahm, M. (2012). *Wenn die Dunkelheit ein Ende findet: Terminale Geistesklarheit und andere Phänomene in Todesnähe.* Crotona.

Nahm, M. (2022a). Terminal lucidity versus paradoxical lucidity: A terminological clarification. *Alzheimer's & Dementia, 18,* 538–539.

Nahm, M. (2022b). The importance of the exceptional in tackling riddles of consciousness and unusual episodes of lucidity. *Journal of Anomalous Experience and Cognition, 2,* 264–296.

Nahm, M. (2023). Climbing mount evidence: A strategic assessment of the best available evidence for the survival of human consciousness after permanent bodily death (revised version). In Bigelow Institute for Consciousness Studies (BICS) (Eds.), *Winning essays 2023: Proof of survival of human consciousness beyond permanent bodily death* (vol. 3, pp. 107–203). BICS.

Nahm, M. (2024a). Defining terminal lucidity: Taking the need for accuracy and integrity seriously. *Journal of Near-Death Studies, 42,* 70–78.

Nahm, M. (2024b). *The arcane nexus: Assessing the roots of non-local consciousness.* Available at: https://noetic.org/prize-2024/

Nahm, M., & Weibel, A. (2020). The significance of autoscopies as a time marker for the occurrence of near-death experiences. *Journal of Near-Death Studies, 38,* 26–50.

Nahm, M., Greyson, B., Kelly, E. W., & Haraldsson, E. (2012). Terminal lucidity: A review and a case collection. *Archives of Gerontology and Geriatrics, 55,* 138–142.

Nahm, M., Lawrence, M., van Lommel, P., Alon Konichezky, S., & Shamir, E.-H. (2025). Lucid awareness in nonresponsive patients: A "locked-in experience" and its implications. *Journal of Scientific Exploration,* in press.

Nahm, M., Rousseau, D., & Greyson, B. (2017). Discrepancy between cerebral structure and cognitive functioning: A review. *Journal of Nervous and Mental Disease, 205,* 967–972.

Ohkado, M. (2014). Children with life-between-life memories. *Journal of Scientific Exploration, 28,* 477–490.

Orange, R. (2014). Swedish stroke patient hears doctors discuss removing his organs. Telegraph. https://www.telegraph.co.uk/news/worldnews/europe/sweden/10745138/Swedish-stroke-patient-hears-doctors-discuss-removing-his-organs.html

Osterman, J. E., Hopper, J., Heran, W. J., Keane, T. M., & van der Kolk, B. A. (2001). Awareness under anesthesia and the development of posttraumatic stress disorder. *General Hospital Psychiatry, 23,* 198–204.

Owen, A. (2017). *Into the gray zone. A neuroscientist explores the border between life and death.* Scribner.

Parnia, S., Shirazi, T. K., Patel, J., Tran, L., Sinha, N., [...] & Deakin, C. D. (2023). AWAreness during REsuscitation – II: A multi-center study of consciousness and awareness in cardiac arrest. *Resuscitation, 191,* 109903.

Pearce, A., & Pearce, B. (2024). Coma and near-death experience: *The beautiful, disturbing, and dangerous world of the unconscious.* Park Street Press.

Rady, M. Y., & Verheijde, J. L. (2010). General anesthesia for surgical procurement in no-heart-beating organ donation: Why we should care. *Anesthesia & Analgesia, 111,* 1562.

Rivas, T., Dirven, A., & Smit, R. H. (2023). *The self does not die: Verified paranormal phenomena from near-death experiences* (2. ed.). International Association for Near-Death Studies.

Roehrs, P., Fenwick, P., Greyson, B., Kellehear, A., Kothe, K., Nahm, M., Roe, C., Tassell-Matamua, N., & Woollacott, M. (2024). Terminal lucidity in a pediatric oncology clinic. *Journal of Nervous and Mental Disease, 212,* 57–60.

Sebel, P. S., Bowdle, T. A., Ghoneim, M. M., Rampil, I. J., Padilla, R. E., Gan, T. J., & Domino, K. B. (2004). The incidence of awareness during anesthesia: A multicenter United States study. *Anesthesia and Analgesia, 99,* 833–839.

Welch, K., & Penfield, W. (1950). Paradoxical improvement in hemiplegia following cortical excision. *Journal of Neurosurgery, 7,* 414–420.

Woerlee, G. M. (2011). Could Pam Reynolds hear? A new investigation into the possibility of hearing during this famous near-death experience. *Journal of Near-Death Studies, 30,* 3–25.

Chapter Six

Near-Death Experiences: A Glance Beyond the River Styx

MARIETA PEHLIVANOVA
& BRUCE GREYSON

Abstract

This chapter explores the phenomenology, impact, and broader implications of near-death experiences (NDEs). These are subjective experiences that individuals sometimes report while they are close to death or in critical medical condition. We survey relevant literature from decades of academic research on these experiences, including explanatory models for their occurrence. In particular, we consider whether these experiences challenge strictly physicalist interpretations of consciousness, including the assumption that consciousness is solely a product of brain activity and ceases entirely at death. NDEs hold the potential not only to transform individuals who experience them, but also to influence societal perspectives on life and death, as well as our understanding of the nature of human consciousness.

Introduction

One of the most intriguing phenomena on the spectrum of end-of-life experiences is the near-death experience (NDE). NDEs have captivated scientists, philosophers, and popular audiences alike with their potential to reveal transcendent aspects of death and what may lie beyond it, as well as profound lessons on how to live a meaningful life. Importantly, along with other phenomena explored in this collection, NDEs may offer evidence for the potential independence of consciousness from the brain and its continuity beyond bodily death. These subjective and often mystical experiences are reported by some individuals who were physiologically (or sometimes only psychologically) close to death, including clinical death and subsequent resuscitation (Holden et al., 2009; Moody, 1975; Parnia et al., 2001; van Lommel et al., 2001). As indicated in the Introduction of this book, they therefore offer a glance beyond the River Styx, the Greek mythological boundary between the lands of the living and of the dead.

While there is currently no clinical definition of NDEs, these experiences commonly feature feelings of peace and unconditional love, though some may be distressing (Greyson, 2023). Other typical features include a sensation of existing outside of one's body, heightened sensory perception, and an apparent awareness beyond physical circumstances, including encounters with deceased spirits, a sense of visiting a mystical realm, a review life, or witnessing events displaced in space and time (Greyson, 1983b; Moody, 1975; Zingrone & Alvarado, 2009). Certain features of these experiences—particularly corroborated reports of events and deceased individuals unknown to the experiencer—challenge prevailing materialist views that reduce consciousness solely to physical processes (Greyson, 2010a; Kelly et al., 2007).

Research interest in NDEs has burgeoned in the past five decades (Sleutjes et al., 2014), but reports of this phenomenon date back to antiquity, for example in the writings of Ancient Greek philosophers. An early autobiographical description of an NDE, along with a collection of similar accounts, was published by Swiss geologist Albert Heim in 1892 (translated into English by Noyes & Kletti, 1972). The English term "near-death experience" was introduced by psychiatrist Raymond Moody (1975), who identified 15 prominent characteristics commonly reported by more than 100 individuals he interviewed about episodes of proximity to death.

Universality of the Experience

NDEs appear to be universal experiences, occurring across a wide range of individuals who come close to death (Holden et al., 2009; Moody, 1975), with reports documented in diverse cultures across the world (Kellehear, 2009). Those who experience and report NDEs represent a diverse cohort with respect to age (Britton & Bootzin, 2004; van Lommel et al., 2001; for NDEs of children see Morse, 1994), sex (Greyson, 2003; Parnia et al., 2007), race (Greyson, 2003; McClenon, 2005), education or socio-economic status (Greyson, 1997), religion (McClenon, 2006), or sexual orientation (Dale, 2006). Although most NDE research has been conducted in Western populations (Greyson, 2003; Holden et al., 2009; Martial et al., 2024; Parnia et al., 2007; van Lommel et al., 2001), a growing number of studies from other cultures indicates that NDEs occur across cultures and often share common phenomenological features and psychological outcomes (Álvarez et al., 2024; Fracasso et al., 2010; Nahm & Nicolay, 2010; Kellehear, 2009; Tassell-Matamua et al., 2018). Notably, there can also be subtle differences in the perception and interpretation of specific NDE features, and even impacts that may be influenced by culture, including religion and language (Belanti et al., 2008; Jahromi & Long, 2020; Tassell-Matamua et al., 2018). For example, in Iranian NDEs, the common element of encounters with religious spirits is preserved, but these figures are more likely to be culturally specific, such as Shia Imams (Jahromi & Long, 2020).

Medical Circumstances

In addition to the demographic diversity among individuals reporting NDEs, the medical circumstances that can lead to an NDE are also wide-ranging. These include surgery, cardiac arrest, childbirth, accidents or injuries, acute or chronic illness, drowning, suicide, violence (including military combat), among others (Greyson, 1986, 2001, 2003; Greyson et al., 2009; Moody, 1975; Parnia et al., 2001; van Lommel et al., 2001; Zingrone & Alvarado, 2009). In some cases, individuals have been pronounced clinically dead and were subsequently resuscitated, with the likelihood of an NDE increasing with proximity to death (Greyson, 2003). While there are typical NDE features, each experience is an idiosyncratic blend unique to the individual and their circumstances. Notably, research suggests that the nature of the medical event that led to the NDE may be linked to particular features. For example, NDEs resulting from sudden or unexpected events, compared to anticipated medical conditions, are more likely to include so-called "cognitive" features, such as a life review and distortion of time perception (Greyson, 1985).

Incidence

Estimates of how common NDEs are vary depending on medical circumstances and method of assessment, but these experiences are not rare and occur consistently in certain contexts. Prospective observational studies with cardiac arrest patients indicate that between 10% and 23% of these patient cohorts report an NDE (Greyson, 2003; Klemenc-Ketis et al., 2010; Parnia et al., 2001; Schwaninger et al., 2002; van Lommel et al., 2001). Two prospective multi-center studies of cardiac arrest found NDEs in 9% and 21% of survivors (Parnia et al., 2014, 2023; and a recent study with survivors of prolonged critical illness in the ICU estimated the incidence of NDEs in this population at 15% (Rousseau et al., 2023). Data from prospective studies in other contexts reveal even higher rates; for example, 26% among survivors of suicide attempts (Greyson, 1986).

Impact

Regardless of the scientific explanations of these fascinating experiences, some of which we will briefly explore later in this chapter, near-death experiencers (NDErs) tend to consider these experiences as real, deeply meaningful, and vividly memorable even decades after they happen (Greyson, 2007, 2022; Moore & Greyson, 2017). NDEs can lead to profound transformations in values, spirituality, relationships, and outlook on life (Greyson, 1983a; Greyson & Khanna, 2014; Long & Woollacott, 2024; Noyes et al., 2009; van Lommel et al., 2001; Woollacott, 2024). Specifically, NDErs report a greater sense of purpose, appreciation of life, self-esteem, compassion for others, desire to serve others, a focus on spirituality, as well as decreased materialistic attitudes (Noyes et al., 2009).

While many of the profound transformations reported by NDErs relate to how they live in the present and how they engage with their environments, some changes concern their perception of the boundary between life and death. One of the most prominent NDE impacts is a decrease in the fear of death, occurring in almost all cases described by Moody (1975), and subsequently documented in various studies using validated psychometric assessments (Greyson, 1992; Pehlivanova et al., 2023; Sabom, 1982). This decrease in fear of death seems to intensify over time (van Lommel et al., 2001), and is positively associated with the intensity/depth of the NDE (Bianco et al., 2024).

In addition to their association with a reduction of negative death-related attitudes, NDEs have also been shown to stimulate positive death-related attitudes, such as death acceptance and particularly the tendency to view death as a gateway to a pleasant afterlife. Among individuals who have had a near-death episode, those who experienced an NDE showed higher death acceptance than those who did not (Greyson, 2003; Pehlivanova et al., 2023). This effect may be attributable to the creation of a psychological association between death and positive feelings, which could be elicited by pleasant NDE aspects (Pehlivanova et al., 2023). Relatedly, many NDErs report a strongly heightened belief in life after death and the continuation of consciousness beyond death (van Lommel et al., 2001), and this shift has been hypothesized as a potential mediator in the relationship between NDEs and reduced fear of death (Moody, 1975).

Can (Neuro-)Physiological Explanations Adequately Account for NDEs?

From both psychological and spiritual perspectives, NDEs are powerful experiences due to their potential to deeply transform experiencers' lives and worldviews. Beyond their personal impact, NDEs also potentially hold significant implications for our scientific understanding of the mind-brain relationship and the nature of human consciousness, including the provocative possibility of the continuation of consciousness beyond death. As a result, various models have been proposed to explain the occurrence and features of NDEs in physiological terms, which is a reasonable approach given that NDEs are most commonly triggered by physiological events, such as severe illness or trauma. However, due to the wide range or proposed explanatory models, it is impossible to explore each in depth within the scope of this chapter.

Some authors have attempted to combine multiple physiological models to support the argument that NDEs are simply "the manifestation of normal brain function gone awry" (Mobbs & Watt, 2011, p. 447). This perspective, however, has been criticized for ignoring aspects of NDEs—such as veridical perceptions without sensory input or encounters with deceased individuals whose deaths were previously unknown to the experiencer—that cannot be explained by the mechanisms proposed (Greyson et al., 2012).

As research in this area evolves, new studies have proposed additional physiological explanations for NDEs (Chawla et al., 2009; Vicente et al., 2022). Notably, a recent review article that has garnered considerable attention attempts to integrate disparate evidence from various physiological models into a unified neuroscientific theory (Martial et al., 2025). In their synthesis, Martial et al. (2025, p. 2) specifically take a materialist perspective, stating "We have excluded dualistic theories from our discussion owing to the lack of empirical neuroscientific evidence and the fact that a fundamental tenet of neuroscience asserts that human experience arises from the brain."

Such initiatives are valuable, as scientists continue to investigate the (likely multifactorial) causes and implications of these experiences. However, we would like to raise concerns about the validity and completeness of Martial et al.'s (2025) proposed theory, focusing on several salient mechanisms they propose, while acknowledging that space constraints prevent us from addressing all of them and in depth. Many such concerns have been raised previously, and we encourage readers to consult with other book chapters for a comprehensive treatment of this material, including perspectives that extend beyond materialism (Greyson, 2021; Kelly et al., 2007).

Theories related to changes in blood gases—specifically reduced oxygen levels and increased carbon dioxide levels—are among the earliest physiological models of NDEs. These theories are generally grounded in the association between cardiac arrest (a common circumstance of NDEs) and such physiological changes, or in the purported similarities of their impact with the phenomenology of NDEs. This reasoning is also endorsed by Martial and colleagues (2025) and these neurobiological changes constitute an initial stage in their cascade of physiological events proposed to trigger NDEs. However, empirical studies, including in cardiac arrest patients, show that patients who report NDEs tend to have either decreased or comparable carbon dioxide levels compared to comparison patients (Parnia et al., 2001; Sabom, 1982).

Some explanatory models have attempted to link NDEs to specific anatomical brain structures. Martial et al. (2025) argued that a preponderance of the evidence implicates the temporal lobe in the production of NDEs, citing studies involving electrical stimulation of the temporal lobe and those with patients with temporal lobe seizures. The authors referenced two studies to support the claim that activation of the temporoparietal junction (TPJ) may be responsible for OBEs (Arzy et al., 2006; De Ridder et al., 2007).

However, the purported OBEs reported in these studies differ significantly from OBEs commonly described in NDEs. In cases of TPJ activation, the center of consciousness remains inside the physical body, and perception of the environment occurs from the normal, internal-to-the-body visual perspective, rather than from the external vantage as reported in NDE-related OBEs. In addition, in TPJ activation, there is a sense of disembodiment without actually seeing a disembodied image, or, if seen, the disembodied image is static and does not move. In contrast, NDE-related OBEs often involve a mobile, disembodied center of consciousness that appears to move independently of the physical body (Greyson et al., 2008). Patients experiencing TPJ activation perceive the event as illusory, whereas those reporting NDEs describe the event as profoundly real (Greyson et al., 2008). Further challenging the claim that electrically induced bodily illusions are similar to spontaneous OBEs during NDEs are NDE cases in which individuals report veridical perceptions of events occurring at a distance, and later corroborated by external sources (Holden, 2009; Rivas et al., 2023).

In supporting the implication of the temporal lobe, Martial et al. (2025) also cited a study by Britton & Bootzin (2004), reporting that NDErs tend to have more subclinical temporal lobe epileptiform EEG activity and report more temporal lobe epileptic symptoms than matched controls without NDEs. However, a study with 100 epileptic patients with partial complex temporal lobe seizures show that none of the patients' experiences met standard criteria for a mystical experience, nor were they associated with the TPJ or any specific brain lobe (Greyson et al., 2015). Mysticism Scale scores were not significantly associated with seizure characteristics, including localization and type of seizures.

In the same sample, seven patients reported at least one seizure-associated experience involving a vague sense of being unaware of their bodies (Greyson et al., 2014). However, these patients did not differ from others in terms of seizure type or location. The one patient who reported a sense of exiting her body and visualizing her body from a disembodied perspective had a lesion that did not involve the TPJ.

Taken together, the conflicting evidence regarding temporal lobe involvement, including the phenomenological differences between disembodiment as reported by NDErs and that produced by temporal lobe stimulation or dysfunction, weakens the hypothesis that the temporal lobe may produce NDEs (Greyson et al., 2008; Greyson, 2021).

One of the more recent categories of physiological explanatory models relates to reports of brief spikes of electrical activity near or at the time of death. An early study proposed to support this theory, and cited by Martial et al. (2025), is a case series of seven patients whose life support was withdrawn as a result of serious illness (Chawla et al., 2009). None of the patients in this and other recent studies (Vicente et al., 2022; Xu et al., 2023) were reported to have any subjective conscious experience or behavioral observations suggestive of such—much less so the often hypervivid perceptions during of an NDE—that would correspond to these brief surges of electrical activity.

Martial and colleagues argue that the evidence presented in Vicente et al. (2022) and Xu et al. (2023) suggests an increase in functional activity across the brain in the human dying brain. Notably, neither of these studies involved patients whose hearts had actually stopped. Xu et al. (2023) monitored comatose patients after the withdrawal of mechanical ventilation, but cardiac activity persisted throughout the EEG monitoring period, and no signs of consciousness were observed (van Lommel & Greyson, 2023). Vicente et al. (2022)

reported a single case study of an elderly patient with severe brain damage, in whom cardiac activity also persisted for the entire duration of the cerebral electrical activity monitored via EEG. Furthermore, the patient had a number of confounding conditions that could have affected the EEG, including a recent traumatic brain injury and subdural hematoma. Importantly, there was no comparison recording of the patient's normal brain activity prior to his brain injury and unconsciousness, making it difficult to interpret the findings in context. Most critically, despite Vicente et al.'s (2022) claim that they were monitoring electrical activity "in the dying brain," the patient's heart was still showing normal cardiac activity at the time of the reported EEG changes. Although such studies provide food for speculation, they fall short of providing convincing evidence of coordinated brain activity after cardiac arrest (Greyson et al., 2022). As such, the hypothesis that such brain activity could explain NDEs remains highly speculative, if not implausible.

Veridical Perceptions During the Out-of-Body State

Regardless of their merits, these physiological explanations cannot adequately account for certain NDE features. Notably, many NDErs describe observing their bodies from a vantage point outside of them, during periods of unconsciousness, including under general anesthesia. These accounts sometimes involve witnessing events happening around their bodies or even at a distance. Examples include describing the actions, statements, or distinguishing features of medical personnel (including emergency resuscitation efforts; for a recent example see Woollacott & Peyton, 2021) or relatives waiting elsewhere in the hospital (for an overview, see Rivas et al., 2023).

While most of these accounts remain subjective, there are well-documented cases in which such reports have been corroborated by independent sources and witnesses (Rivas et al., 2023). Importantly, perceptions of events are reported as occurring in the absence of sensory input (e.g., visual, auditory) that could conventionally account for the perceptions, and the information could not have been deduced through inference—therefore precluding brain mediation and challenging purely brain-based explanations. Holden (2009) analyzed 93 published accounts containing such potentially verifiable reports of perceptions about events in the physical world perceived via non-conventional means. This detailed review revealed that 92% of the cases included evidence that the perceptions were accurate, and of those, 41% (38% of total) were corroborated by independent sources, typically medical personnel and/or medical records (Holden, 2009, p. 197). More recently, Rivas et al. (2023) published the most extensive collection to date of veridical NDE perceptions. Strikingly, veridical visually-based perceptions have even been reported among blind individuals who have had NDEs (Ring & Cooper, 1997).

Holden (2009, p. 196) acknowledged that there may be a "file drawer effect," whereby NDE perceptions that are inaccurate are less likely to be published. Nonetheless, the existence of any corroborated accounts, especially those occurring during cardiac arrest and with concurrent EEG monitoring showing no cerebral electrical activity (Sabom, 1998), should cast serious doubt on interpretations that attribute the vivid and accurate perceptions during NDEs (or their occurrence) to residual electrical activity in the brain (Angeli-Faez et al., 2025; Greyson, 2010a; Kelly et al., 2007).

Some researchers have argued that the timing of NDEs cannot be ascertained, implying that they might occur either before or after cardiac arrest, rather than during it, when brain function is significantly compromised (Martial et al., 2025). However, corroborated reports of veridical perceptions occurring during a complete loss of consciousness serve as "time anchors," allowing researchers to infer the exact time of the NDE (Greyson, 2010a; Kelly et al., 2007, p. 419; van Lommel et al., 2001). This kind of "real time model" for NDEs is supported by additional arguments building on empirical findings and theory (Nahm & Weibel, 2020). Overall, such accounts provide evidence for the possibility that consciousness may function independently of the brain, violating a key tenet of physicalism (Greyson, 2010a; Kelly et al., 2007).

Veridical Perceptions Suggesting Continuity of Consciousness Beyond Death

Another intriguing NDE feature that poses a challenge to physicalist explanatory models is the occurrence of perceived encounters with deceased individuals, whose deaths were unknown to experiencers prior to the NDE, but were later confirmed (Greyson, 2010a, 2010b; Kelly et al., 2007; Nahm, 2011).

Reported encounters with deceased spirits are among the 16 core NDE features included in the NDE Scale (Greyson, 1983b), which is commonly used to characterize typical NDE features and provide a measure of NDE intensity. Approximately 40% of cases in the large NDE database maintained at the University of Virginia Division of Perceptual Studies include perceived encounters with deceased individuals, with published estimates ranging from 32% (van Lommel et al., 2001) to 52% (Greyson, 2003). These encounters with deceased spirits are intriguing because they typically involve deceased relatives (Kelly, 2001), and are often perceived as emotionally significant—offering comfort, reconciliation, the chance to say goodbye or hello (after a long period of physical separation), or even warnings not to proceed further into the experience if one wishes to "come back" to life.

Because of the comfort these encounters may provide, along with religious or cultural influences and the hope of being reunited with deceased loves around or after death, this NDE feature has often been interpreted as a hallucination shaped by prior expectations. When examining different characteristics of these encounters and the NDEs that include them, such explanations may not be satisfactory (Kelly, 2001). Kelly analyzed a collection of NDEs including encounters with deceased spirits (detailing how this feature typically manifests) and compared them to NDEs without it. She concluded that some aspects of these cases may be consistent with both the expectation hypothesis and the hypothesis of the continuation of consciousness beyond death. For example, one notable finding was that individuals who are physiologically closer to death are more likely to report encounters with deceased persons. However, a significant portion of these encounters are unexpected—experiencers may meet deceased individuals they did not anticipate or hope to see, or even with unidentified deceased persons. Kelly interpreted these findings as evidence challenging the expectation hypothesis, suggesting that not all encounters with deceased spirits can be explained by prior beliefs or desires.

NDEs in which experiencers encounter a recently deceased person of whose death neither they nor anyone around them had any knowledge exclude the possibility that the vision was a hallucination related to the experiencer's expectations, and may bear most directly on the question of postmortem continuity of consciousness. Such NDEs include those in which the deceased person seen had died some time before the vision, although that death was unknown to the experiencer; those in which the deceased person seen had died at the time of, or immediately before, the NDE, thus not allowing any possibility for the experiencer to have learned of the death; and those in which the deceased person seen was someone whom the experiencer had never known. In some of these NDEs, the encounter suggests strong motivation on the part of the deceased individual to communicate a message, providing additional evidence for the ontological reality of deceased spirits (Greyson, 2010b; Kelly, 2001).

Among the varied phenomenology of NDEs, the most compelling evidence for a reality transcending materialism comes from reported veridical features of NDEs, such as perceptions without sensory input and information received from or about individuals perceived as deceased. While not every NDE features such potentially verifiable components, and corroboration can be difficult or even impossible, due to availability of witnesses, or the nature and timing of the reports (Holden, 2009), the existence of well-documented cases and the convergence of multiple lines of evidence remain significant and should not be dismissed (Holden, 2009; Kelly et al., 2007; Rivas et al., 2023). Although a post-materialist explanation of the full range of NDE phenomenology remains provocative and challenges prevailing scientific consensus—and the commonly proposed psychological and physiological theories—it warrants serious consideration in light of the accumulated research.

Does NDE Phenomenology Reflect the Dying Process?

Although NDEs occur in a variety of medical crises, many are reported in close proximity to death or even in documented cases of clinical death followed by successful resuscitation. This raises the intriguing question of whether these experiences may be intrinsic to the dying process itself. Although some physiological explanations attribute NDEs to electrical surges in the dying brain (Martial et al., 2025; Vicente et al., 2022; Xu et al., 2023), in our view, the evidence supporting this interpretation is strongly overstated, and fails to account for the full range of NDE phenomenology, including hyper-vivid cognition and veridical perceptions.

Regardless of potential physiological processes that may be associated with NDEs, it is intriguing that the well-documented phenomenology of NDEs parallels perceptual features reported in other end-of-life experiences. Among those are so-called "near-death visions," a phenomenon less thoroughly researched, primarily because it occurs shortly before death and with individuals who are actively dying (Kerr et al., 2014; see also Chapter 9 of this book). In these visions, which become more common as death approaches, the dying appear to see or interact with entities not physically present, typically deceased relatives, or to visit another realm—features also commonly reported in NDEs. Similarly to NDEs, these visions sometimes include deceased individuals whose death had not been known to the dying (Greyson, 2010b; Nahm, 2011).

However, a related class of experiences bears phenomenological resemblance to NDEs and occurs in cognitively healthy individuals at the time of another's death. In "shared-death experiences" (SDEs), individuals report a subjective experience of accompanying a dying person on their transition to death, whether in physical proximity to them (e.g., in the same room) or from a great distance (Shared Crossing Research Initiative, 2021; see also Chapter 10 of this book).

Academic research on SDEs is only in its infancy, and public awareness of their occurrence and phenomenology remains limited compared to widely known NDEs. Therefore, it is unlikely that individuals merely experience and report SDEs based on preconceived expectations about the dying process.

Implications

Why do NDEs matter? NDEs can change our understanding of human consciousness and even suggest the possibility that consciousness may continue beyond death. While this proposition is profound in science and humanity's ongoing search for the truth of our existence, it is also powerful in shaping how we live our lives. NDEs—especially intense ones—can redirect experiencers toward a more compassionate, less materialistic, and more spiritually-focused way of life. But what if NDEs can also impact society as a whole, especially in today's world in profound need of healing?

Merely learning about NDEs without having one can help individuals embrace more compassion and reduce fear of death (Foster et al., 2009). NDEs may also impact how we die, perhaps encouraging us to value quality of life over its mere prolongation, and to approach death not with fear, but with openness to the insights offered by these fascinating experiences at the boundary between life and death.

References

Álvarez, A. A., Arriola-Godoy, R., & D'León, R. (2024). Near-death experiences, post-traumatic stress, and supernormal abilities in a Latin American sample. *Journal of Near-Death Studies, 41,* 40–66.

Angeli-Faez, B., Greyson, B., & van Lommel, P. (2025). Near-death experience during cardiac arrest and consciousness beyond the brain: A narrative review. *International Review of Psychiatry*, 1–12.

Arzy, S., Thut, G., Mohr, C., Michel, C. M., & Blanke, O. (2006). Neural basis of embodiment: Distinct contributions of temporoparietal junction and extrastriate body area. *Journal of Neuroscience, 26*, 8074–8081.

Belanti, J., Perera, M., & Jagadheesan, K. (2008). Phenomenology of near-death experiences: A cross-cultural perspective. *Transcultural Psychiatry, 45*, 121–133.

Bianco, S., Testoni, I., Palmieri, A., Solomon, S., & Hart, J. (2024). The psychological correlates of decreased death anxiety after a near-death experience: The role of self-esteem, mindfulness, and death representations. *Journal of Humanistic Psychology, 64*, 343–366.

Britton, W. B., & Bootzin, R. R. (2004). Near-death experiences and the temporal lobe. *Psychological Science, 15*, 254–258.

Chawla, L. S., Akst, S., Junker, C., Jacobs, B., & Seneff, M. G. (2009). Surges of electroencephalogram activity at the time of death: A case series. *Journal of Palliative Medicine, 12*, 1095–1100.

Dale, L. (2006). Experiences of light in gay and lesbian near-death experiences. *Journal of Near-Death Studies, 24*, 175–178.

De Ridder, D., Laere, K. V., Dupont, P., Menovsky, T., & Heyning, P. V. de. (2007). Visualizing out-of-body experience in the brain. *New England Journal of Medicine, 357*, 1829–1833.

Foster, R., James, D., & Holden, J. M. (2009). Practical applications of research on near-death experiences. In J. M. Holden, B. Greyson, & D. James (Eds.), *The handbook of near-death experiences: Thirty years of investigation* (pp. 235–258). Praeger.

Fracasso, C., Aleyasin, S. A., Friedman, H., & Young, M. S. (2010). Near-death experiences among a sample of Iranian Muslims. *Journal of Near-Death Studies, 29*, 265–272.

Greyson, B. (1983a). Near-death experiences and personal values. *American Journal of Psychiatry, 140*, 618–620.

Greyson, B. (1983b). The near-death experience scale. Construction, reliability, and validity. *Journal of Nervous and Mental Disease, 171*, 369–375.

Greyson, B. (1985). A typology of near-death experiences. *American Journal of Psychiatry, 142*, 967–969.

Greyson, B. (1986). Incidence of near-death experiences following attempted suicide. *Suicide and Life-Threatening Behavior, 16,* 40–45.

Greyson, B. (1992). Reduced death threat in near-death experiencers. *Death Studies, 16,* 523–536.

Greyson, B. (1997). The near-death experience as a focus of clinical attention. *Journal of Nervous and Mental Disease, 185,* 327–334.

Greyson, B. (2001). Posttraumatic stress symptoms following near-death experiences. *American Journal of Orthopsychiatry, 71,* 368–373.

Greyson, B. (2003). Incidence and correlates of near-death experiences in a cardiac care unit. *General Hospital Psychiatry, 25,* 269–276.

Greyson, B. (2007). Consistency of near-death experience accounts over two decades: Are reports embellished over time? *Resuscitation, 73,* 407–411.

Greyson, B. (2010a). Implications of near-death experiences for a postmaterialist psychology. *Psychology of Religion and Spirituality, 2,* 37–45.

Greyson, B. (2010b). Seeing dead people not known to have died: "Peak in Darien" experiences. *Anthropology and Humanism, 35,* 159–171.

Greyson, B. (2021). Near-death experiences. In E. F. Kelly & P. Marshall (Eds.), *Consciousness unbound. Liberating the mind from the tyranny of materialism.* (pp. 17–56). Rowman & Littlefield.

Greyson, B. (2022). Persistence of attitude changes after near-death experiences: Do they fade over time? *Journal of Nervous and Mental Disease, 210,* 692–696.

Greyson, B. (2023). The darker side of near-death experiences. *Journal of Scientific Exploration, 37,* 683–698.

Greyson, B., Broshek, D. K., Derr, L. L., & Fountain, N. B. (2015). Mystical experiences associated with seizures. Religion, *Brain & Behavior, 5,* 182–196.

Greyson, B., Fountain, N. B., Derr, L. L., & Broshek, D. K. (2014). Out-of-body experiences associated with seizures. *Frontiers in Human Neuroscience, 8,* 65.

Greyson, B., Holden, J. M., & Van Lommel, P. (2012). 'There is nothing paranormal about near-death experiences' revisited: Comment on Mobbs and Watt. *Trends in Cognitive Sciences, 16,* 445.

Greyson, B., Kelly, E. W., & Kelly, E. F. (2009). Explanatory models for near-death experiences. In J. M. Holden, B. Greyson, & D. James (Eds.), *The handbook of near-death experiences: Thirty years of investigation* (pp. 213–234). Praeger.

Greyson, B., & Khanna, S. (2014). Spiritual transformation after near-death experiences. *Spirituality in Clinical Practice, 1,* 43–55.

Greyson, B., Parnia, S., & Fenwick, P. (2008). Visualizing out-of-body experience in the brain. *New England Journal of Medicine, 358,* 855–856.

Greyson, B., van Lommel, P., & Fenwick, P. (2022). Commentary: Enhanced interplay of neuronal coherence and coupling in the dying human brain. *Frontiers in Aging Neuroscience, 14,* 899491.

Holden, J. M. (2009). Veridical perception in near-death experiences. In J. M. Holden, B. Greyson, & D. James (Eds.), *The handbook of near-death experiences: Thirty years of investigation* (pp. 185–211). Praeger.

Holden, J. M., Long, J., & MacLurg, J. (2009). Characteristics of Western near-death experiencers. In J. M. Holden, B. Greyson, & D. James (Eds.), *The handbook of near-death experiences: Thirty years of investigation* (pp. 109–133). Praeger.

Jahromi, A. G., & Long, J. (2020). The phenomenology of Iranian near-death experiences. *Journal of Near-Death Studies, 38,* 180–200.

Kellehear, A. (2009). Census of non-Western near-death experiences to 2005: Observations and critical reflections. In J. M. Holden, B. Greyson, & D. James (Eds.), *The handbook of near-death experiences: Thirty years of investigation* (pp. 135–158). Praeger.

Kelly, E. F., Kelly, E. W., Crabtree, A., Gauld, A., Grosso, M., & Greyson, B. (Eds.). (2007). *Irreducible mind: Toward a psychology for the 21st century.* Rowman & Littlefield.

Kelly, E. W. (2001). Near-death experiences with reports of meeting deceased people. *Death Studies, 25,* 229–249.

Kelly, E. W., Greyson, B., & Kelly, E. F. (2007). Unusual experiences near death and related phenomena. In E. F. Kelly, E. W. Kelly, A. Crabtree, A. Gauld, M. Grosso, & B. Greyson (Eds.), *Irreducible mind: Toward a psychology for the 21st century* (pp. 367–421). Rowman & Littlefield.

Kerr, C. W., Donnelly, J. P., Wright, S. T., Kuszczak, S. M., Banas, A., Grant, P. C., & Luczkiewicz, D. L. (2014). End-of-life dreams and visions: A longitudinal study of hospice patients' experiences. *Journal of Palliative Medicine, 17,* 296–303.

Klemenc-Ketis, Z., Kersnik, J., & Grmec, S. (2010). The effect of carbon dioxide on near-death experiences in out-of-hospital cardiac arrest survivors: A prospective observational study. *Critical Care, 14,* R56.

Long, J., & Woollacott, M. (2024). Long-term transformational effects of near-death experiences. *Explore, 20,* 103030.

Martial, C., Fritz, P., Cassol, H., Gosseries, O., Lambermont, B., Misset, B., & Rousseau, A.-F. (2024). Phenomenological memory characteristics and impact of near-death experience in critically ill survivors: Observations at discharge and after a 1-year follow-up. *International Journal of Clinical and Health Psychology, 24,* 100478.

Martial, C., Fritz, P., Gosseries, O., Bonhomme, V., Kondziella, D., Nelson, K., & Lejeune, N. (2025). A neuroscientific model of near-death experiences. *Nature Reviews Neurology, 21,* 297–311.

McClenon, J. (2005). Content analysis of a predominantly African-American near-death experience collection: Evaluating the ritual healing theory. *Journal of Near-Death Studies, 23,* 159–181.

McClenon, J. (2006). Origins of belief in life after death: The ritual healing theory of near-death experiences. In L. Storm & M. Thalbourne (Eds.), *The survival of human consciousness: Essays on the possibility of life after death* (pp. 242-261)). McFarland Press.

Mobbs, D., & Watt, C. (2011). There is nothing paranormal about near-death experiences: How neuroscience can explain seeing bright lights, meeting the dead, or being convinced you are one of them. *Trends in Cognitive Sciences, 15,* 447–449.

Moody, R. A. (1975). *Life after life.* Mockingbird Books.

Moore, L. E., & Greyson, B. (2017). Characteristics of memories for near-death experiences. *Consciousness and Cognition, 51,* 116–124.

Morse, M. L. (1994). Near-death experiences of children. *Journal of Pediatric Oncology Nursing, 11,* 139–144.

Nahm, M. (2011). Reflections on the context of near-death experiences. *Journal of Scientific Exploration, 25,* 453-478.

Nahm, M., & Nicolay, J. (2010). Essential features of eight published Muslim near-death experiences: An addendum to Joel Ibrahim Kreps's "The search for Muslim near-death experiences". *Journal of Near-Death Studies, 29,* 255-263.

Nahm, M., & Weibel, A. (2020). The significance of autoscopies as a time marker for the occurrence of near-death experiences. *Journal of Near-Death Studies, 38,* 26-50.

Noyes, R., Fenwick, P., Holden, J. M., & Christian, S. R. (2009). Aftereffects of pleasurable Western adult near-death experiences. In B. Greyson & D.

James (Eds.), *The handbook of near-death experiences: Thirty years of investigation* (pp. 41–62). Praeger.

Parnia, S., Keshavarz Shirazi, T., Patel, J., Tran, L., Sinha, N., [...] & Deakin, C. D. (2023). AWAreness during Resuscitation – II: A multi-center study of consciousness and awareness in cardiac arrest. *Resuscitation, 191,* 109903.

Parnia, S. Spearpoint, K., de Vos, G., Fenwick, P., Goldberg, [...] & Schoenfeld, E. R. (2014). AWARE – AWAreness during Resuscitation – a prospective study. *Resuscitation, 85,* 1799–1805.

Parnia, S., Spearpoint, K., & Fenwick, P. B. (2007). Near death experiences, cognitive function and psychological outcomes of surviving cardiac arrest. *Resuscitation, 74,* 215–221.

Parnia, S., Waller, D. G., Yeates, R., & Fenwick, P. (2001). A qualitative and quantitative study of the incidence, features and aetiology of near death experiences in cardiac arrest survivors. *Resuscitation, 48,* 149–156.

Pehlivanova, M., Carroll, A., & Greyson, B. (2023). Which near-death experience features are associated with reduced fear of death? *Mortality, 28,* 493–509.

Ring, K., & Cooper, S. (1997). Near-death and out-of-body experiences in the blind: A study of apparent eyeless vision. *Journal of Near-Death Studies, 16,* 101–147.

Rivas, T., Dirven, A., & Smit, R. H. (2023). *The self does not die: Verified paranormal phenomena from near-death experiences* (2nd ed.). International Association for Near-Death Studies.

Rousseau, A.-F., Dams, L., Massart, Q., Choquer, L., Cassol, H., Laureys, S., Misset, B., Dardenne, N., Gosseries, O., & Martial, C. (2023). Incidence of near-death experiences in patients surviving a prolonged critical illness and their long-term impact: A prospective observational study. *Critical Care, 27,* 76.

Sabom, M. (1998). *Light and death: One doctor's fascinating account of near-death experiences.* Zondervan.

Sabom, M. B. (1982). *Recollections of death: A medical investigation.* Harper & Row.

Schwaninger, J., Eisenberg, P. R., Schechtman, K. B., & Weiss, A. N. (2002). A prospective analysis of near-death experiences in cardiac arrest patients. *Journal of Near-Death Studies, 20,* 215–232.

Shared Crossing Research Initiative. (2021). Shared death experiences: A little-known type of end-of-life phenomena reported by caregivers and loved ones. *American Journal of Hospice & Palliative Care, 38,* 1479–1487.

Shared Crossing Research Initiative. (2022). Comparing near-death experiences and shared death experiences: An illuminating contrast. *Journal of Near-Death Studies, 40,* 77–94.

Sleutjes, A., Moreira-Almeida, A., & Greyson, B. (2014). Almost 40 years investigating near-death experiences: An overview of mainstream scientific journals. *Journal of Nervous and Mental Disease, 202,* 833–836.

Tassell-Matamua, N. A., Steadman, K. L., & Frewin, K. E. (2018). Does cultural context influence descriptions of change after a near-death experience? Exploratory findings from an Aotearoa New Zealand sample. *Journal of Near-Death Studies, 36,* 193–218.

van Lommel, P., & Greyson, B. (2023). Invited commentary: Critique of recent report of electrical activity in the dying human brain. *Journal of Near-Death Studies, 41,* 3–8.

van Lommel, P., van Wees, R., Meyers, V., & Elfferich, I. (2001). Near-death experience in survivors of cardiac arrest: A prospective study in the Netherlands. *Lancet, 358,* 2039–2045.

Vicente, R., Rizzuto, M., Sarica, C., Yamamoto, K., Sadr, M., Khajuria, T., Fatehi, M., Moien-Afshari, F., Haw, C. S., Llinas, R. R., Lozano, A. M., Neimat, J. S., & Zemmar, A. (2022). Enhanced interplay of neuronal coherence and coupling in the dying human brain. *Frontiers in Aging Neuroscience, 14,* 813531.

Woollacott, M. (2024). Near-death experience: Memory recovery during hypnosis. *Explore, 20,* 103036.

Woollacott, M., & Peyton, B. (2021). Verified account of near-death experience in a physician who survived cardiac arrest. *Explore, 17,* 213-219.

Xu, G., Mihaylova, T., Li, D., Tian, F., Farrehi, P. M., Parent, J. M., Mashour, G. A., Wang, M. M., & Borjigin, J. (2023). Surge of neurophysiological coupling and connectivity of gamma oscillations in the dying human brain. *Proceedings of the National Academy of Sciences, 120,* e2216268120.

Zingrone, N. L., & Alvarado, C. S. (2009). Pleasurable Western adult near-death experiences: Features, circumstances, and incidence. In J. M. Holden, B. Greyson, & D. James (Eds.), *The handbook of near-death experiences: Thirty years of investigation* (pp. 17–40). Praeger.

Chapter Seven

Alternate Lives During Medically Induced Comas

ALAN PEARCE

Abstract

This chapter explores the phenomenon of consciousness during medically induced comas, challenging the assumption that patients in such a coma experience no meaningful conscious activity. As detailed in a previous book for which we interviewed patients who survived induced comas (Pearce & Pearce, 2024), their accounts frequently describe extended states of awareness and altered cognition, raising questions about the nature of consciousness under deep sedation. While many medical professionals dismiss these experiences as false memories or hallucinations, research suggests that sedatives used in intensive care units (ICUs) suppress REM sleep, leading to acute brain dysfunction. In this chapter, I broach specifically what we described as alternate lives that appear to take place in alternate realities. These experiences are often extremely terrifying and traumatize the experiencers. There is a pressing need to make these kinds of coma experiences better known and acknowledge that they can have profound and long-lasting impacts on those who experience them. Studies into EEG patterns, post-ICU cognitive function, and neurochemistry are crucial for a deeper understanding of these phenomena. Parallels between these experiences and psychedelic DMT-induced visions suggest that endogenous DMT may play a role in shaping coma-induced consciousness. This chapter calls for further research to better understand the nature of these enigmatic and often harrowing kinds of coma experiences.

Introduction

The word "coma" comes from the Greek *kōma*, meaning deep sleep and refers to a prolonged state of deep and unresponsive unconsciousness, either brought about by illness, injury or medically induced by anesthetics similar to those used in surgery. In essence, coma is a profound shutdown of brain function. But when giving sedatives to induce coma, no medical practitioner can be sure just how far they are pushing the patient as the effects of the different sedatives vary from person to person. In an effort to determine the depth of his patients' sedation when inducing comas, Dr E. Wesley Ely, director of medicine at Vanderbilt University Medical School, connected his patients to an EEG device to measure and display their brain's activities when he put them into coma. He was astonished by what he found: "Some sank all the way down to zero." In these cases, the monitors displaying the rippling horizontal lines that represent brain activity in waking states gradually turned into a long flat line that signified complete inactivity of the measured brain regions. He added: "Now I knew where my patients were when they were unconscious, and it was near death" (Ely, 2022, p. 126).

It defies current medical or scientific understanding that it is possible to be conscious within a medically induced coma. Of those that return from the supposed depths of unconsciousness, many tell of alternate realities and parallel universes, some staggeringly beautiful, others defying all imagination in the depth of their horror. Most doctors dismiss these accounts as false memories or drug-induced hallucinations. The term "ICU Delirium" has become a universal diagnosis, perceived as a seemingly mild affliction that will soon fade away.

Despite a wealth of evidence to the contrary, most doctors believe that once comatose the patient is at total rest. The brain is off-line. The event will be a blank in their lives. And while many a doctor will tell families that the comatose patient is resting and that the sedatives aid a deeper sleep, multiple research papers and a growing number of studies have shown that the sedatives employed disrupt brain activity so severely that REM sleep is not possible, leading to acute brain failure. General anesthetics, such as isoflurane, can strongly inhibit REM sleep. For instance, research involving anesthetized mice demonstrated a substantial REM sleep deficit post-anesthesia, indicating that these agents do not replicate natural sleep patterns and may lead to a need for REM sleep recovery afterward (Moore et al., 2012; Pick et al., 2011). Propofol, a commonly used anesthetic for inducing deep sedation, has been associated with the suppression of REM sleep stages. In critically ill patients receiving propofol for sedation, studies have observed a decrease in REM sleep, further deteriorating the already poor sleep quality in these individuals (Kondili et al., 2012).

Alternate Reality Experiences in Coma

Coma survivors sometimes describe experiences reminiscent of classic NDEs, including: bucolic landscapes, meeting with dead relatives, and standing at the threshold of this life and next. Many others recount far darker experiences, more resembling hell than any concept of heaven. Some survivors tell of being stuck in loops, reliving one appalling event over and over. Others are able to count off one death after another, often horrifyingly violent. Although distressing NDEs have also been reported, albeit less so than pleasant NDEs, it seems with medically induced comas, experiences of the distressing type are more commonly reported. Isobel Wells from South Africa recounted for us numerous lives, all ending in rape and murder. James Morrall from the United Kingdom recalled a series of deaths, mostly involving water and air flight.

> "I lived a whole other life whilst in the coma, spanning many different eras. I was a Spitfire pilot and I crashed in the Thames and drowned. I was locked in a box as punishment and it was filled with water and I drowned. I was a fisherman and was involved in an accident while unloading fish and I drowned. I was flying a really, really old plane over what I assume was the Caribbean when we lost power and crashed into the sea. And I drowned."

Alternate lives—lived in rich detail, minute by minute—feature large in coma survivor accounts. Nick MacDonald from the USA was able to recall an entire life, ending sometime in the late 1970s.

> "It feels like my consciousness, spirit or soul packed and went to another world just like this one and picked up a life there," he told us. "It still blows my mind to recall that place. I was in a world just like this but just slightly different. The atmosphere was slightly orange instead of ours which is blue. There was still a lot of the same places but they were not the same or in the same location as they are here. It was like the United States but not like the United States on a map. It was just mixed up. The two weeks I was in coma felt to me like twenty years. I lived a whole other life while I was under. So much so that when I finally was brought back to this world, realm, dimension, or whatever you want to call it, I was actually sad I was awake and didn't get to see how my other life there played out. I literally missed it, the people, the experiences; the

things I learned. I feel these emotions very strongly to this day. As far as meaningful relationships, yes, I had several. Sometimes I feel like I had more there than I do here. And they were pretty deep, too. Three years later and I still feel that emotion from love and loss. I don't like to say this was a dream because these experiences were so real to me. The vividness was so clear. I just can't explain a dream like that. It's weird but I now know how to do things I learned there. I had new skills when I woke up that I didn't have before. I was able to fix my fiancé's old-school HVAC (heating, ventilation and air conditioning) system at her house. I can't really tell you how. Similar story with the neighbor's push mower and my car. So that's eerie. Before coma—I call it BC—I wouldn't have even looked at it. Was it stuff I learned in my other life and was now applying here? I'm now taking on bigger issues like my car, and was successful in fixing it a few times. I kind of enjoy it, actually."

Unlike dreams, these memories from within coma rarely fade. They remain a constant presence in the survivor's life. Survivor Deborah Mayo from the United Kingdom told us:

"The memories are all so vivid and they stay with me. Which is real? Am I awake or still in my coma? Now, I get them as flashbacks—the smells, the sounds, the feelings, the emotions—and then I'm back there. This is my loop, my hell. And that's how I experienced my coma, the same dreams looping and looping. It was just horrific. I was assaulted. I was raped. I was cast in fiberglass. I was abandoned. I was placed in a water tank with my Dad's decomposing corpse. I was told my husband didn't love me anymore by two actors employed by the nurse who was actually the Angel of Death in disguise.

For the longest loop, I was in this serial killer-themed pub and they decided that they wanted it to be totally realistic and use real people as murder victims, and I was one of the living murder victims because I was in a coma and they could do whatever they wanted to me. Throughout the years, they would spray me with lacquer or a cotton candy type of fiberglass to keep me preserved. I remember the smell even now. And they kept making it more and more realistic. So, they went from having actors and actresses playing these serial killers to then having real-life serial killers, actual people released from prison, to reenact some of their murders on me and on the other people, the other bodies being kept alive. I was raped which was just horrific. I had three children. Years passed, decades. I became encased in so much fiberglass it was like golden rock, like amber. But the pub was due to be demolished and they didn't know what to do with me. I'd been there eighty years. They eventually sold me to an organ harvesting facility where I was placed in the tank.

I spent the first two months after my coma convinced I had died. And still, I have to check I am actually alive. I tell people I was in my coma for eighty years because that's what happened. I think my nightmares were my personal hell."

Almost all coma survivors are left to puzzle these events alone; unable to process the clinical explanations that dismiss these experiences outright, leaving many to feel belittled or insulted. Many are left to question their sanity. As part of a rare study, Dr Leanne Boehm, Assistant Professor at Vanderbilt University School of Nursing, interviewed around forty coma survivors to learn how they were faring after discharge (e.g., Sevin et al., 2021). She told us:

"And sometimes after those interviews, I would feel like I needed some therapy myself. They look okay, but they are not okay. And people don't understand that, even the patients and family members don't understand. They are just alone and isolated and so it's very heartbreaking to hear about all of those things."

Rory Atherton, a coma survivor from the United Kingdom, spent seven days in a medically induced coma after suffering a violent and life-threatening assault. He told us that the coma experiences were infinitely worse.

"My therapy did very, very little to help me with my PTSD or the trauma of my coma experience. I was alone on this hospital bed and this little effeminate doctor with a big black moustache was wiring me up to something. He was telling me, Don't worry, this won't hurt. It will be over soon. He then pulled a lever and I felt my body leap off the hospital bed. My body then began to grow and swell in size, massively swell and start to turn orange and grow huge spikes until I was the size of a car. And then these doctors were laughing, saying it should have killed me and how strange the side-effects were.

Then they left the room and naked teenage boys started stabbing me with knives, trying to finish me off. It didn't work so they began to drink my blood from the wounds. Now, at this point, I believed I was actually dying because my vision was fading in and out, and all I was seeing was a very bright light. This was never a dream. It was one-hundred percent real to me. It was really happening. The coma has absolutely changed my views on life and death. Sometimes, I'm in a total state of panic, believing I'm still in the coma and this life isn't real. I never thought about death or dying before, I just enjoyed my life. Now, I am absolutely terrified of dying and think about it all the time. I don't honestly think doctors have the first clue about what it is like to be in a coma. The only people who really know are the ones who have suffered through it themselves."

Occasionally, medical personnel find themselves undergoing prolonged deep sedation. Isobel Wells is a health care professional working in one of South Africa's top hospitals in Cape Town. She was reluctantly placed into a coma by her colleagues during the COVID-19 pandemic.

"So I was put into a coma. And my reality changed," she told us. "I woke up in an organ harvesting facility. They'd found a way to kill me and regrow my organs over and over again. And that went on for four years and I was kept in a coffin. All of my organs were harvested over and over again. And each time I woke up into a different life—die, wake up, have another life, then die again and wake up. Each time I was murdered, I was raped and my organs harvested. Sometimes I starved to death.

They were just countless, these lives. And in every reality I was paralyzed. I had another reality where I spent one-hundred-thousand years on the top and bottom levels of existence. On the upper levels it was all ones and zeros. And on the bottom was the sediment and different layers of life throughout the years. And you switch between the two. You know, people like to think these are just like dreams. But I remember it as a memory. I can give all kinds of detail. These are clear memories."

When Isobel felt strong enough, she went back to see her colleagues at the ICU. She needed them to understand what she had just experienced.

"I tried to tell them about my experiences inside coma, and everyone was like, That's weird. Oh, really? And when I saw my surgeons and my anesthetist, no one could understand what I was talking about. It was only when I went to rehab and spoke to the trauma counsellor and told her that no one knows about this and she said, Well, I do. We get this all the time. I told her I work at the hospital. We have the best doctors in the country, they really know their stuff. We've been intubating and sedating patients for years, why is this not known? She told me she thought everyone knew about it."

Altered States of Consciousness in Dark Retreats

A patient sick enough to be placed into a medically induced coma may find themselves in the deepest state of sensory deprivation, deprived of all contact with the world around them. Buddhist monks and others say that the withdrawal from the physical world opens the doorway to the spiritual world and by taking such a step one is entering a death-like existence, with the six stages of Bardo to explore. To experience these six states, death is not imperative. It is possible to step across the threshold after years of intense meditation or by literally jumping off the deep end into the most extreme state of grace imaginable, the Dark Retreat.

As Taoist Master Mantak Chia explains in a guide to dark retreats (Chia, n. d., p. 2):

> "Complete darkness profoundly changes the sensibilities of the body and brain. Darkness shuts down major cortical centers in the brain. Emotions and feelings are enhanced. Dream states manifest in our conscious awareness. We descend into the void, into the darkness of deep, inner space."

Since the dawn of time, mystics have taken themselves off to the darkest recesses of caves seeking a spiritual connection. Today, such ascetic delights can be booked online. Emma Carruthers runs the Hermitage Solitary and Dark Retreat Center on the shores of Lake Atitlan in the highlands of Guatemala. We thought to show her some of the coma accounts that we had gathered. At first, she laughed.

> "All of those sound like the experiences that I personally have had in dark retreats, and I've done over ten," she told us. "I've heard the same from the people who have run through our dark retreats, and we've had close to five-hundred now. We talk individually to every single one afterwards. We are really fascinated with these alternate lives. People [in

dark retreat] tend to see it as visiting their past lives. Often within coma, people are having alternate lives, but they are set in the past, sometimes not so far back."

Emma says that the ultra-vivid nightmare-like events experienced during coma are a common early feature once one begins a dark retreat. "People also have projections about the future. People see a lot of other people in the room. Depending on their belief, they may see the Virgin Mary or Buddha. Sometimes they see an angel or they see other beings and even aliens."

Kalianey, a French software developer who undertook a 40-day retreat in Guatemala found herself sleeping a lot with intensely lucid dreams. As the dark days wear on, she first saw highly-detailed geometric patterns. She went on to tell us:

> "And then, the vision of a beautiful, bright white moon and castle in the sky appeared, and very pictorial visions never stopped again until the end of my retreat, only growing stronger and brighter as time passed. The visions were quite varied from cartoon-like Technicolor movies to a 360° immersion in a beautiful purple or turquoise landscape with characters moving around, interacting with me, from flying boats filled with kittens wearing hats to huge stone faces starring at me."

As Kalianey entered her third week, she experienced intense visions and a sense of vast energy, together with transcendental feelings of universal love and compassion.

> "My body is shaking more and more from inside in meditation, and I really feel an inner tremor growing as I go deeper inside. I do not see the darkness anymore, as everything is so colorful and bright most of the time. It was quite challenging sometimes as the room was by moment crowded and I had to pass through all these characters and animals, even walls, to go from one side of the room to the other. I got scared a few times by very dark floating shadows or characters coming from horror movies, not so much from their presence—although my first reaction was fear, I decided very firmly from the beginning that I would not be scared by my own mind—but from their sudden movements. It is already a bit unsettling to be doing your yoga, trying not to watch the tortured woman from the Martyr movie crawling towards you. But I really jumped in shock when she suddenly extended her arm to touch me!"

The Role of DMT in Altered States of Consciousness

Precisely why events such as these happen cannot be easily explained. The most likely explanation is that N, N-dimethyltryptamine (DMT), a naturally-occurring psychedelic compound found in most mammals, is released by certain triggers, including utter isolation and death. Such experiences, as recounted by coma survivors and by those in dark retreats, closely match accounts recorded by Dr Rick Strassman when he submitted volunteers to the first trials of intravenously-introduced DMT in the late 1990s. Strassman concluded that DMT is likely released in significant quantities at the time of death and that this release is responsible for the spiritual experiences that people report both in DMT trials and NDEs (Strassman, 2000).

Emma Carruthers thinks that the release of DMT in dark retreats can be responsible for a lot of the visions. She likens this intentional DMT experience to a form of conscious unconsciousness, with the ability to process the events from a clear, rational perspective. Unlike those entering a medically induced coma, people on dark retreats or undergoing DMT trials spend time preparing themselves for the experience and often have others with whom to discuss the strange happenings, removing the fear not only of being alone but also that their minds may actually be permanently damaged. In the case of coma patients, if they are undergoing a DMT release, no one has prepared them for the experience and few ever get the opportunity to analyze the events later with knowledgeable counsellors, leaving so many to question their sanity. The suppressed REM sleep in medically induced comas might increase the occurrence of horrific experiences further.

> "I think spiritual, DMT or coma experiences can be very difficult to integrate for everyone," maintains Kalianey. "It is why traditionally long dark retreats and intense spiritual practices were always done under the direction of a master who could guide the disciple, reassure him when needed and dismissing fanciful interpretations of these experiences. For an uninitiated person, these intense experiences can be very unsettling without guidance."

The Need for Further Research

Some doctors argue that the powerful mix of medications in the coma cocktail can explain the highly detailed accounts that survivors provide. But there are no known medicinal drugs that can induce an alternate life spanning decades while mere days or weeks pass in this world. If there were, we would all know about it. However, we do know that the human body produces its own psychedelic DMT. It has also been demonstrated that DMT is released at the point of death in the brain of rats, and therefore, very likely also in the human brain (Dean et al., 2019). When a person is placed into a coma, it is fair to say that they are so seriously ill that they are already close to death, and that the heavy sedation pushes them even further. It is likely that DMT has a role to play in coma experiences but further research in this field is complicated by ethical considerations.

For the time being, no one can definitively say where or how we produce DMT in our system, nor what its precise role may be. Similarly, no one can safely say what happens at the point of death, nor beyond. But it does seem certain that the human body is capable of producing its own cocktail of chemicals that may either be Nature's way of taking the sting out of death to ease our passing or, perhaps, to open a doorway to what lies ahead.

When working on our previous book (Pearce & Pearce, 2024), we have spoken with many who felt they had died within their comas and yet returned. They tell of something that lies beyond, of other levels of consciousness yet to be explored, and of other dimensions previously recounted by countless others across time, continents and cultures. When so many appear to offer highly lucid accounts, it becomes harder to dismiss these coma events out of hand, as so many doctors do; obliged to use seemingly convenient labels such as false memories, hallucination or delirium, while steadfastly refusing to explore other possibilities. The suppression of REM sleep, coupled with potential endogenous DMT activity, may explain the vivid alternate realities experienced by many coma patients. Further research into EEG patterns, post-ICU cognitive function, and psychedelic neurochemistry is crucial for a deeper understanding of these phenomena.

Conclusion

The consciousness occurring during medically induced coma remains an enigma. While mainstream medicine assumes deep sedation equates to unconsciousness, this may only apply to some patients, but certainly not to all of them. The coma survivor accounts suggest otherwise. There are no accurate statistics on the number of people globally that are placed into medically induced comas, although the number is likely to run into the tens of millions. And very many of the survivors have stories to tell. Dismissing coma narratives as the result of mere hallucinations does a disservice to survivors and impedes progress in understanding the complexities of human consciousness.

References

Chia, M. (n. d.). *Darkness technology: Darkness techniques for enlightenment.* Universal Tao Publications.

Dean, J. G., Liu, T., Huff, S., Sheler, B., Barker, S. A., Strassman, R. J., Wang, M. M., & Borjigin, J. (2019). Biosynthesis and extracellular concentrations of N,N-dimethyltryptamine (DMT) in mammalian brain. *Scientific Reports, 9,* 9333.

Ely, W. (2022). *Every deep-drawn breath: A critical care doctor on healing, recovery, and transforming medicine in the ICU.* Scribner.

Kondili, E., Alexopoulou, C., Xirouchaki, N., & Georgopoulos, D. (2012). Effects of propofol on sleep quality in mechanically ventilated critically ill patients: A physiological study. *Intensive Care Medicine, 38,* 1640–1646.

Moore, J. T., Chen, J., Han, B., Meng, Q. C., Veasey, S. C., Beck, S. G., & Kelz, M. B. (2012). Direct activation of sleep-promoting VLPO neurons by volatile anesthetics contributes to anesthetic hypnosis. *Current Biology, 22,* 2008–2016.

Pearce, A., & Pearce, B. (2024). *Coma and near-death experience: The beautiful, disturbing, and dangerous world of the unconscious.* Park Street Press.

Pick, J., Chen, Y., Moore, J. T., Sun, Y., Wyner, A. J., Friedman, E. B., & Kelz, M. B. (2011). Rapid eye movement sleep debt accrues in mice exposed to volatile anesthetics. *Anesthesiology, 115,* 702–712.

Sevin, C. M., Boehm, L. M., Hibbert, E., Bastin, A. J., Jackson, J. C., Meyer, J., Quasim, T., Bakhru, R. N., Montgomery-Yates, A., Slack, A., Still, M., Netzer, G., Mikkelsen, M. E., Iwashyna, T. J., Haines, K. J., & McPeake, J. (2021). Optimizing critical illness recovery: Perspectives and solutions from the caregivers of ICU survivors. *Critical Care Explorations, 3,* e0420.

Strassman, R. (2000). DMT. *The spirit molecule: A doctor's revolutionary research into the biology of near-death and mystical experiences.* Park Street Press.

Chapter Eight

Implications of Medically Induced Comas in Intensive Care Units

KALI DAYTON

Abstract
This chapter examines the implications of medically induced comas in intensive care units (ICUs), focusing on their association with delirium and ICU-acquired weakness. It defines delirium, outlines its symptoms, and discusses its causes, including common sedatives like propofol and benzodiazepines, which disrupt brain function and exacerbate patient outcomes. The chapter highlights the alarming statistics surrounding delirium, such as its correlation with increased mortality and long-term cognitive impairments. It further critiques the cultural standardization of sedation practices initiated in the 1990s, which initially provided a false sense of safety for healthcare providers. The "ABCDEF Bundle" is introduced as a transformative approach aimed at keeping patients awake and mobile, thus reducing the negative consequences of prolonged sedation. Studies supporting the efficacy of this bundle in improving recovery outcomes and decreasing hospitalization costs are reviewed. The chapter also addresses barriers to implementing awake and walking ICUs, such as knowledge deficits and ingrained practices among clinicians. Ultimately, it calls for a paradigm shift in ICU care, advocating for enhanced patient autonomy and communication, and emphasizes the need for collaborative efforts among healthcare providers, survivors, and policymakers to revolutionize critical care practices.

Introduction
Most chapters in this book focus on end-of-life experiences and their implications for consciousness studies as well as spiritual questions that arise for the experiencers and those who witness these phenomena. This chapter takes a different approach and focuses on very practical and clinical matters of coma patient care, specifically regarding medically induced comas in intensive care

units (ICUs). In recent years, it has become increasingly recognized that the bodies of patients, and often also their minds, are not at all in peaceful rest during medically induced comas. Instead, medically induced comas imply significant stress and patients may suffer from long-lasting negative after-effects. It is vital that more and more people, including medical professionals, become aware of the adverse implications of medically induced comas and contribute to advancing alternative and much more sustainable methods of caring for critically ill patients. After all, all of us might one day be in a situation in which we directly or indirectly need to deal with medically induced comas. The following sections introduce important key terms, the mentioned negative implications of medically induced comas, and possible solutions for improving patient care in ICUs.

Medically Induced Comas

Medically induced comas have been a common practice in intensive care units (ICUs) for patients with breathing tubes on ventilators for decades. Despite the prevalence of this treatment, it comes with significant costs related to delirium and ICU-acquired weakness.

Delirium

During illness, patients are at risk of suffering from "delirium," a term that encompasses a spectrum of symptoms that are usually attributed to brain dysfunction. Symptoms can include altered levels of arousal, ranging from lethargy (hypoactive delirium) to severe agitation (hyperactive delirium), and can fluctuate as "mixed delirium." Patients also commonly experience inattention, confusion, delusions, and hallucinations (Wilson et al., 2020). The causes of this brain disruption can include numerous predisposing factors such as inflammation, infection, sleep deprivation, conditions affecting blood and oxygen flow to the brain (e.g., stroke, low oxygen saturation), medications, etc. (Mei et al., 2023).

Delirium is distressing for patients, loved ones, and caregivers as patients' behavior drastically changes from their normal demeanor. Hyperactive delirium can increase the risk of violence and harm to oneself or others during this state of hyper-vigilance, fear, and impulsiveness as patients respond to vivid hallucinations and alternative realities. Hypoactive delirium can appear as "sleep, rest, drowsiness" with high risks of misdiagnosis and is associated with worse outcomes (Hosker & Ward, 2017).

Risks of delirium are particularly high in ICUs due to the complexity of conditions and complications during critical illness. On average, patients arrive at the ICU with 11 risk factors for delirium (Ely et al., 2001), and they are at high risk of receiving interventions that can independently cause delirium. Delirium doubles the risk of dying in the hospital (Ely et al., 2004), and for every day of delirium, there is a 10% increased risk of death.

Sedatives used in the ICU to place patients into medically induced comas such as propofol and benzodiazepines, disrupt brain activity and prevent REM cycles 3 and 4, exacerbating sleep disruption and deprivation and further increasing delirium risks (Telias & Wilcox, 2019). Continuous intravenous sedation is a key modifiable risk factor for delirium and alone increases the risk by 214%. If patients are sedated, restrained, and in an ICU bed for over seven days, their delirium risks increase by over 3,000% (Pan et al., 2019).

While patients are sedated in medically induced comas, they are chemically restrained and unable to move their bodies and express what they are experiencing. They can often hear and feel their surroundings and what is happening to them but are unable to interact with their environment while in the comatose state. In the setting of acute brain failure (delirium), this sensory input can be twisted into graphic and alternative realities. This can lead to the misinterpretation of chest tubes, catheters, etc. being "gun shot wounds during battle", kidnapping of their children (Richards, 2023), abduction and torture with nurses as the perpetrators (Dayton et al., 2023), or being cannibalized by a deceased father on repeat for days (Dayton, 2023b). Instrumental music in the room can be interpreted as being in a morgue about to be buried alive (Dayton, 2020), and hearing visitors who spend comfort at the bedside, such as spouses, can be interpreted as if they are planning to harvest organs to be sold (Dayton, 2023a).

The coma experiences described in Chapter 7 of this book are often subsumed under the umbrella term of ICU delirium as well (see also Pearce & Pearce, 2024). Even after the sedatives are off and patients are aroused from their coma, the acute brain dysfunction can persist for days to weeks to months leading to ongoing symptoms of confusion, hallucinations, etc. The brain damage occurring during delirium can also lead to long-term cognitive impairments similar to mild Alzheimer's and moderate traumatic brain injury three and 12 months after discharge, regardless of age (Pandharipande et al., 2013). The horrors vividly experienced during delirium carry high risks of post-ICU post-traumatic stress disorder (PTSD), with one-third of delirium survivors having PTSD (Grover et al., 2019; see also Chapter 7).

ICU-Acquired Weakness

While patients are motionless during medically induced comas, their brains are not the only organ system under attack. The musculoskeletal system can suffer life-threatening and life-altering damage. The musculoskeletal system is vital for survival. Muscles play a role in the function of most other organ systems. Even the simple act of independent breathing requires engagement, strength, and stamina from the abdominal, chest, neck, back, and intercostal muscles as well as the diaphragm.

During critical illness, the body is likely to use its own muscle for energy to fight the illness (van Gassel et al., 2020), leading to rapid muscular atrophy. When patients are sedated, their entire bodies are immobilized, meaning they are not contracting any muscles or lifting limbs. Adding to the problem, propofol disrupts the sodium channels of the muscle, leading to disruption in neuromuscular transmission (Liu et al., 2019). Propofol is also a mitochondrial toxin that contributes to the dysfunction of skeletal muscle (Abdelmalik & Rakocevic, 2017). Its toxic effects may explain why propofol alone can cause diaphragm dysfunction (Bruells et al., 2014).

As critically ill patients lay motionless while the ventilator does the work of breathing and they receive myotoxic sedatives that lead to diaphragm dysfunction, patients can face prolonged time on the ventilator, increased risk of tracheostomy, extensive rehabilitation, and increased risk of dying in the hospital by 3.6 times (Hermans et al., 2014), plus a 30% increased risk of dying within two years after discharge (Saccheri et al., 2020). The longer patients remain in medically induced comas, the higher their risk of losing the ability to sit, stand, walk, swallow, and even breathe independently (Hermans & van den Berghe, 2015).

The Cultural Standardization of Medically Induced Comas

The practice of automatically inducing comas for all intubated patients on ventilators began in the 1990s during experimentation with Acute Respiratory Distress Syndrome (ARDS). The sight of patients lying still with their eyes closed instilled a false sense of success and safety among nurses and doctors. The common belief was that patients were "sleeping, unaware of the breathing tube, and comfortable" while sedated, and this practice became the cultural norm for all patients on ventilators (Dayton et al., 2025).

As research reviewed the outcomes of ARDS patients treated with prolonged sedation, it was discovered that, although their lungs had recovered, they experienced persistent cognitive, psychological, and physical impairments even five years after ICU discharge known as "Post-ICU Syndrome" (Herridge et al., 2011). These impairments are now known as post-ICU syndrome and show a strong correlation to sedation, immobility, delirium, and ICU-acquired weakness (Herridge & Azoulay, 2023).

It was realized that benzodiazepines such as lorazepam and midazolam are very dangerous. Lorazepam increases the risk of delirium by 20% per 1 mg (Pandharipande et al., 2006), while midazolam triples the risk of delirium per 5 mg (Zaal et al., 2015) and increases the risk of prolonged time on the ventilator and death (Lonardo et al., 2014). Furthermore, sedation levels that leave patients unable to respond to voice are an independent predictor of death (Shehabi et al., 2012).

We learned that mechanical ventilation and an endotracheal tube do not automatically require patients to be comatose; only about 10% of patients have actual indications for continuous sedation. Patients who receive no sedation are off the ventilator 4.2 days sooner and do not have an increased risk of PTSD (Strom et al., 2010). Ultimately, real and factual memories of the ICU experience when patients were awake and free of delirium during their ICU stay are protective against post-ICU PTSD (Long et al., 2014). Avoiding sedation while on a ventilator can protect patients from delirium, ICU-acquired weakness, and post-ICU syndrome.

The ABCDEF Bundle and Awake and Walking ICUs

Amidst these discoveries, it was determined that a protocolized process of care should be created to guide ICU clinicians away from medically induced comas and to keep patients as awake, communicative, autonomous, and mobile as possible, even while on ventilators. This care bundle is called the "ABCDEF Bundle", with each letter representing an element of care needed to protect patients from delirium (Balas et al., 2013). The bundle was inspired by an "Awake and Walking ICU" in Salt Lake City, Utah, founded by visionary nurse Polly Bailey and other revolutionary clinicians (Dayton et al., 2025).

This ICU, alongside a few others, allows patients to be awake and communicate directly after intubation and to perform their highest level of mobility within 12 hours after intubation unless there is a medical need for them to be comatose or unable to mobilize.

Polly Bailey published a study proving that it is safe and feasible for patients with breathing tubes on the ventilator to be awake and walking, even with severely sick lungs, with an adverse event rate of 0.6% (Bailey et al., 2007). This inspired further research demonstrating that mobilizing patients within 48 hours after intubation decreased delirium, reduced time on the ventilator and in the ICU by two days, and increased the likelihood of returning to baseline functional status by 24% by hospital discharge, compared to patients who remained in bed while on the ventilator (Schweickert et al., 2009).

A study in 2019 showed that even at lower doses, in which patients are lightly sedated with minimal or no benzodiazepines, the ABCDEF Bundle has the potential to decrease 7-day mortality by 68%, coma and delirium by 25–50%, discharges to care facilities other than home by 36%, and hospital readmissions by 46%. The more elements of the bundle patients receive, the more likely they are to survive and thrive (Pun et al., 2019). It was also noted that the ABCDEF Bundle decreases hospitalization costs by 30% (Hseih et al., 2019). These findings spotlight the avoidable harm and dangers of medically induced comas, providing compelling evidence to steer care toward keeping patients awake and mobile on ventilators instead of in comas.

However, a study in 2021 found that 64% of COVID patients on mechanical ventilation were receiving continuous intravenous drips of benzodiazepines (Pun et al., 2021). Despite decades of compelling research, 66% of nurses still believe that sedation is necessary for patient comfort and that limiting patients' recall is a desired outcome of sedation (Guttormson et al., 2020). In one study in 2022, despite orders for patients to be able to open their eyes to voice, over 70% of patients were sedated and responsive only to touch or even unresponsive (Rasulo et al., 2022).

Some of the ongoing barriers preventing the standardization of Awake and Walking ICUs include knowledge gaps, clinician skills, culture, and staffing. When patients are automatically sedated after intubation and develop delirium, it becomes a significant challenge to turn sedation off and mobilize the patient later. During periods of confusion, agitation, panic, and impulsiveness, patients are at high risk of pulling out their breathing tubes (Kwon & Choi, 2017) and may exhibit violent behavior toward themselves or clinicians (Tachibana et al., 2021). Patients who have been immobilized and sedated for days or longer are likely to experience impaired cognitive and fine motor skills, along with profound weakness. This leads to difficulty utilizing nonverbal communication tools, such as a pen and paper, leaving the patient unable to express their needs or questions, which further exacerbates their frustration and agitation.

The "culturally normal" response is to resume and even increase sedation (Mehta et al., 2008) as well as to administer wrist restraints. Clinicians are largely untrained to keep patients awake and mobile early on and are often unprepared to manage the delirium, agitation, and weakness that frequently occurs following prolonged sedation. Thus, sedation and agitation remain the primary barriers to getting patients awake and mobile in the ICU after they have received sedation for extended periods (TEAM Studies Investigators et al., 2022).

In an Awake and Walking ICU, clinicians expect patients to be awake, communicative, autonomous, and mobile, and they possess the skills and knowledge to help manage patients' anxiety, pain, fear, and discomfort. In such an environment, continuous sedation to induce a coma is reserved for exceptional circumstances, such as when seizures, elevated intracranial pressure, or severe instability requiring restricted movement are necessary to save a patient's life. Otherwise, once the breathing tube is placed, patients are allowed to wake up from the procedure and can use their cell phones to text or a pen and paper to express their needs, wants, questions, and desires. Their loved ones are at the bedside, helping them communicate and providing comfort and reassurance.

Patients are allowed to see their endotracheal tube with a mirror and provide feedback to clinicians about which position of the tube or setting on the ventilator is the most comfortable. Unless the patient is unsafe or unable to tolerate movement, they are permitted to sit up at the side of the bed, stand, walk themselves to a chair, use the commode, and even walk around the ICU with the breathing tube and ventilator. This approach helps patients acclimate to the challenge of breathing with a tube and ventilator and can help prevent and address anxiety related to being reclined in bed for extended periods.

Patients are informed of their condition and involved in decision-making regarding their care and pain management as much as possible. Once they understand and are cautious with their breathing tube, they can often be unrestrained, use the call light, and communicate freely with staff and their loved ones. Their dignity, autonomy, and independence are preserved as much as possible during what can be pivotal, vulnerable, and potentially final moments of their lives.

This approach humanizes care in the ICU. Clinicians can understand and connect with patients beyond their diagnoses and physical conditions, addressing what matters to each individual. Patients are allowed to engage actively in the fight for their lives, thus enhancing their chances of returning to the lives they knew before.

If survival is not a possibility, patients can have the highest likelihood of making their own care decisions, connecting with their loved ones, finalizing their affairs, and having the opportunity to say their goodbyes. These precious privileges are routinely removed during medically induced comas.

The Revolution

Updating these long-held and dangerous practices requires more than compelling research. It demands a transformation of education, knowledge, beliefs, perspectives, training, leadership, accountability, and culture. It requires engagement from revolutionaries on all sides of the hospital bed. Survivors, loved ones, future and current patients, clinicians, hospital leadership, and lawmakers must join together to advocate for the responsible use of sedation in the ICU. Together, we can revolutionize critical care medicine and standardize Awake and Walking ICUs.

References

Abdelmalik, P. A., & Rakocevic, G. (2017). Propofol as a risk factor for ICU-acquired weakness in septic patients with acute respiratory failure. *Canadian Journal of Neurological Sciences, 44,* 295–303.

Bailey, P., Thomsen, G. E., Spuhler, V. J., Blair, R., Jewkes, J., Bezdjian, L., Veale, K., Rodriquez, L., & Hopkins, R. O. (2007). Early activity is feasible and safe in respiratory failure patients. *Critical Care Medicine, 35,* 139–145.

Balas, M. C., Burke, W. J., Gannon, D., Cohen, M. Z., Colburn, L., Bevil, C., Franz, D., Olsen, K. M., Ely, E. W., & Vasilevskis, E. E. (2013). Implementing the awakening and breathing coordination, delirium monitoring/management, and early exercise/mobility bundle into everyday care:

Opportunities, challenges, and lessons learned for implementing the ICU Pain, Agitation, and Delirium Guidelines. *Critical Care Medicine, 41*(9 Suppl 1), S116–S127.

Bruells, C. S., Maes, K., Rossaint, R., Thomas, D., Cielen, N., Bergs, I., Bleilevens, C., Weis, J., & Gayan-Ramirez, G. (2014). Sedation using propofol induces similar diaphragm dysfunction and atrophy during spontaneous breathing and mechanical ventilation in rats. *Anesthesiology, 120,* 665–672.

Dayton, K. (2020). *Walking home from the ICU. Episode 4: Sedation is not sleep.* Dayton ICU Consulting. Podcast: https://daytonicuconsulting.com/walking-home-from-the-icu-podcast/walking-home-from-the-icu-episode-4-sedation-is-not-sleep/

Dayton, K. (2023a). *Walking home from the ICU. Episode 119: The trauma of delirium after a traumatic birth.* Dayton ICU Consulting. Podcast: https://daytonicuconsulting.com/walking-home-from-the-icu-podcast/walking-home-from-the-icu-episode-119-the-trauma-of-delirium-after-a-traumatic-birth/

Dayton, K. (2023b). *Walking home from the ICU. Episode 157: Sedation is sleep-deprivation.* Dayton ICU Consulting. Podcast: https://daytonicuconsulting.com/walking-home-from-the-icu-podcast/walking-home-from-the-icu-episode-157-sedation-is-sleep-deprivation/

Dayton, K., Hudson, M., & Lindroth, H. (2023). Stopping delirium using the awake-and-walking intensive care unit approach: True mastery of critical thinking and the ABCDEF Bundle. *AACN Advanced Critical Care, 34,* 359–366.

Dayton, K., Lindroth, H., Engel, H. J., Fuchita, M., Gonzalez, P., Nydahl, P., Stollings, J. L., & Boehm, L. M. (2025). Creating a culture of an awake and walking intensive care unit: In-hospital strategies to mitigate post-intensive care syndrome. *Critical Care Clinics, 41,* 121–140.

Ely, E. W., Shintani, A., Truman, B., Speroff, T., Gordon, S. M., Harrell, F. E., Jr, Inouye, S. K., Bernard, G. R., & Dittus, R. S. (2004). Delirium as a predictor of mortality in mechanically ventilated patients in the intensive care unit. *JAMA, 291,* 1753–1762.

Ely, E. W., Siegel, M. D., & Inouye, S. K. (2001). Delirium in the intensive care unit: An under-recognized syndrome of organ dysfunction. *Seminars in Respiratory and Critical Care Medicine, 22,* 115–126.

Grover, S., Sahoo, S., Chakrabarti, S., & Avasthi, A. (2019). Post-traumatic stress disorder (PTSD) related symptoms following an experience of delirium. *Journal of Psychosomatic Research, 123,* 109725.

Guttormson, J. L., Chlan, L., Tracy, M. F., Hetland, B., & Mandrekar, J. (2019). Nurses' attitudes and practices related to sedation: A national survey. *American Journal of Critical Care, 28,* 255–263.

Haeseler, G., Störmer, M., Bufler, J., Dengler, R., Hecker, H., Piepenbrock, S., & Leuwer, M. (2001). Propofol blocks human skeletal muscle sodium channels in a voltage-dependent manner. *Anesthesia and Analgesia, 92,* 1192–1198.

Hermans, G., & Van den Berghe, G. (2015). Clinical review: intensive care unit acquired weakness. *Critical Care, 19,* 274.

Hermans, G., van Mechelen, H., Clerckx, B., Vanhullebusch, T., Mesotten, D., Wilmer, A., Casaer, M. P., Meersseman, P., Debaveye, Y., van Cromphaut, S., Wouters, P. J., Gosselink, R., & van den Berghe, G. (2014). Acute outcomes and 1-year mortality of intensive care unit-acquired weakness. A cohort study and propensity-matched analysis. *American Journal of Respiratory and Critical Care Medicine, 190,* 410–420.

Herridge, M. S., Tansey, C. M., Matté, A., Tomlinson, G., Diaz-Granados, N., Cooper, A., Guest, C. B., Mazer, C. D., Mehta, S., Stewart, T. E., Kudlow, P., Cook, D., Slutsky, A. S., Cheung, A. M., & Canadian Critical Care Trials Group (2011). Functional disability 5 years after acute respiratory distress syndrome. *New England Journal of Medicine, 364,* 1293–1304.

Herridge, M. S., & Azoulay, É. (2023). Outcomes after Critical Illness. *New England Journal of Medicine, 388,* 913–924.

Hosker, C., & Ward, D. (2017). Hypoactive delirium. *BMJ, 357,* j2047.

Hsieh, S. J., Otusanya, O., Gershengorn, H. B., Hope, A. A., Dayton, C., Levi, D., Garcia, M., Prince, D., Mills, M., Fein, D., Colman, S., & Gong, M. N. (2019). Staged implementation of awakening and breathing, coordination, delirium monitoring and management, and early mobilization bundle improves patient outcomes and reduces hospital costs. *Critical Care Medicine, 47,* 885–893.

Kwon, E., & Choi, K. (2017). Case-control study on risk Factors of unplanned extubation based on patient safety model in critically ill patients with mechanical ventilation. *Asian Nursing Research, 11,* 74–78.

Liu, Q. Z., Hao, M., Zhou, Z. Y., Ge, J. L., Wu, Y. C., Zhao, L. L., Wu, X., Feng, Y., Gao, H., Li, S., & Xue, L. (2019). Propofol reduces synaptic strength by inhibiting sodium and calcium channels at nerve terminals. *Protein & Cell, 10,* 688–693.

Lonardo, N. W., Mone, M. C., Nirula, R., Kimball, E. J., Ludwig, K., Zhou, X., Sauer, B. C., Nechodom, K., Teng, C., & Barton, R. G. (2014). Propofol is associated with favorable outcomes compared with benzodiazepines in ventilated intensive care unit patients. *American Journal of Respiratory and Critical Care Medicine, 189,* 1383–1394.

Long, A. C., Kross, E. K., Davydow, D. S., & Curtis, J. R. (2014). Posttraumatic stress disorder among survivors of critical illness: creation of a conceptual model addressing identification, prevention, and management. *Intensive Care Medicine, 40,* 820–829.

Mehta, S., Burry, L., Martinez-Motta, J. C., Stewart, T. E., Hallett, D., McDonald, E., Clarke, F., Macdonald, R., Granton, J., Matte, A., Wong, C., Suri, A., Cook, D. J., & Canadian Critical Care Trials Group (2008). A randomized trial of daily awakening in critically ill patients managed with a sedation protocol: A pilot trial. *Critical Care Medicine, 36,* 2092–2099.

Mei, X., Liu, Y. H., Han, Y. Q., & Zheng, C. Y. (2023). Risk factors, preventive interventions, overlapping symptoms, and clinical measures of delirium in elderly patients. *World Journal of Psychiatry, 13,* 973–984.

Pan, Y., Yan, J., Jiang, Z., Luo, J., Zhang, J., & Yang, K. (2019). Incidence, risk factors, and cumulative risk of delirium among ICU patients: A case-control study. *International Journal of Nursing Sciences, 6,* 247–251.

Pandharipande, P., Shintani, A., Peterson, J., Pun, B. T., Wilkinson, G. R., Dittus, R. S., Bernard, G. R., & Ely, E. W. (2006). Lorazepam is an independent risk factor for transitioning to delirium in intensive care unit patients. *Anesthesiology, 104,* 21–26.

Pandharipande, P. P., Girard, T. D., Jackson, J. C., Morandi, A., Thompson, J. L., Pun, B. T., Brummel, N. E., Hughes, C. G., Vasilevskis, E. E., Shintani, A. K., Moons, K. G., Geevarghese, S. K., Canonico, A., Hopkins, R. O., Bernard, G. R., Dittus, R. S., Ely, E. W., & BRAIN-ICU Study Investigators (2013). Long-term cognitive impairment after critical illness. *New England Journal of Medicine, 369,* 1306–1316.

Pearce, A., & Pearce, B. (2024). *Coma and near-death experience: The beautiful, disturbing, and dangerous world of the unconscious.* Park Street Press.

Pun, B. T., Balas, M. C., Barnes-Daly, M. A., Thompson, J. L., Aldrich, J. M., Barr, J., Byrum, D., Carson, S. S., Devlin, J. W., Engel, H. J., Esbrook, C. L., Hargett, K. D., Harmon, L., Hielsberg, C., Jackson, J. C., Kelly, T. L.,

Kumar, V., Millner, L., Morse, A., Perme, C. S., ... Ely, E. W. (2019). Caring for critically ill patients with the ABCDEF Bundle: Results of the ICU Liberation Collaborative in over 15,000 adults. *Critical Care Medicine, 47,* 3–14.

Pun, B. T., Badenes, R., Heras La Calle, G., Orun, O. M., Chen, W., Raman, R., Simpson, B.-G. K., Wilson-Linville, S., Hinojal Olmedillo, B., Vallejo de la Cueva, A., van der Jagt, M., Navarro Casado, R., Leal Sanz, P., Orhun, G., Ferrer Gómez, C., Núñez Vázquez, K., Piñeiro Otero, P., Taccone, F. S., Gallego Curto, E., ... Pandharipande, P. P. (2021). Prevalence and risk factors for delirium in critically ill patients with COVID-19 (COVID-D): A multicentre cohort study. *Lancet Respiratory Medicine, 9,* 239–250.

Rasulo, F. A., Badenes, R., Longhitano, Y., Racca, F., Zanza, C., Marchesi, M., Piva, S., Beretta, S., Nocivelli, G. P., Matta, B., Cunningham, D., Cattaneo, S., Savioli, G., Franceschi, F., Robba, C., & Latronico, N. (2022). Excessive sedation as a risk factor for delirium: A comparison between two cohorts of ARDS critically ill patients with and without COVID-19. *Life (Basel), 12,* 2031.

Richards D. (2023). Transitioning to reality: The diary of an ARDS survivor. *Intensive Care Medicine, 49,* 1571–1575.

Saccheri, C., Morawiec, E., Delemazure, J., Mayaux, J., Dubé, B. P., Similowski, T., Demoule, A., & Dres, M. (2020). ICU-acquired weakness, diaphragm dysfunction and long-term outcomes of critically ill patients. *Annals of Intensive Care, 10,* 1.

Shehabi, Y., Bellomo, R., Reade, M. C., Bailey, M., Bass, F., Howe, B., McArthur, C., Seppelt, I. M., Webb, S., Weisbrodt, L., Sedation Practice in Intensive Care Evaluation (SPICE) Study Investigators, & ANZICS Clinical Trials Group (2012). Early intensive care sedation predicts long-term mortality in ventilated critically ill patients. *American Journal of Respiratory and Critical Care Medicine, 186,* 724–731.

Schweickert, W. D., Pohlman, M. C., Pohlman, A. S., Nigos, C., Pawlik, A. J., Esbrook, C. L., Spears, L., Miller, M., Franczyk, M., Deprizio, D., Schmidt, G. A., Bowman, A., Barr, R., McCallister, K. E., Hall, J. B., & Kress, J. P. (2009). Early physical and occupational therapy in mechanically ventilated, critically ill patients: A randomised controlled trial. *Lancet, 373,* 1874–1882.

Strøm, T., Martinussen, T., & Toft, P. (2010). A protocol of no sedation for critically ill patients receiving mechanical ventilation: A randomised trial. *Lancet, 375,* 475–480.

Tachibana, M., Inada, T., Ichida, M., & Ozaki, N. (2021). Risk factors for inducing violence in patients with delirium. *Brain and Behavior, 11,* e2276.

Telias, I., & Wilcox, M. E. (2019). Sleep and circadian rhythm in critical illness. *Critical Care, 23,* 82.

TEAM Study Investigators and the ANZICS Clinical Trials Group, Hodgson, C. L., Bailey, M., Bellomo, R., Brickell, K., Broadley, T., Buhr, H., Gabbe, B. J., Gould, D. W., Harrold, M., Higgins, A. M., Hurford, S., Iwashyna, T. J., Serpa Neto, A., Nichol, A. D., Presneill, J. J., Schaller, S. J., Sivasuthan, J., Tipping, C. J., Webb, S., … Young, P. J. (2022). Early active mobilization during mechanical vVentilation in the ICU. *New England Journal of Medicine, 387,* 1747–1758.

van Gassel, R. J. J., Baggerman, M. R., & van de Poll, M. C. G. (2020). Metabolic aspects of muscle wasting during critical illness. *Current Opinion in Clinical Nutrition and Metabolic Care, 23,* 96–101.

Wilson, J. E., Mart, M. F., Cunningham, C., Shehabi, Y., Girard, T. D., MacLullich, A. M. J., Slooter, A. J. C., & Ely, E. W. (2020). Delirium. *Nature Reviews Disease Primers, 6,* 90.

Zaal, I. J., Devlin, J. W., Peelen, L. M., & Slooter, A. J. (2015). A systematic review of risk factors for delirium in the ICU. *Critical Care Medicine, 43,* 40–47.

Chapter Nine

The Paradox of Dying: Spiritually and Emotionally Alive at the End-of-Life

HANNAH MACIEJEWSKI
& CHRISTOPHER KERR

Abstract

End of life is more than a medical treatise. The notion that nothing valuable can come from the final days and weeks of life truncates the totality of the dying experience. Those facing death reveal that even through the transition from a focus on curative treatment, they discover hope and notions of personal meaning. At the end-of-life, awareness goes beyond the physical dimensions of dying to embrace nonphysical experiences which include remarkable and transformative pre-death dreams and visions. Our research team uses an evidence-based approach and has studied the end-of-life experiences of over 1,400 dying patients and their families. Using quantifiable data, we demonstrate that the majority of dying patients experience pre-death dreams which are described as "more real than real" and increase in frequency as death nears. These dreams and visions typically bring comfort to the patient and their loved ones and often include a transition from distress to acceptance. These inner experiences validate the life that was led, lessen the fear of death, and return them to what and whom they loved the most. Pre-death dreams and visions also confirm that dying can include mechanisms of positive psychological adaptation and spiritual growth, moreover, these benefits can extend from the patient to the bereaved. This is the paradox of dying: despite physical decline, patients are often emotionally and spiritually alive, even enlightened.

Introduction

We have lost our way with dying as it has become easier to live longer but harder to die well. This sentiment was expressed by Irish physician and writer, Dr. Seamus O'Mahony who wrote "death in a modern hospital still has a whiff of an industrial accident" (O'Mahony, 2017). The dying process is now largely hidden in settings such as hospitals and nursing homes, places where strangers provide care, and often fail to acknowledge the entirety of the dying experience including one's personhood and spirituality. Dying is evermore a medical rather than a human event, defined by a technically driven medical culture that has unintentionally created an illusion that death can be denied or defied. The science of medicine has outstripped the art of medicine and with it, our obligation to "cure sometimes, to relieve often, and to comfort always." Instead, modern medicine has become curatively biased and often fails to recognize that dying marks the closing of a life, not merely a medical failure.

Humanizing the dying process requires a shift from a medical paradigm, based on organ systems, to one that acknowledges the view from the bed- the patient's perspective and experience. Dying is a time of introspection, integration, and self-actualization that should be driven by an individual's will and interpretation of what a "good death" is (Cottrell & Duggleby, 2016). It stands to reason that one's inner focus becomes not only reflective but revealing. Dying provides a unique vantage point as changes in perspectives and perceptions unfold. In other words, people don't stop living because they are dying. In fact, profound living occurs within the dying process. The inner world of the dying patient includes rich and meaningful dreams and visions. Such pre-death experiences have been acknowledged across all cultures and throughout time. They are in fact recognized in the religious and sacred traditions of many Indigenous people around the world and integral to humanity's need to maintain connection with the departed (Duggleby et al., 2015; Wills-Brandon, 2010). Our work therefore has never claimed to discover, but only shines a light on something always known and merely lost within our larger culture. From a clinical perspective, others have not only documented the significance of such pre-death experiences but described their profound effect on the dying person and their loved ones (Barrett, 1926; Bennett, 1988; Brayne et al., 2006; Dam, 2016; Fenwick & Brayne, 2011; Mazzarino-Willett, 2010; Santos et al., 2017).

Acknowledgement of the patients' subjective experience is also central to hospice and palliative care as it seeks to relieve suffering in its many manifestations, including physical, psychological, spiritual, and existential forms of suffering. Gaining access to human emotions and experiences, that are not inherently measurable by science, requires the input and synergy of an array of disciplines. In fact, the basis of our work began under the direction of a group of nurses, chaplains, social workers, and volunteers. This diverse team of hospice workers were remarkably attuned and receptive to the experiences of the dying patient. In truth, their ability to understand and interpret the patient's inner experiences aided in their assessment of comfort as well as their ability to prognosticate impending death. This team understood that death was approaching based on the content and frequency of the patient's pre-death dreams and visions. These important bedside observations would be the cornerstone of our work for decades which has sought to validate these clinical interpretations.

The significance of pre-death dreams and visions, although widely accepted within the hospice culture, faced scrutiny and even ridicule when attempts were made to share these observations within mainstream medicine (Betty, 2006; Grant et al., 2014). Although end of life dreams and visions (ELDVs) are well documented within the humanities, acknowledgment within the medical literature was largely based on case reports or surveys of third person observers. Moreover, confounding factors such as delirium and medications needed to be controlled and accounted for. The challenge to provide objective validation became the impetus for our work.

A Series of Five ELDVs Studies
Quantitatively Studying ELDVs
The first study had several goals: 1) document ELDV experiences longitudinally; 2) examine the content, prevalence, and significance of ELDVs over time; and 3) discredit the notion that ELDVs are related to confusion or cognitive decline. This initial study included 59 patients who were aged 18 or older and had the capacity to provide informed consent, patients were screened for delirium and passed a Confusion Assessment Method (CAM) that asserted they were cognitively intact. Eligible participants we required to have a Palliative Performance Scale (PPS) score of 40 or greater to ensure they were able to meet the demands of the study (Anderson et al., 1996), did not have a psychotic disorder as per the Diagnostic and Statistical Manual for Mental Disorders (DSM-IV), and did not have a barrier of language or communication. Participants engaged in a standardized interview almost daily, as to quantify changes in the end-of-life process over time.

These 59 patients completed a total of 453 interviews, averaging eight interviews per person. A vast majority of our sample (88%) reported experiencing at least one dream or vision. Most participants reported a single ELDV event daily (81%), with multiple ELDV events occurring daily with less frequency. The sleeping/ waking states in which ELDVs took place were 45% when asleep, 16% when awake, and 39% while asleep and awake. The content of ELDVs was coded on a simple checklist consisting of eight categories. Patients reported that ELDV content included reunions with deceased friends or relatives (72%), going or preparing to go somewhere (39%), living friends or relatives (17%), other people (10%), deceased/living pets or animals, religious figures, past meaningful experiences, and other content (a combined 35%). These categories were not mutually exclusive. The degree of realism for nearly all ELDV events (99%) were reported to "feel more real than real." Participants also rated the comfort/distress that ELDVs brought them on a 5-point scale, with 1 being the most distressing and 5 being the most comforting. The mean distress/comfort score for all dreams was 3.6, with 60% percent of ELDVs rated as comforting or extremely comforting, and 19% rated distressing or extremely distressing. Dreams or visions involving content of previously deceased individuals were associated with the highest level of comfort (mean = 4.1). Additionally, the frequency of end-of-life experiences increased as participants became closer to death, and the most prevalent ELDV content during this time involved reunions with the deceased. This trend suggests that as a patient grows closer to death, they experience more ELDVs that are progressively more comforting in content. This pattern disrupts the common perception that dying involves increasing distress and again emphasizes the vast difference in the dying process we imagine or are socialized to believe, versus the death experienced (Kerr et al., 2014).

> At 95, Frank was still completely aware of his surroundings and loved a good conversation. Most of which had to do with the lifetime worth of baseball lore he had collected. Despite his incredible recall and engagement, when Frank closed his eyes, his room became crowded with dead relatives. His body was shutting down, but his mind had not lost consciousness. One of the visitors in this room was Uncle Harry who died 46 years ago and who "wouldn't shut up." Over time, Frank's inner-world experiences returned him to what he treasured most in life, his wife's love. He dreamt of her more, felt her presence more, and became more peaceful. Frank finally requested that treatment was discontinued. As is so often the case, the patient recognized medical futility before the physician. Frank wanted to join "Ruthie in heaven." He died with the

beauty and grace with which he lived. As his organs failed, his senses, perceptions, and awareness did not. In fact, all signs pointed to the fact that Frank's soul was very much alive. In contrast to the notion of "raging against the dying of the light", Frank, like many patients under these circumstances, was fighting towards it. The "towards" he was drawn to, within his ELDV, a warm familiar love. (Kerr, 2021)

A video of Horace similarly captures a dying patient fighting towards the familiar love of his deceased wife (Video 1, Horace; see below for the internet links to the videos referenced in this text).

Qualitatively Studying ELDVs

The quantitative study of ELDVs provided evidence for their trademark characteristics: sleeping/waking state, vividness, prevalence, comfort, and general themes. The subsequent research became more focused on investigating qualitative content. After patients were deemed eligible, using the same stringent inclusion criteria as the first study, semi-structured interviews were conducted with 63 hospice patients. Participating individuals were interviewed daily for as long as they were able. Participants were simply asked to recount their dreams and visions in as much detail as possible. The results revealed six major themes within ELDVs.

1. Comforting Presence: The presence of deceased or living friends, relatives, and animals who appeared to materialize for the sole purpose of providing comfort was illustrated heavily within the data (Video 2, Florence). One example included a patient who had a sense that "I am not going alone [my sister] will be with me" due to dreams she frequently had of her deceased sister sitting beside her bed. Several patients dreamed of their deceased mothers who provided messages of "everything will be okay" and "I love you". In one dream, the patients mother appeared so vividly that beyond being able to hear her voice, he could smell her perfume. These ELDVs were overwhelmingly described as comforting.

2. Preparing to Go: The act of preparing to go or the act of travelling somewhere, often with an unknown destination, was prevalent in ELDV descriptions. Seeing family members or friends in dreams with the feeling that "I know we are going somewhere, but I don't know where" was a shared experience for many. One patient dreamed of boarding an airplane with her living son but had no sense of where they were head-

ing, another dreamed of driving around his town but again could not determine what his destination was. This type of content was reported as distressing at times because patients felt "hurried", however overall this content was described as comforting.

3. Watching or Engaging with the Dead: Participants recognized others in their dreams as simply being there to watch over, or interact with them as they normally would (Video 3, Jeanne). In one instance, a patient reported that her two aunts would watch over her while she was lying on the couch. Another patient dreamed of being hugged by her deceased father and brothers. Instances of sitting down for a meal or playing games with loved ones were reported along with recollections of playing with pets who had passed away. This type of content was largely reported as comforting.

4. Loved Ones Waiting: Dead relatives and friends in some cases would appear to be waiting for the patient (Video 4, Alice). In one instance, a patient had up to six deceased family members in her room "waiting for her". In another case, a woman recognized her husband who was waiting for her at the bottom of a staircase while she stood at the top. The presence of these dead friends and family members was primarily comforting, however some patients expressed discomfort with this type of content in that they were not ready to die, and the perception that the dead were "waiting" for them was unsettling.

5. Distressing Experiences: There were ELDVs that depicted negative content, commonly related to traumatic life experiences (Video 5, Dwayne). ELDVs reminiscent of abusive childhood memories, difficult relationships, or challenging situations were documented. One patient had graphic dreams of previous war experiences. Another patient had distressing dreams of his family being critical of him, and another patient had dreams of threatening coworkers. While the distressing content was not necessarily enjoyable for patients, distressing dreams often afforded an opportunity for supported discussion in processing these events, life review, and newfound perspectives.

6. Unfinished Business: This category of ELDVs revolved around patients' fears of no longer being able to do things or leaving things unfinished (Video 6, Jennifer). Specifically for parents of young children, distress-

ing dreams of not being able to fulfill parental obligations such as paying bills, getting kids ready for school, and driving to practices were common. Similarly, while these dreams are not as comforting to the patient, they may provide the opportunity for individuals to plan and come to terms with these stressors before their death (Nosek et al., 2015).

Pediatric Accounts

The third publication in regard to this work on ELDVs was a pediatric case series. The study of end-of-life dreams and visions typically focuses on adults; however, children with terminal diagnoses also have these experiences, further delineating that these experiences are related to the psychological and emotional transition to death and not to aging or physical decline. Children and adolescents experience of illness and impending death calls on them to grapple with fears, existential questions, and spiritual concerns much like adults. However, in contrast to older individuals, the lived experiences and the language to discuss such topics is limited for children, making it especially difficult for clinicians to engage in conversations about end-of-life and ELDVs. In the cases documented below, ELDVs brought comfort to the dying process, not by refuting death but by informing and enriching the transition.

> Ginny was a 15-year-old girl whose dreams and visions heavily impacted her dying process (Video 7, Ginny). With exceptional detail, Ginny recounts a dream in which she is in a beautiful castle that has enveloped her with warmth and light, playing dolls and singing songs with her deceased aunt. In her own words, Ginny describes the castle as a "safe place" and emphasizes that she is "not alone." In addition to her aunt, the castle is home to numerous deceased family pets that now appear alive, healthy, and playful. Upon waking, Ginny found meaning in her ELDV experience, telling her mother, "I'm going to be okay, I'm not alone." (Levy et al., 2020)

Four days before Ginny's death, her mother, Michele heard a peculiar conversation through a baby monitor that was kept on Ginny's bedside table. When Michele asked Ginny whom she was talking to, Ginny responded, "I was talking to God." She added "He's old, but he's kinda cute." She said to her mother, "I'm not going to be sick; you know where I'm going. You know, to the castle" (Levy et al., 2020).

Another pediatric case was that of thirteen-year-old Jessica (Video 8,

Jessica).

> She dreamed in ways that she was aware of her impending death but also secured in love. Jessica did not pause to mourn the life she would not get to live, she had no regrets to mull over, she was living in the now, and her ELDVs were part of that present, an extension of the life she was living. Jessica was raised by a single mother and her concern was how would she go on without her mother. Near death, Jessica began to dream of a mother figure, her mother's friend Mary who died at 35, when Jessica was only 8: "Mary is one of my mom's best friends who passed away from leukemia. I think I was pretty close to her, and she was very close to my mom." The vision of this mother surrogate, her mother's best friend, brought tremendous peace to her. She felt "relief and happiness". She continued, "Mary was a very strong person, and I know that I am strong, and my mom tells me all the time that I am like her." Kristin, who never left her daughter's side, reminded her that "You told me all the time that: 'Mom I saw an angel,' and then you were able to go to sleep." "Yes," Jessica nodded, "I was able to go to sleep... it was really comforting, and I was not afraid of it at all." Jessica also spoke often of dreams of her deceased dog Shadow. Shadow's presence was so vivid that she often struggled to determine whether, "it was real or imagined." (Kerr, 2021)

The knowledge of death that adults first experience as grief and sadness is not afforded to children in the same way. The difference in children's end of life experiences is often the innocence, the lack of questioning, the naive way that they do not become focused on the boundaries between life and death. Children do not have complex vocabularies or fully formed theories on life or death, yet they remain impacted and transcended by the richness of an ELDV experience (Kerr, 2021).

Growth at the End of Life

ELDVs demonstrate that beyond the physical symptomology of dying, there is a profound multidimensional inner process that reaffirms life. This life affirming experience points out again the clear paradox within the dying process that there is space for spiritual and emotional growth even at life's end. The ability to acknowledge one's own end-of-life can be extremely difficult or traumatic, however the ability to overcome such a harsh reality with positive psychological change is possible, and is defined with the term posttraumatic growth (PTG). The fourth study begged the question of whether the experience of ELDVs enabled PTG to take place, easing and expanding the depth of the transition from life to death. Individuals who were having ELDVs were compared to those who were not, it was anticipated that those having ELDVs would be afforded more opportunities for PTG.

Participants over the age of 18, with a minimum PPS score of 30, who were free of cognitive diagnoses and had the ability to communicate and give informed consent were enrolled in this study. Once enrolled, participants completed demographic measures, the Confusion Assessment Method (CAM), the post-traumatic growth inventory (PTGI), and a brief dream interview with the researcher. Every day following the initial visit, verbal consent was reobtained, and participants were asked to complete the CAM, PTGI, and dream interview again. Patients were interviewed daily until they no longer wanted to participate, could no longer participate, or were discharged from hospice.

Of the 70 participants recruited, 35 had experienced at least one ELDV, while the other 35 had not. Independent statistical t-tests between ELDV and non-ELDV participants revealed significant findings. Participants were compared across five domains of PTG: Relating to Others, New Possibilities, Personal Strength, Spiritual Change, and Appreciation for Life. There were significant differences between groups on the factors of personal strength and spiritual change, as well as overall PTG, in that patients who had ELDVs reported significantly higher scores than patients who didn't have ELDVs.

These results suggest that while ELDVs are themselves a vehicle for garnering comfort and meaning at the end of life, they also promote positive psychological growth in respect to certain dimensions of PTG. These findings quantify the expanded insight, understanding, and growth that can come from experiencing ELDVs (Levy et al., 2020).

The Impact on Bereaved Families

People die within the context of their lives, which of course includes those they love. In return, how family and loved ones observe or interpret the death of a loved one impacts how they will grieve and remember. In the fifth study, we investigated if the positive and comforting psychological features of ELDVs extend from the patient to the family at the bedside. It was hypothesized that the bereaved family member's interpretation and perception of ELDVs would correlate to their attitude and impact their journey through bereavement.

Five hundred family caregivers (FCGs) of patients who died under hospice care were recruited for this study. The survey results suggested that openness to ELDV experiences positively correlated with comfort for both patients and bereaved FCGs, and negatively with fear and anxiety surrounding ELDV experiences. Positive general attitudes towards ELDVs and positive ELDV perceptions were correlated with better bereavement outcomes. Additionally, individuals with positive attitudes and perceptions saw ELDVs as a natural part of the dying process. In contrast, negative perceptions, such as attributing the ELDVs to medication side effects or delirium, affected grief negatively, in that accepting the loss or maintaining a connection with the deceased was more difficult.

How a family caregiver makes sense of their loved one's ELDVs actually matters little. The grief experience, much like the dying experience, is multidimensional, flexible, and subjective to the person. What is important however, is the higher level of acceptance achieved by the dying and bereaved alike when they

> "When he told me that he saw his favorite sister (deceased) hold out her hands to him, it made me feel comforted because I knew it comforted him. [...] He did find comfort talking to and seeing people who passed before him. He was not afraid or scared—he had told me." (Kerr, 2021)

These experiences embody for caregivers as much as for the dying, the possibility of being reunited, and it allows them to adjust to life without their loved one while maintaining a continuing bond (Video 9, Dianne). The bereaved find serenity and reassurance in the knowledge that their family members felt at ease and loved in their last moments (Video 10, Norb). This work underlines the need for patient and family education on ELDVs that focuses on awareness and understanding of ELDVs in order to enhance their positive impacts (Grant et al., 2021).

Implications for Practice

A principal obligation of the care team is to help translate the dying process and to lessen the obstacles between patients and those at the bedside. As shown in the previous study, caregivers preconceived notions regarding dreams, directly correlated to their interpretation and their degree of peace as they navigated grief. It is important that the care team help by validating and normalizing the near universality of ELDVs. Unfortunately, without such explanation, ELDVs are often interpreted by family as a side effect of medication, brain disease, or manifestations of a patient's fear of dying.

The results of these studies have important implications for caregivers as well as all disciplines providing care for patients at the end of life. Dying is often lonely and isolating and perhaps more so when the patients' inner experiences are invalidated or dismissed. The challenge from a pure medical perspective is that such experiences are subjective and reference an unshared reality for which there are no means to objectively measure or validate. Too frequently such experiences are dismissed as "delirium" and of course medications used to treat this "delirium" may sterilize or blunt the patient from such transformative experiences within the dying process. This again underscores the need to de-medicalize the dying process in a way that allows for acknowledgement of the patients' experience. The clinical importance of ELDVs continues to build momentum from multiple studies (Hession et al., 2024; Nyblom et al., 2022; Rabitti et al., 2024; Santos et al., 2017). The best ways to support patients and families, and continue this important work is by validating, building rapport, utilizing active listening, allowing for self-interpretation of these experiences, and normalizing their occurrence (Grant et al., 2023).

Recently, we were in the room of an older dying patient who, with eyes closed, was speaking in her childhood language of Polish. Her daughter sat uncomfortably in the corner of the room with her hands on her lap. She was justifiably unsettled by her mother's ongoing conversations with numerous people, all unseen. We explained to the daughter that the dying process included progressive sleep, as well as changes to sleep cycles and architecture and that often, patients experience vivid dreams that feel near virtual, overwhelmingly comforting and often focus on those they loved during life. When we rounded the next day, the daughter had a new place sitting beside her mother's bed with a notepad in hand. The daughter was documenting her mother's experiences including references to early life, childhood friends, family, pets, and memorable experiences.

Most of us can relate to the daughter of the Polish immigrant. As we sat at the bedside of those we love, we struggle with uncertainty—are they at peace or are they alone now that they are beyond our reach? Perhaps we should accept that dying is a mystery and that we don't have answers to all the unknown. What matters though is that we have reverence for the patient's experience. Within the obvious tragedy and suffering of dying, are unseen processes that hold meaning. The dying patient often experiences a growing sense of belonging that leaves us more connected than alone.

Links to Videos

Video 1, Horace:	youtu.be/Ssfw-sRiNuo
Video 2, Florence:	youtu.be/oz_YWPomLdc
Video 3, Jeanne:	youtu.be/ECmFizzZEg0
Video 4, Alice:	youtu.be/V4PzG8BFECM
Video 5, Dwayne:	youtu.be/1B05llRYXeI
Video 6, Jennifer:	youtu.be/InncrCm_O18
Video 7, Ginny:	youtu.be/hykQVBYDmsM
Video 8, Jessica:	youtu.be/qCMtnkoxgs0
Video 9, Dianne:	youtu.be/88fJDXZ7sg4
Video 10, Norb:	youtu.be/3cmo7UyFBwY

References

Anderson, F., Downing, G. M., Hill, J., Casorso, L., & Lerch, N. (1996). Palliative performance scale (PPS): A new tool. *Journal of Palliative Care, 12*, 5–11.

Barrett, W. (1926). Death-bed visions. Methuen & Co. Available at: https://babel.hathitrust.org/cgi/pt?id=inu.39000005818419&seq=7

Bennett, G. (1988). [Review of Death-bed visions, by W. Barrett]. *Folklore, 99*, 132–132.

Betty, L. S. (2006). Are they hallucinations or are they real? The spirituality of deathbed and near-death visions. *Omega, 53*, 37–49.

Brayne, S., Farnham, C., & Fenwick, P. (2006). Deathbed phenomena and their effect on a palliative care team: A pilot study. *American Journal of Hospice and Palliative Medicine, 23*, 17–24.

Cottrell, L., & Duggleby, W. (2016). The "good death": An integrative literature review. *Palliative and Supportive Care, 14,* 686–712.

Dam, A. K. (2016). Significance of end-of-life dreams and visions experienced by the terminally ill in rural and urban India. *Indian Journal of Palliative Care, 22,* 130–134.

Duggleby, W., Kuchera, S., MacLeod, R., Holyoke, P., Scott, T., Holtslander, L., Letendre, A., Moeke-Maxwell, T., Burhansstipanov, L., & Chambers, T. (2015). Indigenous people's experiences at the end of life. *Palliative and Supportive Care, 13,* 1721–1733.

Fenwick, P., & Brayne, S. (2011). End-of-life experiences: Reaching out for compassion, communication, and connection – meaning of deathbed visions and coincidences. *American Journal of Hospice and Palliative Care, 28,* 7–15.

Grant, P. C., Levy, K., Lattimer, T. A., Depner, R. M., & Kerr, C. W. (2021). Attitudes and perceptions of end-of-life dreams and visions and their implication to the bereaved family caregiver experience. *American Journal of Hospice and Palliative Medicine, 38,* 778–784.

Grant, P. C., Levy, K., Rossi, J. L., & Lattimer, T. A. (2023). End-of-life dreams and visions: Initial guidelines and recommendations to support dreams and visions at the end of life. *Journal of Palliative Medicine, 26,* 684–689.

Grant, P., Wright, S., Depner, R., & Luczkiewicz, D. (2014). The significance of end-of-life dreams and visions. *Nursing Times, 110,* 22–24.

Hession, A., Luckett, T., Currow, D., & Barbato, M. (2024). Nurses' encounters with patients having end-of-life dreams and visions in an acute care setting – A cross-sectional survey study. *Journal of Advanced Nursing, 80,* 3190–3198.

Kerr, C. (2021). Experiences of the Dying: Evidence of Survival of Human Consciousness. Available at: https://www.bigelowinstitute.org/wp-content/uploads/2022/10/kerr-experiences-dying.pdf

Kerr, C. W., Donnelly, J. P., Wright, S. T., Kuszczak, S. M., Banas, A., Grant, P. C., & Luczkiewicz, D. L. (2014). End-of-life dreams and visions: A longitudinal study of hospice patients' experiences. *Journal of Palliative Medicine, 17,* 296–303.

Levy, K., Grant, P. C., Depner, R. M., Byrwa, D. J., Luczkiewicz, D. L., & Kerr, C. W. (2020). End-of-life dreams and visions and posttraumatic growth: A comparison study. *Journal of Palliative Medicine, 23,* 319–324.

Levy, K., Grant, P. C., & Kerr, C. W. (2020). End-of-life dreams and visions in pediatric patients: A case study. *Journal of Palliative Medicine, 23,* 1549–1552.

Mazzarino-Willett, A. (2010). Deathbed phenomena: Its role in peaceful death and terminal restlessness. *American Journal of Hospice and Palliative Medicine, 27,* 127–133.

Nosek, C. L., Kerr, C. W., Woodworth, J., Wright, S. T., Grant, P. C., Kuszczak, S. M., Banas, A., Luczkiewicz, D. L., & Depner, R. M. (2015). End-of-life dreams and visions: A qualitative perspective from hospice patients. *American Journal of Hospice and Palliative Care, 32,* 269–274.

O'Mahony, S. (2017). *The way we die now: The view from medicine's front line.* St. Martin's Publishing Group.

Rabitti, E., Cavuto, S., Díaz Crescitelli, M. E., Bassi, M. C., & Ghirotto, L. (2024). Hospice patients' end-of-life dreams and visions: A systematic review of qualitative studies. *American Journal of Hospice and Palliative Medicine, 41,* 99–112.

Santos, C. S. D., Paiva, B. S. R., Lucchetti, A. L. G., Paiva, C. E., Fenwick, P., & Lucchetti, G. (2017). End-of-life experiences and deathbed phenomena as reported by Brazilian healthcare professionals in different healthcare settings. *Palliative and Supportive Care, 15,* 425–433.

Wills-Brandon, C. (2010). *One last hug before I go: The mystery and meaning of deathbed visions.* Simon and Schuster.

Chapter Ten

The Shared Death Experience: Expanding the Scientific and Philosophical Understanding of Consciousness and Death

WILLIAM J. PETERS, MONICA WILLIAMS & NANCY PHILPOTT

Abstract

The shared death experience (SDE) is an increasingly recognized phenomenon that challenges conventional materialist paradigms of consciousness and the nature of death. During SDEs, people feel that they have participated in a dying person's transition to a post-mortem existence. Unlike near-death experiences (NDEs), which often occur when individuals are in very severe health crises and seemingly unconscious, SDEs are reported by caregivers, loved ones, or bystanders who are not in a health crisis but perceive themselves as participating in the transition of another person from life to death. This chapter examines the historical and phenomenological foundations of the SDE, drawing primarily from qualitative research and end-of-life studies. It explores SDE typologies and features and discusses implications for consciousness studies and post-materialist science.

Introduction

Death remains one of the most profound and mysterious aspects of human existence. Across cultures and historical periods, individuals have reported extraordinary experiences surrounding the transition from life to death, suggesting that consciousness may not be confined to the brain nor extinguished at the moment of physical death. Among these phenomena are shared death experiences (SDEs). They can be defined as particularly compelling events in which loved ones, caregivers, or bystanders report that they are sharing in a dying person's transition to a benevolent postmortem existence (afterlife).

The dominant motif in the SDE appears to be "journey." Movement, often ascension, frequently toward "the light," is a common characteristic. The dominant themes expressed by experiencers are that during their SDE, they possessed heightened knowledge, a sense of profound belonging, and ineffable feelings of love. The relationship or bond between the experiencer and the dying person appears central to the SDE. The possible features in the SDE are similar, if not identical, to the near-death experience (NDE). Numerous elements reported from NDEs, such as the separation of consciousness from the body, the perception of a mystical or transcendent light, encountering mystical or deceased beings as well as heavenly realms, and alterations of space and time are reported from both kinds of experiences, albeit with different prevalence (Shared Crossing Research Initiative, 2022). This suggests that the SDE and NDE reflect a common post-human death experience (Shared Crossing Research Initiative, 2021).

Like NDEs, which are well-documented in clinical and anecdotal literature, SDEs challenge conventional neuroscientific models. But whereas NDEs often occur under conditions of severe impairment of brain functions, SDEs generally occur in the healthy body and minds of unsuspecting others, who are often but not always loved ones, and who are either fully conscious or in a sleep state at the time of the experience. It is therefore difficult to attribute the experience of NDE-like features in SDEs to compromised brain functions. By examining the paradigm-challenging nature of these experiences, we aim to situate the SDE within a broader framework of consciousness studies and post-materialist science. In this chapter, we explore the historical and phenomenological foundations of the SDE by drawing primarily upon qualitative research findings and end-of-life studies.

The SDE has been documented for centuries in the literature, although it has been described under different terminologies. In the late 19th and early 20th centuries, researchers from the Society for Psychical Research (SPR), including Frederic Myers and Sir William Barrett, collected numerous accounts of apparitions around the time of death, in which healthy individuals perceived the transition of a loved one at a distance. Myers' 1903 publication, Human Personality and Its Survival of Bodily Death, described these cases where individuals reported telepathic or visionary experiences coinciding with the death of a loved one.

Based on such reports, authors such as Ernesto Bozzano (1923) and Barrett (1926) documented numerous cases of visions around the time of death.

A review of the 58 death-related vision accounts contained in Barrett's book finds that 17 of these can be classified as SDEs. In these accounts, caregivers and family members witness the departure of a dying person's consciousness, often accompanied by visions of deceased relatives or luminous beings. Later researchers such as Karlis Osis and Erlendur Haraldsson (1971) contributed to the broader study of deathbed visions, though they did not explicitly identify the SDE as a distinct experience. During the recent years, authors made more explicit mention of them. For example, Yvonne Kason (2000) referred to the SDE by the term "death watch experiences", Phyllis Atwater (2007) referred to the SDE as an "empathic death experience", and Pim van Lommel as "empathetic NDE" (van Lommel, 2010).

Also in 2010, Raymond Moody, who coined the term "near-death experience" in 1975, formally introduced the term "shared death experience" into the literature. He highlighted SDEs as a unique phenomenon distinct from NDEs because they are experienced by healthy bystanders but not by people in health crises (Moody, 2010).

In recent years, the Shared Crossing Research Initiative, led by William Peters, has conducted groundbreaking research, focusing specifically on SDEs and their therapeutic implications, collecting more than 600 cases to date, largely unpublished. This initiative has helped establish a structured framework for understanding and categorizing these experiences. Peters published the first research-based, general-public book that features 28 SDE accounts worldwide (Peters, 2022).

Recent research further indicates that SDEs are reported across various cultures and among those with diverse belief systems. Tressoldi et al. (2023) published a survey of culturally diverse populations regarding SDEs and after-death-communications (ADCs) which included but was not limited to: Taiwanese Buddhists, Mexican and Italian participants with a Catholic religious cultural background, and Brazilian spiritists. Participants were randomly sampled and were self-selected with a final total of 121 respondents reporting 146 experiences. The largest percentage of participants, 27% of the sample, identified themselves as not following any religion at all. The next largest groups of respondents identified themselves as Spiritual 17%, Catholic 15%, and Kardecist Spiritism 14%. SDEs reported among divergent religious and cultural populations suggest that they are not merely cultural or religiously conditioned expectations but rather consistent transpersonal experiences that reveal deeper aspects of human consciousness.

Phenomenological Core Features of the Shared Death Experience

Moody (2010) originally identified seven core features that he referred to as elements of the SDE. Recent research conducted by the Shared Crossing Research Initiative has confirmed and expanded upon Moody's foundational research and identified additional core phenomenological features of the SDE, many of which closely resemble NDEs. In the following, we provide examples of eleven identified core features (see also Table 1 below).

1. *A vision of the dying:* Seeing some sort of physical form of the person who is dying.

   Adela, at the time of her father's death: "I think he's gone; he's not breathing. I walked in, and he was not in his body anymore. But I saw him as clearly as I see you now, slightly elevated but in the corner of the room, a light behind him. I said to him, 'Go to the light,' and I smiled. He started laughing. It was the most beautiful, amazing moment between us, so many rich layers of things coming together right then. I was laughing, he was laughing, and then he turned and he went. He was gone" (Peters, 2022, p. 51).

2. *Heightened awareness:* SDErs express that they possessed a kind of higher knowledge, often about the higher meaning or purpose of human existence and consciousness itself. Some say they accessed the ultimate reality.

   Ida, at her mother's death, recalls: "I was floating upward, and we went farther up. She was ahead of me, and we entered this black void or darkness. It was as huge as the sky, but it was an intimate feeling. I felt there were other souls there. We were floating around in this realm, and every question I ever had was answered. I had the answer to everything. I felt connected with the souls around me and this Divine Being and my mother. I felt like we were one. 'We're all one' was the strongest message I was given out of this" (Peters, 2022, p. 60).

3. *Encounters with spirit beings:* Experiencers frequently report seeing deceased relatives or spiritual beings who appear to welcome or guide the dying person. Some describe beings of light or angels.

   Leslie, when her father died, said, "I had this image of this golden light and Dad with his two brothers and his mom and their arms around each other, walking away, and he was looking back over his shoulder like, Yeah, it's okay, I'm good" (Peters, 2022, p. 164).

4. *Witnessing a transcendent light:* A frequent number of experiencers report seeing or sensing a radiant, loving light, often described as a gateway to another dimension.

   Christina, at her mother's bedside, recalls, "I saw her going towards a bright light. I knew it was her because, in those exact moments, I said, "I'm here, God's here, and that's when I saw the light. I saw her go towards the light. It felt like when you're drinking water and you can feel it, and you're still drinking water. It was white and really bright. I can compare it to the sun, the sunlight" (C. Coyne, personal communication, 1/2/19).

5. *Alterations in the perception of time and space:* The realization that time has slowed, stopped, or been undiscernible. Physical environments warp or transform out of three-dimensional reality.

   Karla, at her husband's deathbed, recalls, "He came right up to my face and showed me his face and his happiness. Then the hospital wall, it's hard to describe, it like it disappeared. There should have been a room right next to us, but instead, we were at the edge of the building" (Peters, 2022, p. 196).

6. *Seeing spirit leave the body:* SDErs describe witnessing a mist, light, or energetic form rising from the form of the dying body.

   Sallie, at the bedside when her mother died, described seeing a "membranous, mist-like substance rise from her mother's body at the moment of death. She later felt a powerful wave of love and peace, reassuring her mother was safe" (S. Light, personal communication, 10/29/19).

7. *Appearance of heavenly realms:* A vision of beautiful environments often described as hyper-alive and pulsing with energetic vitality.

   Alice recalls, "I found myself behind my husband, who is going up in the blue sky. And there is this feeling of perfect beatitude. It was perfect, perfect peace, kind of what I saw on his face when I walked into his room that morning. In this experience, I couldn't see his face exactly. It wasn't as if I could see my husband physically, but I was following him into the heavenly spheres, into blue light and white clouds. I don't know how high I was, but I was up there with him, and I kept following him and following him. And at one point, I made the decision to come back. I'm sure I didn't actually have the choice; I think I had to come back. If I didn't, I would have to die" (Peters, 2022, p. 188).

8. *A boundary the experiencer cannot cross:* A point where the experiencer realizes they cannot go any further and immediately finds themselves back in their physical human body.

   Gail remembers clearly, "I was with my dad when he suddenly began to have a seizure, and I screamed for help. The medical team descended quickly, and a nurse escorted me down the hallway to a small room with a desk and a couple of chairs. I remember sitting down. Then quite unexpectedly, I was in two places at once. I was sitting in that little hospital waiting room, but I was also outside on this incredibly beautiful day, walking down a road. I didn't see anyone, but I knew I wasn't alone. I had a feeling I was on a journey and I was escorting someone somewhere. We came to a huge gate and behind this gate was a gigantic mansion. I heard voices saying, 'Hurry! Hurry! Walter's almost here!' Walter was my dad's name. I felt this presence go through the gate—It was my dad! I wanted to go with him, but I knew that I wasn't allowed to. I looked around; then, immediately, I was back in that little room. The very next minute, the doctor walked in looking sad and said, 'I'm sorry, he's gone'" (Peters, 2022, p. 5).

9. *Sensing unusual energy:* Feelings of strong energy described as vibration, buzzing, higher frequency, or electrical in nature. This energy is often felt as a connection to a higher source.

   Sonya, at the time her friend Denni died, recounts, "Then I started having this sensation of just an intense electrical sensation in my body. It was so strong it felt like it was waking me up; as I was waking up, I became…I don't know what happened. But I literally felt like I was being pulled into an upright position" (S. Fairbanks, personal communication, 6/23/20).

10. *Overpowering emotions:* Being completely overwhelmed by the most desirable feelings and emotions. Often described as the most profound sense of connection, belonging, or expression of love one has ever experienced.

    Brian, at his wife's deathbed, remembers, "I'm lying there holding her, and she's on my right side, and I start feeling this opposite of sadness. I start feeling this feeling, and it's very distinctly coming from my right side into me. It's a feeling of joy, love, and uplift. And it was a little bit dissonant in my mind because I was grieving already that she was dying. But I couldn't, couldn't really hold on to that" (B. Sackett, personal communication, 5/26/20).

11. *Physical sensations:* Actual physical, bodily responses that seem to mimic the sensations of the dying around their time of death.

Sarah recalls, "I woke up abruptly with a severe cramp in my leg. I've had cramps before but nothing like this. I leaped out of bed and began jumping up and down. I woke up my husband. What came next was terrifying. This is the part I don't remember. I was stiff and seizing. My eyes were rolling back in my head. My husband called for my kids to call 911. I woke up and told everyone I was okay. My daughter canceled the ambulance. I looked at my son and said, 'That was the strangest experience. That's what it feels like to die.' I then began to sweat profusely. I drenched the sheets for about two hours and then vomited. I called my sister, and she said I should go to the doctor. But I felt normal other than being wiped out. Twenty minutes later, my sister called and said my niece had died. She had snorted fentanyl-laced heroin" (Peters, 2022, p. 115).

Table 1: Eleven core SDE features and their prevalence (Peters, 2022, p. 238). Percentages relate to a sample of 164 cases.

A vision of the dying person	51%
Heightened awareness	37%
Encounters with spirit beings	29%
Witnessing a transcendent light	25%
Alterations in the perception of time and space	19%
Seeing the spirit leave the body	15%
Appearance of heavenly realms	12%
A boundary the experiencer cannot cross	11%
Sensing unusual energy	20%
Overpowering emotions	29%
Physical sensations	9%

Two Shared Death Experience Typologies
William Peters furthermore developed two distinct typologies to classify SDEs. The first classification, or the Main Typological Classification, includes a proximity classification with two subtypes concerning the time of the SDE in relation to the death and the number of experiences. The second typological classification, termed Modes of Participation, concerns four distinct but non-exclusive kinds of SDEs. These different types and subtypes of SDEs are described below in more detail.

1. Main Typological Classification: Location and Proximity to the Dying
The proximity of the SDEr to the dying is the first classification for which there are two designations: Bedside or Remote. Bedside SDEs occur when the experiencer is located in the same physical location (at the bedside, in the same room, or within visual sight) of the dying person. They account for 36% of all experiences and represent typical examples of SDEs as introduced by Moody (2010) in which, for example, bystanders at bedsides co-experience NDE-like elements along with the dying person.

Remote SDEs occur when the experiencer is not in the same physical location as the dying. The experiencer can be in the next room, across town, or on the other side of the globe. These SDEs account for 64% of experiences (SCRI, 2021). They concern typical examples of experiences described in the earlier literature on death-related experiences by Myers (1903) and which include what has been called "crisis telepathy" and "crisis apparitions", for example apparitions of the dying who seem to inform loved ones at a distance about their demise and transition.

But SDEs can further be classified by the element of time, which is referred to as the sub-type Time Variation of the Main Typological Classification:

1a. Time Variation
Most SDEs transpire very close to the observed time of death, while 7% occur a few hours or, in rare cases, a few days before death. This tends to occur when moribund individuals are declining. These SDEs are referred to as Early SDEs. Additionally, 14% occur a few hours or a few days after death. These are referred to as Delayed SDEs (SCRI, 2021). In these cases, people experience being in contact with the recently deceased individual and the SDEr expresses that they are being informed of or observing their (ongoing) transition. Most SDEs occur within a set period of time, typically a few moments to

minutes, but SDEs may also occur over a longer period of time, and these are referred to as Gradual SDEs (W. Peters, personal communication, 08/16/2020). In other contexts, delayed and gradual SDEs have previously been discussed as after-death communications (ADCs; e.g., Penberthy et al., 2023; Woollacott et al., 2022). Whereas the emphasis of the term ADC lies on the fact that these experiences occur after somebody has died, the emphasis of the latter two terms lies on the feature of sharing an experience with the deceased including the elements of transition with movement and journey motif operative.

1b. Quantity of SDErs (Single or Multi-Person) per Death

Another sub-type of the Main Typological Classification of SDEs relates to the quantity of SDErs for a particular death. The vast majority of SDErs report that, to the best of their knowledge, they were the only experiencer at the time of a particular death. However, transition-related phenomena that are experienced by more than one person around the time somebody dies have been reported as well (Barrett, 1926; Bozzano, 1923). The Shared Crossing Research Initiative has collected many dozens of multi-person SDEs and thus classifies these experiences as the Multi-person SDE sub-type (W. Peters, personal communications, 08/16/2020).

2. Secondary Typological Classification: Modes of Participation

The Modes of Participation (MOP) assesses the qualitative experience reported by the shared death experiencer (SDEr). There are four distinct and nonexclusive modes of participation: remotely sensing a death, witnessing unusual phenomena attributed to death, accompanying the dying in a visionary realm, and assisting the dying in transitioning (SCRI, 2021).

2a. MOP 1: Remotely Sensing a Death

Remotely sensing a death occurs in about 20% of SDE accounts when the experiencer has brief thoughts, feelings, or a sense of the dying's presence around the time of death (SCRI, 2021). Dawn recalls remotely sensing the death of her son Sean a few days before his wedding.

> "I was home, hot-gluing flowers on this big selfie board for the wedding. I was texting Sean's fiancé, Tessa, saying, 'Do you like this? Do you know what this is?' And she said, 'Is that tissue paper?' And I was writing her back saying, 'Yes.' And I was writing, Y-E-S. And I got the Y out, and then suddenly, I couldn't see the phone. I couldn't see anything. My feet came

off the floor. I felt like I was gonna pass out, and I got really nauseated. I scooted this bench up under me, and I looked behind me because we had all these flowers on the kitchen floor through the hallway, and real strong; all of a sudden, I felt Sean was dead. In my mind, I said, 'We're wasting our time.' At 10:31, I got a call from Tessa to tell me that Sean had been hit by a car, and I said to myself, 'This happened at 10:27.' Nearly five minutes before" (Peters, 2022, p. 111).

2b. MOP 2: Witnessing Unusual Phenomena Attributed to a Death

Witnessing unusual phenomena is the most common MOP and occurs in 88% of SDE accounts (SCRI, 2021). Scott witnessed unusual phenomena associated with the death of his stepson Nolan.

What Scott saw, as Nolan's heart stopped beating on the monitor, "was Mary Fran coming and scooping Nolan up out of his physical body. Mother and son embraced, and then they turned to Scott, and embraced me. And then the three of us merge into the clear light." Scott describes the light as an "all-encompassing, hugely bright light. Everything around you just exudes the light of the universe. So, the table, the chairs, you, me, everything. All of a sudden, you begin to see it with these eyes that are aware that we're all made of exactly the same stuff. And it is the love of the universe. You are the light." Scott describes it as being both in the room and in another dimension, "I'm in the room, but I have also entered into another dimension that is simultaneous with the one that I am in." He was aware of the grief around him, but at the same time, "I'm with Mary Fran and Nolan, and we're having this moment of unity. I'm with them, and they're with me, and I'm one with everything. And it's incredibly heart-centered. You really are just immersed in the love of the universe." Five or ten minutes passed until "Mary Fran and Nolan turned and left" (Peters, 2022, p. 81).

2c. MOP 3: Accompanying the Dying

Accompanying the dying occurs in 15% of SDE accounts (SCRI, 2021). Experiencers report that they unexpectedly found themselves in another postdeath experience with the dying, or perhaps more accurately stated, the transitioning person. SDErs express that they accompanied the deceased on a beautiful journey. In MOP 2, experiencers may have contact with the recently departed and observe a variety of SDE phenomena but they do not join the recently deceased in their transition journey. MOP 3 experiencers accompany their departing loved ones and at some point, they encountered a limit or boundary. They realized that while their deceased loved one would continue, they could not and suddenly found themselves back in their human life. Cynthia accompanied her husband when he was dying and reported the following:

> "I remember lifting up out of my form, my body, and taking my husband by the hand and pulling him up. Then I pulled him up past me, and then he pulled me up past him, and we kept doing that for a long time. The sensation was very freeing. He was fully intact, you know. He wasn't mentally compromised then. There was no sensation of constraint or discomfort from anyone's body, and then I saw the light. I feel almost corny saying that, but I saw the light, and you know it's not a pinpoint of light. It's a huge light, and I told him, 'Look, there's the light,' and we both turned towards it and went towards it, and his mother appeared. In the experience of the light, here was a complete wholeness sensation for me. A freedom was in that. Any of my own psychology wasn't there. None of that was there. It was just an opportunity to experience that. Then his mother reached for him, and he reached for her, and he looked. He was still holding her hand, and he looked back at me and said, 'But I want to stay with you,' and then he slipped away" (C. Vitale, personal communication, 1/7/2019).

2d. MOP 4: Assisting the Dying in Transitioning

Assisting the dying in transitioning occurs in about 9% of SDE accounts (SCRI, 2021). Experiencers report that they suddenly find themselves with a recently deceased person and realize that they need to assist them with their transition. These experiences are similar to MOP 3, but the experiencers are more involved, often reminding the deceased that they have indeed died and need to orient themselves to their new reality. Experiencers report providing a variety of assistance and, in some cases, describe physically supporting the deceased along their journey and serving as guides. Experiencers often express that the knowledge of how to assist the transitioning person arose at the moment of their encounter, and they were unsure of the source of that knowledge. Mark described assisting his father in his transition, saying:

"I felt an overwhelming need to check in on him. So, I sent myself, my spirit to the hospital where I knew he was. And I get there, and he was just a wraith of a man. My dad was a big guy... Nothing physically was ever daunting to him. But now he was emaciated. I remember going to him at his bedside and speaking to him and saying, 'Dad, why don't you just let go? Mom's going to be all right. All of us kids are going to be all right. You can go. There's nothing holding you here anymore.' And he looks at me, and there's no surprise in his face that I was actually there talking to him, but there was puzzlement, and he said, 'I don't know how. I don't know how.' " Mark had studied a meditation around life and death, specifically about bringing someone near death into the light. "I knew right away, as soon as I was there with my dad, that that's exactly what I needed to do. And I picked him up, and he was as light as a feather. Like there was almost nothing to him. I started that meditation, walking down this particular trail, and then at a certain point, turning, stepping up these stairs, and walking towards the light" (Peters, 2022, p. 91).

Conclusion and Outlook

Shared death experiences provide experiential and phenomenological evidence challenging the notion that consciousness is a result of purely physiological processes—particularly the ability to remotely sense a death or witness another person's transition without previous knowledge that the person was dying. The materialist view that consciousness is solely a byproduct of brain activity is inadequate to explain such phenomena.

Of course, critics of these views can argue that SDEs are hallucinations. However, if they were purely hallucinatory, we would expect random or meaningless experiences rather than consistent patterns, and a lack of verifiable elements; yet many SDE reports include accurate descriptions of distant death events. Therefore, these aspects suggest something more than just an internal brain-generated illusion.

Shared death experiences, like NDEs, present anomalous data that challenge the mainstream neuroscientific view of consciousness. If they are genuinely nonlocal in nature, they could point toward a post-materialist paradigm where consciousness is fundamental or, via alternative mechanisms, operate in ways that defy the present understanding of consciousness as a mere byproduct of brain activity alone. As post-materialist sciences continue to evolve, SDEs offer a crucial lens through which we may redefine the nature of consciousness, death, and human connection. They offer fascinating research avenues for future studies that can enhance our understanding of the dying process and contribute to removing the taboo that often surrounds the topic of death.

References:

Atwater, P. M. H. (2007). *The big book of near-death experiences: The ultimate guide to what happens when we die.* Hampton Roads Publishing.

Barrett, W. (1926). *Death-bed visions.* Methuen and Co LTD.

Bozzano, E. (1923). *Phénomènes psychiques au moment de la mort.* BPS.

Kason, Y. (2000). *Farther shores: Exploring how near-death, kundalini, and mystical experiences can transform ordinary lives.* HarperCollins.

Moody, R. (2010). *Glimpses of eternity: Sharing a loved one's passage from this life to the next.* Guideposts.

Moody, R. A. (1975). *Life after life: The investigation of a phenomenon – survival of bodily death.* Mockingbird Books.

Myers, F. W. H. (1903). *Human personality and its survival of bodily death.* Longmans, Green, and Co.

Osis, K., & Haraldsson, E. (1971). *At the hour of death: A new look at evidence for life after death.* Avon Books.

Penberthy, J. K., St Germain-Sehr, N. R., Grams, G., Burns, M., Lorimer, D., Cooper, C. E., Roe, C. A., Morrison, S., & Elsaesser, E. (2023). Description and impact of encounters with deceased partners or spouses. *Omega,* 302228231207900.

Peters, W. (2022). *At heaven's door.* Simon & Schuster.

Shared Crossing Research Initiative. (2021). Shared Death Experiences: A little-known type of end-of-life phenomena reported by caregivers and loved ones. *American Journal of Hospice & Palliative Care, 38,* 1479–1487.

Shared Crossing Research Initiative. (2022). Comparing near-death experiences and shared death experiences: An illuminating contrast. *Journal of Near-Death Studies, 40,* 77–94.

Tressoldi, P., Alvarez, A. A., Facchin, N., Frullanti, M., Liberale, L., Saad, M., Shiah, Y.-J., & Testoni, I. (2023). Shared death experiences: A multicultural survey. *American Journal of Hospice & Palliative Medicine, 40,* 79–86.

van Lommel, P. (2010). *Consciousness beyond life*. HarperOne.

Woollacott, M., Roe, C. A., Cooper, C., Lorimer, D., & Elsaesser, E. (2022). Perceptual phenomena associated with spontaneous experiences of after-death communication: Analysis of visual, tactile, auditory and olfactory sensations. *Explore, 18,* 423–431.

Chapter Eleven

End-of-Life Experiences in Animals

MICHAEL NAHM, PAM SMART
& RUPERT SHELDRAKE

Abstract

There has recently been an increased interest in end-of-life experiences (ELEs) in humans, but ELEs in non-human animals have not yet been assessed. In this chapter, we summarize findings from a study we performed to collect and analyze reports about remarkable behavioral aspects of animals during their last phase of life. After public appeals in which we asked for reports about ELEs in animals, we received numerous responses from pet owners. We were able to group these experiences into specific categories, which we termed *the last goodbyes, last visits, last rally, retreating into solitude, unusual premonitions of death, somatic surprises, terminal lucidity in animals, and potential near-death visions in animals*. We present representative reports pertaining to these different categories and show that many of them show striking similarities to remarkable behavior reported by dying people. The similarity between animal and human ELEs could increase the recognition that animals share an inner life similar to that of humans during all phases of life. However, as our study was of a preliminary character and only the first of its kind, we encourage further systematic research in this field. Such studies would help to understand facets of the dying process in animals, and especially pets, better. This could lead to a more respectful treatment of pets, as well as of animals in farms, zoos, and in the wild.

Introduction

Numerous treatises on exceptional experiences of humans published in the 19th and 20th centuries covered unusual death-related phenomena. Nevertheless, only in recent decades have spontaneous phenomena that occur around the time somebody dies aroused the interest of scientists in mainstream medical settings. The variety of death-related occurrences has become known by different names, such as death-bed phenomena, end-of-life phenomena, or end-of-life experiences (Brayne et al., 2008; Claxton-Oldfield et al., 2020; dos Santos et al., 2017; Shared Crossing Research Initiative, 2024). They include near-death visions (Claxton-Oldfield & Dunnett, 2018; Depner et al., 2020; Klein et al., 2018; Morita et al., 2016) and terminal lucidity (Claxton-Oldfield & Dunnett, 2018; Nahm, 2012; Nahm et al., 2012; Nahm, 2022, 2024). The study of end-of-life experiences (ELEs) can help to improve our understanding of human nature, advance our knowledge about the dying process, and offer perspectives for dealing with spontaneous and often emotionally intense phenomena in near-death states.

Although unusual death-related experiences have also been reported from non-human animals, research into animal ELEs is lacking almost completely. In order to raise awareness about them, we recently provided the first case compilation regarding phenomena reported to occur when animals die (Sheldrake et al., 2023). The present book chapter is a shortened and revised version of this publication. At the time of writing it, our data base contained about 150 entries of varying quality in which people described behavior of animals that seemed to be related to their impending death. Of these, 114 case reports were sufficiently detailed and appropriate to be considered in our collection. They contain features that allowed us to group them into specific categories. Notwithstanding that some cases could be allocated to more than one category, we classified them into groups with the following names: Last goodbyes (53 case reports), last visits (6), the last rally (28), retreating into solitude (10), unusual premonitions of death (5), somatic surprises (2), terminal lucidity (7), near-death visions (3).

In the following, we present accounts that illustrate typical examples of these types of ELE behavior. More information about the acquisition of the case reports as well as additional examples can be found in our original publication (Sheldrake et al., 2023) and at the website of Rupert Sheldrake (https://www.sheldrake.org/research/end-of-life-experiences). But we also included two new accounts that were sent to us after the original study was published. They demonstrate that many more of these observations must have been made already. These two cases are marked with an asterisk in brackets (*) at their beginning.

Case Examples
Last Goodbyes

The dominant feature in many of the case reports is that the pet seeks to say goodbye to their owners or other loved ones. Typically, these pets are already very weak, and they die soon after this final farewell.

> "This is the sad but true story of what our family experienced with our dog Foxi. We all loved the dog because it was so friendly, devoted, and loyal, as well as very watchful and clever. When the dog became old, it could not hear so well anymore, ate less, and became weak. Finally, at the age of 14, it could barely move from its resting place. Then one day, the following happened: The whole family sat at the dinner table when the good dog struggled to its feet, went around from one to the next, sadly looked at everybody, and gave paws to each member of the family. Then it trudged back, slowly lay down—and died. You can believe me, we had tears in our eyes after this goodbye scene. The dog had felt the end and pulled itself together for a final goodbye to all of us."

> "When I was a child, our family inherited my great-grandmother's parakeet, Sugar-bird. Sugar-bird was a light blue parakeet that had suffered a stroke and was no longer able to use his legs to grasp his perch. My dad installed a batten to replace the perch so the bird could still sit in his spot. One day the bird flew from his cage in the family room to the kitchen while the family was eating dinner at the kitchen table. We were all startled by this as he had never flown outside the cage before. The next day he passed away. We thought at the time that the bird must have flown up to the kitchen to say goodbye to all of us as we were all gathered around the table."

Last Visits

In this category, we included accounts in which animals visited loved ones for a last goodbye in a similar manner as in the cases described in the previous section—but this time, the animals crossed a considerable distance between two different locations. In their book on remarkable aspects of animal life, Gaddis and Gaddis (1970) included a case that represented a case of "psi trailing", i.e. a case in which an animal found its owner in a new location that the animal had never visited previously (Rhine & Feather, 1962; Sheldrake, 2011). A dog found a beloved caretaker in a location it had never been to and then died there. The case described below likewise involves the astonishing feature of psi trailing.

> "For many years I had a mongrel dog called Bruce. When I started courting, I spent less time with him, although I still loved him. In turn, he turned his affection toward a girl who lived not very far away who took him for long walks, and occasionally she would ask if she could keep him at weekends. After mother died, my father decided to move to a house several miles away. What to do with Bruce was a problem, which was resolved when my friend said she would love to have him. Many years later, on a lovely summer's evening, I heard scratching outside the bedroom window of my new home. I opened it and looking down, I saw the white-haired face of Bruce. You can imagine the excitement in the household. We made such a fuss over him. However, in the early hours of the morning, he made indications it was time to go. I can still see him walking away over the field, stopping and looking back. I met my friend whilst shopping a few weeks later who informed me Bruce had died. He had gone missing one night, returning early the following day—and had passed away three days later. It is especially remarkable that Bruce had never been to the new address, and we had been parted for over five years. The dog had to cross over a bridge and travel over three miles to find me in my new address."

The Last Rally

In some of the presented cases, the animals appeared to muster an extra strength to say goodbye. A pronounced surge of vitality in animals shortly before dying was, in fact, a frequent feature of the cases reported to us. Therefore, we grouped some of them into a distinct category. Such increased vitality has long been known to occur in dying people. There are various names in different cultures and languages for this remarkable phenomenon. In English, recent terms that are used in the context of palliative and hospice care include the last "rally" before death (Kastenbaum, 2006; Kemp, 1995) or "premortem surge" (Schreiber & Bennett, 2014). We present three examples below.

> (*) "My PhD was in microbiology, but I have also been a registered nurse for 50 years. The phenomenon of the last rally is by no means common, but I too have observed it several times. Having shared my home with many dogs in my 72 years, I also observed it once in a dog! We had a

wonderful Labrador, Max. He was what we call in the UK an 'old soul', he was very wise and kind. He grew old. At the age of 12, he suffered a weak heart, arthritis and a degree of dementia. Max was unable to walk far at all. One morning I took him out for his little toilet visit and he ran away from me! I chased him and he ran to a wooded waterfall walk about a mile away. He ran around, swam in the river, tail wagging the whole time. It was his favorite walk many years ago. We went home, he ate and settled in his bed. Next morning he died. I'm sure on some level Max knew that death was imminent and he chose one last happy gallop around the waterfalls."

"I have a bird story that is almost hard to believe because it is about our family's parakeet who lived 20 years, seemed to adore my mother, and exhibited skills and traits seemingly impossible for a creature with a brain the size of a pea. The years came and went, and I am at a loss to know how to explain all the wonderful things we learned from this cheerful, loving green being. The last day inevitably came, and he sat in a stupor on his perch for hours without eating, drinking, wing-stretching, or chirping. We just sat there by his cage, wondering if he was suffering or if there was something we should do for him. Suddenly he awoke bolt upright, exited the open door of his cage, and managed to fly to my mother's hand. He never moved again. He returned to a stupor state for another two hours as she held him. Then he was gone. We never knew how he found the strength to make that final flight. He knew he was dying, and he wanted to spend his final moments with my mother."

"I run a very large animal sanctuary and oversee every soul who passes. They usually know when they are going. I had a race horse who was dying of snake bite with us frantically trying to save her. Suddenly she got up, and we were able to lead her to a stable. We thought she was healing. But she died the next day. This type of rally, for me, is part of the dying process. Dying animals will get very active. We just lost a beloved old goat who wandered up to the hay shed and gorged himself. We knew it was his last rally."

Retreating into Solitude

Another seemingly typical phenomenon reported from animals is their retreat into solitude before dying. As the following examples from our collection illustrate, animals sometimes gather enough physical strength to bid farewell to their loved ones prior to leaving.

> "We had a Collie many years ago. In the final months and weeks, it was just lying passively on the floor without energy. Then one day it came running to each family member to greet us, jumping like in joy, etc. Then it took off to the woods, where it chose to die in solitude. We found it later the same day. Without a doubt, it knew that now the time had come to say goodbye."

> (*) "I inherited two cows when I bought my property. They responded to being called by name. During a drought period I decided that I would need to start feeding them as everything was really dried up. One of them, Devi, came up to me showing me that she was no longer able to eat. I am not sure how old she was. She had lost her teeth. She came up to me and looked me in the eyes with a sad goodbye-look and then wandered off towards the bushes. She turned around one more time looking at me as if saying thank you and then disappeared. We never found her body until two years later. I still have her horns now and cry every time I tell this story."

Unusual Premonitions of Death

Several of the previous case reports indicated that the moribund animals knew that their lives were about to end. These premonitions are quite remarkable, given that even the minds of higher mammals such as dogs and cats are often thought to be not developed enough to be able to form a concept of dying and their own death. Nevertheless, the animals in the previously presented examples had been very old and/or ill already and might have felt their powers fading. It is, therefore, even more intriguing that we also received reports that concerned comparatively healthy animals that nevertheless seemed to display premonitions of their impending threat to their lives, such as the following two cases.

> "It happened in December 1944 during the Second World War in Houffalize, Belgium. An old man who owned sheep had died. He had no family. My grandfather decided to lead the sheep into his garden and into a kind of veranda or greenhouse near the main building. The sheep didn't have a problem with living in this new environment for a few days. But one

evening, they all began to bleat very loudly all night through. The eight children who lived in the house (including my mother) didn't understand what was happening and considered the sheep's behavior very curious. It was difficult, if not impossible, to sleep. Early in the morning, a bomb hit the greenhouse and killed all sheep. My mother told me this story. It was impossible for her to forget it."

"In the summer of 1997, my daughter was working on a grant under Dr. [...] at a university. Part of her duties was to retrieve the cage with the lab rats. They were part of a cancer research program and, as such, had been injected with live cancer tumors and then different medicines to study the results. Each of the rats was color dotted to determine how long they had been on the medications. And, every so often, the rats would be 'sacrificed' so the cancer and the organs could be studied. My daughter, not really sympathetic to lab rats, became concerned when she noticed a regular phenomenon. On the day the rats were to be sacrificed, unlike days when they were being weighed and measured, the rats would all gather in a corner, heads facing the center of a circle, and they would be squeaking and showing signs of alarm. As my daughter said to me, 'Mom, they know. Somehow, they know.' "

Somatic Surprises

Sometimes, the last rally or terminal vitality goes hand in hand with physical improvements or movements that seemed inconceivable before because of the animals' handicap or injury.

"I have a story about a cat that I found on the road with a broken neck and brought home to die. It was with me three days and never moved, just panted. Just before it died, it got up, stretched, meowed very loud, purred into my hand, and then lay down dead."

Terminal Lucidity in Animals

The mental pendant to the last rally and somatic surprises is terminal lucidity, the already mentioned unexpected improvement of mental clarity shortly before death in creatures that have previously been in a drowsy, confused, or even comatose state. Naturally, somatic surprises and terminal lucidity can occur concomitantly. But because the communication of animals is more difficult to decipher than that of other human beings, it is often difficult to determine whether an animal is confused or demented, and thus, if a last goodbye or rally before death also implied an instance of terminal lucidity. Nevertheless, we received case reports according to which the mental state of the moribund animals was clearly impaired before they seemed to brighten up for a very last time.

> "My pet was a six-year-old Chihuahua that developed a brain tumor. He was basically out of it, did not respond to my wife or me, and was having occasional convulsions. The night before he was to be put down at the vet, he was completely normal for a brief time. He jumped up in my lap, wanted to play like everything was normal, then went to my wife and did the same thing. All of this happened in about a 30-minute time frame, and then he went back into "out of it and convulsing." My wife and I believe he was saying goodbye."

> "My cat Cleo was dying, and I was sitting with her. She was nearly comatose, not moving, her eyes glazed over unseeing. Her legs were very cold. This state had been progressing upon her for days, and because of the coldness of her legs, I felt she might be very close. But I was just sitting there, mostly, not even really petting her. Suddenly she woke up. She put her paw upon my hand and gazed into my eyes with intensity. She was saying goodbye to me. That was perfectly clear. Within an hour, she had passed."

Near Death Visions in Animals?

Among ELEs known from human beings, near-death visions are a prominent feature. In these experiences, sick people report glimpses into what appears to them as a transcendental afterlife realm. Frequently, they perceive apparitions of deceased loved ones or spiritual figures who come to prepare them for their transition (Claxton-Oldfield & Dunnett, 2018; Depner et al., 2020). In the vast majority of cases, these experiences are regarded as very comforting and soothing. Sometimes, near-death visions go hand in hand with terminal lucidity and a transiently improved physical strength. It is intriguing that judging from their behavior, also some of the moribund animals in our reports might have experienced a similar vision. This is particularly evident in the following example (Neppe, n. d.):

> "Our dog Snowy died on 30 June 2004. She was in a coma for several hours: Initially, her level of consciousness fluctuated somewhat, and

she was calmed. Then she fell into a deep coma in which she was unresponsive to sound stimuli, from about noon that day until her eventual death at 11:45 p.m. At about 6 p.m., she was more clearly very weak and had altered consciousness. She did not respond to tactile stimuli, which were not painful (we did not perform painful stimuli for humane reasons). At about 7 p.m., Snowy suddenly sat upright, looked as if she was looking at an object very, very intensely, and followed that object with her eyes, her head moved slightly from side to side. If a dog could smile, she would smile. You could see a certain happiness radiating from her. She started wagging her tail for a few seconds, then collapsed and fell back into a coma. All four members of my family witnessed this. My wife, myself, and two teenagers (my daughter and my son), although I and my daughter were particularly aware of this. We both independently and immediately noticed that it was a very strange thing happening. We spoke almost simultaneously, recording our amazement. I interpreted this as a possible near-death vision."

Discussion

For those familiar with ELEs in human beings, it is intriguing that these ELEs in animals show many parallels to those reported by humans. This concerns especially the *last rally before* death and the additional characteristics that we classified into *last goodbyes, somatic surprises, terminal lucidity,* and potential *near-death visions*. The literature on ELEs in humans describes numerous aspects of this last rally. One of them is an increased desire and renewed ability to eat (Klein et al., 2018; Schreiber & Bennett, 2014). In our collection, we find indications of this behavior in the goat that "gorged" himself before dying and other examples described in our full paper (Sheldrake et al., 2023).

The literature on human ELEs furthermore contains examples of somatic surprises. For example, a man born deaf-mute was said to have uttered his first intelligible words during his last hours (Schubert, 1808); a man suffering from high fever and grave articular rheumatism lost his fever and rheumatism after having had a near-death vision, ate a copious meal and died on the same evening (Geley, 1927); a woman in a nursing home with severe spinal fusion who was able to only look down to the floor for several years noticed one day with surprise that she was able to look out of her room window for the first time—and died soon after (Brayne et al., 2008). In another case, a man dying from lymphatic cancer, who had been unable to move his arm for over a year, moved his arm while he experienced a near-death vision (Fenwick & Fenwick, 2008; for other examples, see Nahm, 2012).

Similarly, the already mentioned unexpected surge of mental clarity before dying—terminal lucidity—has been reported for centuries and across cultures (Claxton-Oldfield & Dunnett, 2018; Lim et al., 2020; Macleod, 2009; Nahm, 2012; Nahm et al., 2012; Nahm & Greyson, 2009). Because terminal lucidity frequently goes hand in hand with near-death visions in humans, it is not too surprising that some pet owners held the opinion that their moribund animals experienced something similar. However, while last goodbyes, last visits, last rallies, somatic surprises, and even terminal lucidity are accessible to external observation and can be documented, it will always remain difficult to gain insight into the mental state of animals that seem to experience near-death visions. It is nevertheless noteworthy that other ELEs known from human life, such as crisis telepathy and crisis apparitions, and even after-death communications, appear to be paralleled in the life of pets as well.

Unfortunately, however, systematic research in these facets of animal life is practically absent, even though respective experiences do not seem to be uncommon. Although there are several popular books on such occurrences, the case collections published by Italian parapsychologist Ernesto Bozzano (1905, 1950) still contain some of the best-documented examples. In order to stimulate future research in these areas, we recently published a new case collection regarding ostensible after-death communications of animals (Matlock et al., 2024).

Regarding the category of *unusual premonitions of death* or of grave danger, the literature on psychical research contains numerous examples already, both in people and in animals. Regarding animals, for example, members of various vertebrate and invertebrate species have been reported to anticipate natural catastrophes such as earthquakes, volcano eruptions, and tsunamis, but also fatal air raids during war (Gaddis & Gaddis, 1970; Pleimes, 1971; Schrödter, 1960; Schul, 1977; Sheldrake, 2005, 2011).

The examples of our animal categories last visits and retreating into solitude appear to be absent in the literature on the death and dying of people in the Western world. At least, we are not aware of reports about sick people who suddenly and unexpectedly showed up at the homes of friends and relatives for a last visit to say goodbye, and died shortly after. In our present Western culture, sick or decrepit people usually stay at home, in nursing homes, or in hospices and are visited by their kin rather than the other way around. Means for arranging visits to sick people are often readily available, and conversations including last goodbyes can also be held via telephone. In addition, family members can live too far apart from each other to enable the old and sick to visit them unexpectedly. Therefore, it is usually neither necessary nor possible to pay unexpected last visits to loved ones. Nevertheless, cases of crisis telepathy and crisis apparitions from dying people sometimes fulfill the role of conveying a last farewell to somebody at a distance (Gurney et al. 1886; Fenwick & Fenwick, 2008; Shared Crossing Research Initiative, 2024).

Similarly, retreating into solitude is hardly possible for terminally ill humans in modern civilizations. Even in the unlikely case that somebody would prefer to die alone somewhere outside, it would be very difficult and often impossible for such a person to suddenly leave their sickbed in order to walk away and find a lonely place where they can lie down and expire. Regarding supposed premonitions of one's death, which may also play a role when animals retreat into solitude, it is of note that they might not only be due to passively received impressions. It is known from tribal human societies that some of their members seem able to induce their own death, e.g., when they think they have been influenced by sorcery or voodoo practices (Kelly, 2007; Rose, 1968). Severe psychologically driven effects on one's body that may even lead to death have also been reported from the West (Kelly, 2007; Nahm, 2012; Reeves et al., 2007). Thus, an active component of psychophysiological influence on the body could also play a role when people and animals seem to anticipate their own death.

As far as we know, our case collection is the first of its kind. It is necessarily limited in its scope. We also made no attempt to verify the contents of these self-selected reports through interviews with witnesses. Still, we consider the data obtained in our survey sufficiently robust to draw the conclusion that ELEs reported from animals are remarkably similar to those reported from human beings. Hence, we believe that further studies into ELEs in non-human animals could elucidate facets of their lives that have so far received only little attention among scientists. At the very least, it would help to understand facets of the dying process in animals, and especially pets, better. It is increasingly recognized that the loss of a beloved companion animal can have considerable adverse mental and physical effects on the bereaved's health (Brown et al., 2023; Kowalski, 2012; Muldoon & Williams, 2024; Wilson et al., 2021; Zoanetti, 2024). Further research in this field is therefore desirable (for some suggestions, see Sheldrake et al., 2023; see also Matlock et al., 2024). It seems certain that performing systematic and large-scale studies in different languages will elicit many more reports about unusual occurrences regarding animals during their last phase of life. We are convinced that there is still a lot we can learn from our animal companions.

References

Bozzano, E. (1905). Animals and psychic perceptions. *Annals of Psychical Science, 2*, 79–120.

Bozzano, E. (1950). *Gli animali hanno un'anima?* Armenia Editore.

Brayne, S., Lovelace, H., & Fenwick, P. (2008). End-of-life experiences and the dying process in a Gloucestershire nursing home as reported by nurses and care assistants. *American Journal of Hospice & Palliative Care, 25*, 195–206.

Brown, C. A., Wilson, D. M., Carr, E., Gross, D. P., Miciak, M., & Wallace, J. E. (2023). Older adults and companion animal death: A survey of bereavement and disenfranchised grief. *Human-Animal Interactions, 2023*, 1.

Claxton-Oldfield, S., & Dunnett, A. (2018). Hospice palliative care volunteers' experiences with unusual end-of-life phenomena. *Omega, 77*, 3–14.

Claxton-Oldfield, S., Gallant, M., & Claxton-Oldfield, J. (2020). The impact of unusual end-of-life phenomena on hospice palliative care volunteers and their perceived needs for training to respond to them. *Omega, 81*, 577–591.

Depner, R. M., Grant, P. C., Byrwa, D. J., LaFever, S. M., Kerr, C. W., Tenzek, K. E., LaValley, S., Luczkiewicz, D. L., Wright, S. T., & Levy, K. (2020). Expanding the understanding of content of end-of-life dreams and visions: A consensual qualitative research analysis. *Palliative Medicine Reports, 1*, 103–110.

dos Santos, C. S., Paiva, B. S. R., Lucchetti, A. L. G., Paiva, C. E., Fenwick, P., & Lucchetti, G. (2017). End-of-life experiences and deathbed phenomena as reported by Brazilian healthcare professionals in different healthcare settings. *Palliative & Supportive Care, 15*, 425–433.

Fenwick, P., & Fenwick, E. (2008). *The art of dying.* Continuum.

Gaddis, V., & Gaddis, M. (1970). *The strange world of animals and pets.* Cowles.

Geley, G. (1927). *Clairvoyance and materialisation.* Fisher Unwin.

Gurney, E., Myers, F. W. H., & Podmore, F. (1886). *Phantasms of the living.* Trübner.

Kastenbaum, R. (2006). *The psychology of death* (4. ed.). Springer Publishing Company.

Kelly, E. W. (2007). Psychophysiological influence. In E. F. Kelly, E. W. Kelly, A. Crabtree, A. Gauld, M. Grosso, & B. Greyson (eds.), *Irreducible mind: Toward a psychology for the 21st century* (pp. 117–239). Rowman & Littlefield.

Kemp, C. E. (1995). *Terminal illness: A guide to nursing care.* Lippincott Williams & Wilkins.

Klein, S. D., Kohler, S., Krüerke, D., Templeton, A., Weibel, A., Haraldsson, E., Nahm, M., & Wolf, U. (2018). Erfahrungen am Lebensende: Eine Umfrage bei Ärzten und Pflegenden eines Spitals für anthroposophisch erweiterte Medizin. *Complementary Medicine Research, 25,* 38–44.

Kowalski, G. (2012). *Goodbye, friend: Healing wisdom for anyone who has ever lost a pet.* New World Library.

Lim, C.-Y., Park, J. Y., Kim, D. Y., Yoo, K. D., Kim, H. J., Kim, Y., & Shin, S. J. (2020). Terminal lucidity in the teaching hospital setting. *Death Studies, 44,* 285–291.

Macleod, A. D. S. (2009). Lightening up before death. *Palliative & Supportive Care, 7,* 513–516.

Matlock, J. G., Hilton, B., Sheldrake, R., Smart, P., & Nahm, M. (2024). After-death communications (ADCs) from non-human animals: Parallels with human ADCs. *Journal of Scientific Exploration, 38,* 61–78.

Morita, T., Naito, A. S., Aoyama, M., Ogawa, A., Aizawa, I., Morooka, R., Kawahara, M., Kizawa, Y., Shima, Y., Tsuneto, S., & Miyashita, M. (2016). Nationwide Japanese survey about deathbed visions: "My deceased mother took me to heaven". *Journal of Pain and Symptom Management, 52,* 646–654.

Muldoon, J., & Williams, J. (2024). 'She has saved my life on many occasions': Care-experienced young women's reflections on the significance of pets and the impact of loss. *Adoption & Fostering, 48,* 30–56.

Nahm, M. (2012). *Wenn die Dunkelheit ein Ende findet: Terminale Geistesklarheit und andere Phänomene in Todesnähe.* Crotona.

Nahm, M. (2022). The importance of the exceptional in tackling riddles of consciousness and unusual episodes of lucidity. *Journal of Anomalous Experience and Cognition, 2,* 264–296.

Nahm, M. (2024). Defining terminal lucidity: Taking the need for accuracy and integrity seriously. *Journal of Near-Death Studies,* in press.

Nahm, M., & Greyson, B. (2009). Terminal lucidity in patients with chronic schizophrenia and dementia: A survey of the literature. *Journal of Nervous and Mental Disease, 197,* 942–944.

Nahm, M., Greyson, B., Kelly, E. W., & Haraldsson, E. (2012). Terminal lucidity: A review and a case collection. *Archives of Gerontology and Geriatrics, 55,* 138–142.

Neppe, V. (n. d.). *Snowy expérience.* Internet source (translated by M. Nahm): https://www.nderf.org/French/snowy_nele.htm

Pleimes, U. (1971). Psi bei Tieren? Teil II. *Zeitschrift für Parapsychologie und Grenzgebiete der Psychologie, 13,* 203–229.

Reeves, R. R., Ladner, M. E., Hart, R. H., & Burke, R. S. (2007). Nocebo effects with antidepressant clinical drug trial placebos. *General Hospital Psychiatry, 29,* 275–277.

Rhine, J. B., & Feather, S. (1962). The study of cases of „psi-trailing" in animals. *Journal of Parapsychology, 16,* 1–22.

Rose, R. (1968). *Primitive psychic power: The realities underlying the psychical practices and beliefs of Australian Aborigines.* New American Library.

Schreiber, T. P., & Bennett, M. J. (2014). Identification and validation of premortem surge: A Delphi study. *Journal of Hospice & Palliative Nursing, 16,* 430–437.

Schrödter, W. (1960). *Tiergeheimnisse.* Baumgartner.

Schubert, G. H. (1808). *Ansichten von der Nachtseite der Naturwissenschaft.* Arnoldische Buchhandlung.

Schul, B. (1977). *The psychic power of animals.* Fawcett Publ.

Shared Crossing Research Initiative. (2024). The spectrum of end-of-life experiences: A tool for advancing death education. *Omega, 88,* 1314–1334.

Sheldrake, R. (2005). Listen to the animals. Why did so many animals escape December's tsunami? *Ecologist, March,* 18–20.

Sheldrake, R. (2011). *Dogs that know when their owners are coming home.* Crown.

Sheldrake, R., Smart, P., & Nahm, M. (2023). Experiences of dying animals: Parallels with end-of-life experiences in humans. *Journal of Scientific Exploration, 37,* 42–58.

Wilson, D. M., Underwood, L., Carr, E., Gross, D. P., Kane, M., Miciak, M., Wallace, J. E., & Brown, C. A. (2021). Older women's experiences of companion animal death: Impacts on well-being and aging-in-place. *BMC Geriatrics, 21,* 470.

Zoanetti, J., Young, J., & Nielsen, T. D. (2024). A scoping review of the risks posed by companion animals to older adults. *Anthrozoös, 37,* 1015–1031.

Chapter Twelve

(Crisis) After-Death Communications: A Universal and Comforting Experience Suggestive of Survival

EVELYN ELSAESSER

Abstract

In this chapter, I present some research findings of a long-term multilingual research project dedicated to the "Investigation of the Phenomenology and Impact of Spontaneous After-Death Communications (ADCs)." A spontaneous and direct ADC occurs when an individual unexpectedly perceives a deceased person through the senses of sight, hearing, smell or touch, or simply senses their presence. ADCs occur during wakefulness, sleep, or while drifting in or out of sleep. Although the ontological status of ADCs has not (yet) been ascertained, experients consider them to be real and draw great comfort and even a degree of emotional healing from them in times of grief. ADCs have a substantial impact on the belief system, and lead to a significant increase in favor of the hypothesis of the survival of consciousness after physical death (Elsaesser et al., 2021). This is a common phenomenon, with an estimated 30-35% of people surveyed reporting one or more ADCs in their lifetime, rising to 70-80% among the bereaved (Streit-Horn et al., 2022). Among the most convincing cases are shared ADCs and contacts during which experients perceive previously unknown information, which can subsequently be corroborated. Crisis ADCs—or ADCs at the time of death—are considered evidential, since experients claim to have been informed of the death of a relative or friend by the deceased themselves, implying that they had no knowledge by conventional means that death had taken place (for examples see e.g., Flammarion, 1922a, 1922b, 1923). Reference is made to historical research into crisis ADCs, with a quote from perhaps the earliest ADC supposed to have occurred in 1963 BCE (Bourke, 2024).

Presentation of After-Death Communications (ADCs)

The notion that a part of us—our essence, our personality, our memories, our emotional ties—survives the bodily death is deeply rooted in the human being. These convictions are born of experiences that people have lived and recounted, seemingly since the dawn of time. Spontaneous contacts with the deceased are one of these powerful experiences allegedly opening the possibility of survival. A spontaneous After-Death Communication (ADC) occurs when a person unexpectedly perceives a deceased person through sight, hearing, smell, or touch. Not all ADCs involve full-blown perceptions—it is quite common to simply sense the presence of the deceased person. ADCs occur during wakefulness, sleep, or while drifting in or out of sleep, in hypnagogic and hypnopompic states of consciousness. The following case is particularly comprehensive—involving the four sensory organs mentioned above—with a significant message accompanying the perceptions (Elsaesser, 2023, p. 53):

> "I was awakened around 6 a.m. in the morning. I saw someone walking on my front porch through my bedroom window. I thought who would be here this early? I got dressed and went to the front door. I opened the door and saw a woman with her back to me on my left, crying. I asked if she was ok. She turned around and it was my grandmother from my father's side of the family. I was in shock to see her. She spoke and asked me for forgiveness and apologized for no longer talking to me after my father had passed away. I told her it was ok, and I forgave her. She walked towards me, and we hugged. I felt her frail body hug me and I hugged her back. I felt her clothes, her smell, and she thanked me as we hugged. I felt this most intense feeling of love. I started to cry. She then started to turn into this bright white light. I had to close my eyes due to it being so bright. I could see the light fading away through my eye lids. The feeling of her started to slowly leave. I opened my eyes and she was gone. I was standing there with my arms still looking like I was hugging someone. [...] My grandmother had been dead for about seven years I and was so in shock from the experience."

Not all ostensible communications with deceased persons would necessarily qualify as ADCs. The term is usually restricted to experiences that are:
- Spontaneous: contacts or communications allegedly initiated by the deceased, without initiation by or solicitation from the experients.

- Direct: without intervention of spirit mediums (channelling), eye movement desensitization and reprocessing (EMDR), hypnosis, psychomanteum, use of devices (e.g. Instrumental Transcommunication, ITC), or an otherwise mediated contact.

This phenomenon is common, with an estimated 30-35% reporting one or more ADCs during their lifetime, rising to 70-80% among those who have suffered a bereavement (Streit-Horn et al., 2022).

ADCs have a profound impact on the belief system of the experients, with a significant increase in favour of the hypothesis of survival of consciousness after physical death. The data collected in our survey (presented in the following section) reveal that, prior to the ADC, 69% of participants believed in life after death, a percentage quite similar to the results of several surveys on this subject. However, following the ADC, 93% believed in life after death, 6% were unsure and only 1% did not believe in it (Elsaesser et al., 2021). One of the most common messages allegedly communicated by the deceased reveals that they have survived the death of the body and are doing well. This information—which comes as a surprise to many experients—gives them a new and gentler conception of death. This is consistent with what Cooper (2013) stated: "The deceased can [...] be understood by the bereaved, not as ceasing to be, but having entered a transformation into what we may call spiritual form" (p. 27). McCormick and Tassell-Matamua (2016, p. 163) reached a similar conclusion in their study with 13 participants on the therapeutic benefits of ADCs: "Eleven participants reported a sense of continued relationship with the deceased and believed this continuation indicated death is not final. Much of the dialogue relating to continuity reflected a belief that the deceased had transformed and that their consciousness or soul continued on another plane of existence". As a result, the fear of their own death is often reduced, and sometimes eliminated (Penberthy et al., 2023).

The effect of ADCs on the grieving process is powerful and lasting. Beyond the brief but striking perception of the deceased, which is in itself quite remarkable, it is the information transmitted and the emotions perceived and felt by the experients during the contact that are an essential element, if not the essence, of these experiences. As a consequence, 73% of our participants reported emotional healing (10% no emotional healing, 8% unsure, and 8% were never in mourning of the perceived deceased person; Elsaesser, 2023, p. 282). The essential element favouring emotional healing following the ADC consists of the conviction—often newly acquired—that the bond with the deceased loved one has survived the death of the body and that a relationship, obviously transformed and metamorphosed, continues with him or her.

ADC Research Project

Thanks to funding from one, and later several, foundations, we have been conducting since February 2018 a long-term multilingual research project entitled "Investigating of the phenomenology and impact of spontaneous After-Death Communications (ADCs)." Our team consists of Professor Chris A. Roe, Associate Professor Callum E. Cooper and Sophie Morrison from the University of Northampton, UK, David Lorimer from the Scientific and Medical Network, UK, and Evelyn Elsaesser (Switzerland). This international survey has three objectives:

1. to describe the circumstances surrounding the occurrence and phenomenology of ADCs, including possible cultural differences between the countries/language groups studied,
2. to analyse the impact of ADCs on the experients, and
3. to disseminate the research findings to the general public and academia.

To achieve the objectives of the project, we developed a very detailed questionnaire with 194 items (including follow-up questions after positive responses), which comprises an initial description, in the respondent's own words, of the after-death communication. The survey was made available via JISC online surveys platform (https://www.jisc.ac.uk/online-surveys).

The original research project received ethical approval from the University of Northampton and was pre-registered with the Koestler Parapsychology Unit registry (KPU 1047). Analysis strategy is as described there and reported in Elsaesser et al. (2021).

Data collected

Participants were recruited using a purposive snowball sampling. Initially, versions of the survey were produced in English, French and Spanish; responses totalled more than two million words just for the full ADC accounts. The English survey was open from August 2018 until January 2019 and produced 416 responses. The French survey was open from September 2018 to March 2019 resulting in 440 responses. The Spanish survey was open from October 2018 to April 2019 and produced 148 responses. The German survey was opened later, from August 2022 to March 2023, resulting in 235 responses. A small collection of Dutch data ran simultaneously from August 2022 to March 2023, resulting in 17 responses. It proved difficult to recruit participants for the Chinese survey—open from September 2023 to June 2024—with a result of 55 responses. To date, our database contains 1,311 completed questionnaires in six languages, making it the most comprehensive multilingual survey of spontaneous ADCs in the world. The next survey will be conducted in India.

In this chapter, I will refer to survey data in English, French, Spanish (total of 1,004 responses) and German (235 responses).

ADCs Over the Centuries

Testimonies collected on all continents and for centuries suggest this phenomenon to be universal and timeless. They have been reported in different cultures and times (Haraldsson, 2012; Sidgwick et al., 1894). Although culturally coloured and expressed with the linguistic specificities of the period under review, the experiences reported are surprisingly stable across time, space and culture. ADC accounts are reflected in the legends, folklore, and (mystical) traditions of most countries and ethnic groups. Crisis apparitions, in particular, not only inform about the death of the person featured, but often also about the cause of death. In ancient times, when sea travel was particularly perilous, people killed at sea often appeared in wet clothes to family and friends, located at a great distance from their tragic death in the water. Daniel Bourke refers to the writings of Ovid (Metamorphosis, 11) to illustrate this type of case: "From the depths of Greek mythology we find Ceyx, ruler of Thessaly, who, after dying at sea, appeared to Alcyone, his lover, with water "dripping from his locks and beard", just as did the saga revenants, the Celtic wraiths, and even the Polynesian spectres" (Bourke, 2024, p. 186).

Perhaps the earliest of all recorded crisis apparitions, supposed to have occurred in 1963 BCE, is presented by Bourke in Apparitions at the Moment of Death. Amenemhat I, the founder of the twelfth dynasty of ancient Egypt, appeared to his son Senwosret at a time when the latter was unaware of his death:

"In a rather dramatic monologue, the Pharaoh Amenemhat returns as a ghost to explain to his son and loyal followers what had happened during their absence from the palace. Senwosret's father gives a detailed account of his murder during a palace coup. "And see what happened, foul murder", cried the pharaoh's ghost to his son, explaining that they had killed him in the night." (Bourke, 2024, p. 8)

Evidential Cases: ADCs at the Time of Death

Living a spontaneous contact with a deceased person is a powerful, intimate, brief, rare, and often deeply transformative experience. An experience is by nature subjective, and therefore seemingly beyond objective scientific verification. Jeffrey Kripal reflects on the mental reality or "subjective" reality:

> "This order of knowledge is also an order of values or ontological judgments. The objective material aspects are considered real, whereas the subjective mental aspects of reality are considered less real, or even unreal. [...] Some go as far as to mock and demean the inside of reality, with their constant refrain that every human experience is nothing but an anecdote, and that many such anecdotes do not add up to evidence." (Kripal, 2024, p. 171)

However, certain types of ADC have evidential value, such as multiple witness cases, when a deceased person is perceived simultaneously by several people gathered in the same place. Among our survey participants, 21% reported shared ADCs. Also, 20% of the respondents were in the company of a pet when the ADC occurred, of whom 25% noted an unusual behaviour of the animal. Roe et al. (2023, p. 102) concluded: "Such instances are a challenge for conventional explanations in terms of misperception or hallucination, since they would need to explain how different persons, and supposedly even an animal, could independently have created the same imagery."

The most evidential type of ADC however involves the perception of previously unknown information that can subsequently be verified and validated. Indeed, 26% of our participants perceived a wide range of previously unknown information, ranging from practical information to the announcement of the imminent death of a friend or relative, as well as information about upcoming events whose accuracy is confirmed by the passage of time.

The most common previously unknown information concerns the death of the perceived person, occurring in a crisis ADC—or ADC at the time of death—which usually takes place at or shortly after the demise. In a few rare cases, they may happen shortly before death, particularly when the person perceived had fallen into a coma and had not regained consciousness before dying. Experients claim to have been informed of the death of a relative or friend *by the deceased themselves*. These experiences *precede* the announcement of the death (by the hospital, family, etc.).

Crisis ADCs have attracted the attention of researchers for centuries. Indeed, historically, it is the type of alleged spontaneous contacts with a deceased person that has been most often studied and brought to public attention. This phenomenon is also known as "crisis telepathy", "crisis apparitions", or "crisis cases", a term first coined by Gurney et al. (1886). The term "death-coincidence" is also used, defined as "a case in which an apparition or other ghostly phenomenon has taken place, at the moment of the death of the person represented by the phantom" (Carrington, 1920, p. 11). When the Society of Psychical Research (SPR) was founded in 1882 and began collecting material, many cases had to do with haunted houses and apparitions, "but the greater number of them hinged around the one point—the coincidence of apparitions with the death of the persons represented" (Carrington, 1920, p. 20).

Crisis ADCs are generally considered to occur in the range of 12 hours before death and 12 hours after death, although Gurney et al. (1886, p. xix) admit it to be an "arbitrary" time frame adopted for their analysis. This definition might benefit from an extension of the strict 12-hour rule after death in order to accommodate experiences occurring relatively soon after death, in the event that the experient has not yet been informed of the death.

Historically, the term "crisis ADC" implied that the experient had no knowledge by conventional means that death has taken place (Flammarion, 1922a, 1922b, 1923), as illustrated by the following account:

> "My mother [...] who lived in Burgundy, heard one Tuesday, between nine and ten o'clock, the door of the bedroom open and close violently. At the same time, she heard herself called twice—'Lucie, Lucie!' The following Tuesday, she heard that her uncle Clementin, who had always had a great affection for her, had died that Tuesday morning, precisely between nine and ten o'clock." (Flammarion, 1900, p. 21)

The following case from our survey fulfils both criteria to qualify as a crisis ADC: The experient was unaware of the death, and the ADC occurred during the night of the death, although the news did not reach the woman until two days later:

> "When my son died abroad, it was around midnight, I was half asleep and I found myself above him, face to face, and I kissed him on the

forehead... In the morning I got up and as I put my feet on the floor to get out of bed I felt a great emptiness, nothingness, an imbalance, something had been taken from me, I knew it was my son... Two days later I was informed of his death. It was the same night I kissed him on the forehead." (F344)

In the following case from our survey, the ADC did indeed occur at the time of death, but the experient was aware that the person was dying, so one of the two elements for this contact to qualify as a crisis ADC is not met. This account is interesting since the deceased seems to have gone through one of his daughters to give a last kiss to his mother-in-law at the very moment of his passing, while asking her to take good care of his family:

"My son-in-law spoke to me right after he passed with leukaemia. I was in the room next to his ward in hospital looking after his two girls aged eight and ten. I sat next to the youngest girl. Suddenly she sat bolt upright, leaned over and kissed me gently on the cheek and I heard my son in law say, 'Lisa (my name is Elizabeth), look after them.' My daughter (his wife) came into the room we were in, crying. He had just passed over. When I asked my granddaughter if she remembered kissing me, she said she didn't." (E240)

Additional Findings from Our Surveys on Crisis ADCs

A total of 21% of our participants (206 respondents to the survey in English, French and Spanish and 53 respondents to the survey in German) have experienced a crisis ADC, i.e. they answered positively to the question: Did you experience an ADC at the moment of death, in other words, the dying/deceased came to you in some form of ADC to tell you they were dying/dead?

Of these participants, 61% (cumulative data) answered in the affirmative when asked if the moment (hour/minute) when they experienced the ADC was later confirmed as the actual hour of death of the person, 17% were unsure, and for 22% concordance was not confirmed. The time of death was subsequently confirmed as the exact time of demise for the following case:

"I awoke suddenly for no reason from a good sleep and saw my grandfather standing at the side of my bed. He seemed slightly younger, healthier and radiating pure love. He smiled at me and said 'I'm going away my wee dove' (his pet name for me). I smiled back at him and looked at my alarm clock — it was 06:00 — then he was gone. It didn't occur to me to ask my grandfather where he was going or why he was in my room at 6 in the morning. I just slipped back into a peaceful sleep. I was later wakened by the telephone ringing and my grandmother sobbing on the phone that papa was dead. His death certificate later stated approx. time of death 06.00." (E274)

For 50%, the demise was predictable or expected (the person was very ill, very elderly, undergoing life-threatening surgery, etc.), 8% were unsure, and for 42% the demise was not predictable or expected. A candle was the vehicle of this experience at the moment of death, which was predictable and expected:

"Grandfather was known to be dying. He was heavily sedated and had terminal cancer. I was informed the previous evening that he had gone downhill and was started on the morphine. I was in another country, a four-hour plane journey away and was distraught at being unable to get there. The earliest flight was the next day. That night I lit a candle for him and went to bed. I didn't sleep well and awoke about half five. The candle was still burning steady, there was no breeze in the room. I was telling myself off for leaving an unwatched candle burning. I was still upset, wishing I was home with my family, just wanting to be there ... I remember just sitting watching the candle, thinking it was way too early to phone home. I was also thinking I should blow the candle out. It was about 5 ft away from me when the flame flickered for a few seconds, went still, then went out... I got a smell of medicine, hospital disinfectant and immediately knew my papa was there with me saying goodbye. I felt a pressure across my shoulders and back like a hug. He was at peace and I was too. I was no longer upset. A short time later I phoned home to be told the news. He had died a few moments before the candle went out." (E285)

At the time of death, 77% were at a distant location, 1% were unsure, and 22% were present when the person died. Here is a case from our database:

"My mother was not anticipated to live more than a few more days. I was in bed around midnight, suddenly sensed her presence at the side of my bed. She spoke my name and patted my shoulder. I felt mom had passed. Within 10 minutes my brother phoned to tell me she had died a few minutes before his call to me." (E410)

Of these participants, 85% knew that the person was deceased at the moment of the ADC, 2% were unsure, and 13% were not informed of the death of the perceived person. Here is a case drawn from our survey:

> "About midnight, sitting on couch. Felt a presence. Saw reflection on TV and saw a human shape walk behind me and down the hallway. I just knew it was my great grandmother. I was hyperventilating and my phone goes off. It was a text from my mom saying that my great grandmother has just passed, 1,000 miles away. I went to bed with my door cracked open. Lying in bed, not yet asleep and my door opens all the way. I felt a warm squeeze on my hand. No one was there. I knew it was her saying goodbye." (E400).

Our data show that 36% had the opportunity to say good-bye or to resolve unfinished business before the perceived person died, 7% were unsure, and 58% did not have this opportunity. The following account sounds like a last-minute attempt at reconciliation on the part of the perceived deceased person:

> "I was estranged from my uncle, and no longer had any contact with him. One day, in the early afternoon, I had the strange impression of receiving what seemed to me to be a thought not modulated in human terms. A thought that I was receiving, and that I had in no way generated. In this thought, my uncle was addressing me, and saying 'this is too stupid.' I dismissed the idea and went about my business. The next day I learned of the man's death, and based on the time of his death (heart attack), I realized that this strange contact had taken place at the time of death." (F041)

Conclusion

Spontaneous after-death communications have been reported and researched over centuries, with the earliest documented crisis ADC purported to have occurred in 1963 BCE (Bourke, 2024). The ontological status of ADCs has not yet been ascertained, although the vast majority of the participants in our English, French and Spanish surveys were convinced of the authenticity of their experience (only 1% answered this question in the negative; Elsaesser, 2023, p. 273). Although personal conviction does not count as evidence, our database contains a number of cases where the experients perceived previously unknown information that proved to be accurate, thus making them more evidential.

Crisis ADCs, also known as "crisis telepathy", "crisis apparitions" or "death-coincidences", are part of these evidential cases, reported by 21% of our survey participants. Although the current state of consciousness research does not (yet) prove the reality of ADCs, these experiences are being lived on a daily basis by a large number of people who consider them to be real and important to them, especially if they are in mourning and have been profoundly comforted and transformed by the experience.

While we have already gained a wealth of knowledge in this phase of our research project, there are still many unanswered questions. We are confident that consciousness research in general and the continuation of our research project, as well as the realisation of similar projects by others in particular, will bring further insights into (crisis) ADCs.

Acknowledgements

We would like to thank the Bial Foundation (Awards number 169/2020 & number 396/2024), the Society for Psychical Research (SPR) and a foundation that does not wish to be named publicly for their support.

References

Bourke, D. (2024). *Apparitions at the moment of death: The living ghost in legend, lyric, and lore.* Destiny Books.

Carrington, H. (1920). *Phantasms of the dead or true ghost stories.* American University Publ. Company.

Cooper, C. E. (2013). Post death experiences and the emotion of hope. *Journal for Spiritual and Consciousness Studies, 36,* 24–28.

Elsaesser, E. (2023). *Spontaneous contacts with the deceased: A large-scale international survey reveals the circumstances, lived experience and beneficial impact of after-death communications (ADCs).* Iff Books.

Elsaesser, E., Roe, C. A., Cooper, C. E., & Lorimer, D. (2021). The phenomenology and impact of hallucinations concerning the deceased. *BJPsychOpen., 7,* e148.

Flammarion, C. (1900). *The unknown.* Harper & Brothers.

Flammarion, C. (1922a). *Death and its mystery: Before death.* Fisher Unwin.

Flammarion, C. (1922b). *Death and its mystery: At the moment of death.* Fisher Unwin.

Flammarion, C. (1923). *Death and its mystery: After death.* Fisher Unwin.

Gurney, E., Myers, F. W. H., & Podmore, F. (1886). *Phantasms of the living* (2 vols.). Trübner & Co.

Haraldsson, E. (2012). *Departed among the living.* White Crow Books.

Kripal, J. (2024). *How to think impossibly.* University of Chicago Press.

McCormick, B. M. E., & Tassell-Matamua, N. A. (2016). After-death communication: A typology of therapeutic benefits. *Journal of Near-Death Studies, 34,* 151–172.

Penberthy, J. K., Pehlivanova, M., Kalelioglu, T., Roe, C. A., Cooper, C. E., Lorimer, D., & Elsaesser, E. (2023). Factors moderating the impact of after death communications on beliefs and spirituality. *Omega, 87,* 884–901.

Roe, C. A., Cooper, C. E., Lorimer, D., & Elsaesser, E. (2023) A critical evaluation of the best evidence for the survival of human consciousness after permanent bodily death. In Bigelow Institute for Consciousness Studies (BICS), *Winning Essays 2023* (vol. 5, pp. 70–149). BICS.

Sidgwick, H., Sidgwick, E., & Johnson, A. (1894). Report on the census of hallucinations. *Proceedings of the Society for Psychical Research, 10,* 25–422.

Streit-Horn, J., Holden, J. M., & Smith, J. E. (2022). Empirically-based best estimates of after-death communication (ADC) phenomena: A systematic review of the research. *Journal of Near-Death Studies, 40,* 141–176.

Chapter Thirteen

The Coherence Enigma: Detecting Non-Local Consciousness Correlates via Random Events Generators (REGs) at Life's Final Edge

VASILEIOS BASIOS

Abstract

In the sterile corridors of intensive care units and the compassionate halls of a hospice, where life's final chapter unfolds, our research has revealed a remarkable phenomenon. Utilising instruments known as "REGs" (Random Event Generators—which employ the quantum phenomenon of tunnelling in an inverse Zener diode setting to produce truly random numbers) our research team of scientists, affectionately known as the "oREGano" research team, has detected measurable deviations from pure chance in the temporal vicinity of the transition from life to death of human consciousness. The present study suggests that the dying process may create detectable ripples in the fabric of randomness itself in a form of non-local consciousness correlates. This finding challenges our understanding of consciousness, death and even the very nature of reality.

Another Frontier of Consciousness Research

For several decades, the scientific community has engaged in profound and sustained interrogation of one of the most profound mysteries of existence: the nature of consciousness. The predominant theory in mainstream neuroscience is that consciousness emerges exclusively from cerebral activity. However, an increasing amount of research suggests an even more intriguing idea: that consciousness could extend beyond the physical boundaries of the skull. This would give rise to "non-local" effects, which have the capacity to influence the physical world in small, subtle yet measurable ways. This investigation into consciousness extends beyond theoretical speculation. Various experiments using REGs have demonstrated the possibility that mental activity, especially intention, attention or emotion, can influence physical systems.

Our approach is founded on the findings of decades of rigorous scientific research conducted by PEAR (the Princeton Research Anomalies Lab, succeeded by ICRL, the International Consciousness Research Lab; see Jahn & Dunne, 1986; Jahn et al, 2007) and the Global Consciousness Project I & II. The Global Consciousness Project is a worldwide network of REGs that has detected anomalous patterns during major global events (Nelson, 2006; Nelson et al. 2002; Radin & Nelson, 1989). Other notable contributions on consciousness affecting REGs come from Dean Radin's meta-analyses with his team at the Institute of Noetic Sciences (IONS; Wahbeh et al., 2022) and Gary E. Schwartz' and his team at the University of Arizona (Schwartz, 2015).

So, our choice of REGs as detectors of non-local consciousness correlates during dying was not arbitrary. Our team's research focuses on random event generators (REGs), which use quantum mechanics to generate random numbers. Unlike computer-generated pseudo-random numbers, these originate from electronic (Zener) diodes. These systems are well shielded and protected against external disturbances. Quantum tunnelling is the only process responsible for producing these random events, this is a well-established fact. The principle behind REG research is simple yet profound: these devices perform many "quantum flip-coin" operations very quickly, producing random streams of data under normal conditions. However, they reveal anomalous correlations and subtle organisation in contexts involving awareness in a measurable way.

Our Journey into an Uncharted Territory

This line of research prompted our international team of researchers to design an unprecedented experiment. Rather than relying on subjective reports or traditional medical monitoring, we decided to use twin-paired-REGs to detect potential anomalous synchronization phenomena during the dying process.

Our bold venture into previously unexplored territory, answered this profound question: does the transition from life to death create detectable changes in the quantum realm? The answer is in the affirmative.

Our research team deployed pairs of REG devices in two distinct environments: the intensive care units (ICUs) at the General University Hospital of Elche and a hospice facility. These "twin REGs" were placed near 64 terminally ill patients—20 in the ICU and 44 in the hospice—recording data continuously throughout the patients' final days. The devices operated entirely passively, requiring no interaction with patients or medical staff, ensuring that the dying process remained undisturbed while the quantum measurements continued silently, and respecting patients' anonymity and medical/ethical standards, in the background.

The experimental design was meticulously crafted to eliminate potential sources of bias. Each REG pair generated two independent streams of random data. We then applied sophisticated statistical analyses (Multivariate Statistics, Fisher-rank type of tests etc.) to detect any deviations from expected randomness, particularly focusing on correlations between the two data streams during the moment of death that should not exist if pure randomness prevailed.

Methodology: Detecting "Signals" in REGs' Quantum Noise

The challenge of detecting consciousness-related effects in this data required innovative analytical approaches. Our research team developed two complementary methods to identify potential anomalies in the REG data streams.

The first approach, called multivariate analysis, divided the data into non-overlapping 24-hour windows centered on each patient's time of death. Within these windows, the researchers calculated 17 different statistical measures—or "channels"—that could reveal departures from randomness. These included measures of correlation between the two REG devices, variations in the distribution of random numbers, and sophisticated tests for independence between the data streams. Each measure was then evaluated to determine whether it showed statistically significant deviations from what would be expected by chance alone.

The second approach, termed rank-based analysis, employed a more sensitive sliding-window technique that could detect brief but intense anomalies. This method searched for the strongest statistical responses within varying time windows, ranking the significance of detected patterns to identify the most improbable occurrences under the assumption of pure randomness.

To ensure scientific rigor, we established strict controls. We analyzed data from 200 randomly selected 12-hour periods when no deaths occurred, providing a baseline against which to compare the death-related data. This control group was essential for distinguishing genuine anomalies from normal statistical fluctuations that occur in any random data stream.

Safeguarding Scientific Rigour: Statistical Validation and Control Measures

Of course, this research, like any that challenges scientific thinking, is open to legitimate criticism. As in other consciousness-related studies that challenge the mainstream group-thinking, skeptical critics worry that data selection and analysis methods may be biased. However, we've taken several steps to address these concerns, including using pre-specified protocols to analyse data, including substantial blind-control data and well-established statistical methods. Most importantly, we found consistent results across different approaches and patient populations.

The control data from periods without deaths consistently showed normal random behavior, confirming that the REG devices were functioning properly and that the anomalies were specifically associated with death events. Moreover, we used "bootstrapping" to generate thousands of simulated control cases to test our analytical methods, confirming a false positive rate of less than 5% of the time in truly random data.

The twin-REG devices were isolated from electromagnetic interference, positioned in relation to the patients, and operated under identical conditions throughout. No correlation was found between the detected anomalies and other physical environmental factors.

Remarkable Discoveries in the Shadow of Death

The findings of this investigation are both unprecedented and statistically robust. Evidence of anomalous patterns in the REG data was detected via both analytical methods during the periods surrounding patient deaths. These patterns were so unlikely to occur by chance that further attention from the scientific community is required.

The multivariate analysis revealed that deviations from expected randomness were most pronounced when the time windows of sampling where around six minutes. During these intervals, statistical measures exhibited values that surpassed the significance threshold, a phenomenon that was particularly evidently revealed by the standard multivariate analysis among patients who succumbed in the ICU. The observed effect was of such potency that the overall probability of these results occurring by chance was less than 5%—thus meeting the "gold standard" for statistical significance in scientific research.

Perhaps most intriguingly, it was discovered that approximately 25% for the ICU, and 28% of the hospice death cases produced what is classified as "highly unlikely" statistical patterns—results with false positive probabilities ranging from 0.0001 to 0.01. From a scientific perspective, the likelihood of such patterns emerging by chance is negligible, with a probability ranging from less than one in 100 to less than one in 10,000 under typical circumstances. Notably, these patterns manifest exclusively around the reported time of death!

The rank-based analysis yielded even more striking results. Upon examination of individual cases, researchers identified a concurrence between REG activity and recorded death events, with some of the highest daily peaks in REG activity almost coinciding with the occurrence of death. In the dataset, four of the seven highest daily peaks on a key statistical channel occurred on days when patients died. The probability calculations for these extreme events were found to be remarkably low, with some reaching probabilities of less than one in a million!

It is most remarkable that these effects appeared to be highly time-sensitive. The most significant anomalies were observed within approximately six-minute periods surrounding the time of death. This specificity suggests that the deviations were directly related to the dying process itself, rather than being due to environmental factors or chance fluctuations.

A particularly intriguing facet of the study emerged from a comparative analysis of the results obtained from the two research sites. Patients who died in the hospice environment produced anomalous signals that were significantly stronger, when the rank-based analysis method was employed, and more consistent than those who died in the ICU, viewed under the same rank-based method. This discrepancy cannot be attributed merely to variations in sample size or measurement techniques; it indicates fundamental differences in the dying process itself between these two environments.

ICU patients are typically in coma, sedated and connected to life support systems. Hospice patients often die more naturally, often remaining conscious and surrounded by family. We can reasonably posit that this affects such non-local consciousness-related phenomena during death.

Such an environmental difference aligns with existing research on end-of-life experiences. Numerous studies have shown that patients in more natural dying environments often report profound experiences—terminal lucidity, visions, sensations of leaving their body, or encounters with deceased relatives—that are less commonly reported by heavily sedated ICU patients. Our twin-REG data suggests that these experiential differences might have measurable physical yet non-local correlates.

Implications for Understanding Consciousness and Death

The results of laboratory studies on the direct mental influence exerted on REGs have provided compelling evidence. The present study investigates the most profound human experience, namely the moment of death. Our findings carry profound implications for our understanding of both consciousness and the dying process. These findings represent a substantial challenge to the prevailing view that the domains of mind and matter are entirely separate. Instead, they propose a more integrated understanding, suggesting that consciousness might be a fundamental feature of reality rather than merely an emergent property of complex brain activity.

It is important to note that, at this stage, this research is not capable of making clinical recommendations. However, it does suggest that circumstances surrounding death, including medical intervention, patient consciousness and family presence, might influence measurable physical phenomena associated with the transition from life to death.

While these findings are remarkable, it is important to acknowledge certain limiting factors and areas for future investigations. The present study was conducted using a relatively small sample size, particularly in the context of ICU patients, and was conducted in only two locations. It is recommended that replication of the findings be undertaken via inter-hospital studies, with the participation of a greater number of institutions. This would serve to strengthen confidence in the findings and facilitate the determination of their persistence and the nature of their universality.

It is also noted by the research team that current methods can't distinguish between explanations for the detected anomalies. Are these patterns from the deceased's consciousness influencing quantum processes in the REG devices? Alternatively, are they indicative of the emotional state of the dying, their family and medical staff? Or represent an unknown physical process associated with death that affects quantum systems in ways science hasn't yet understood?

Future studies could assess the emotional engagement of family members and staff, and monitor patients' brain activity (EEG), heart rate (ECG) and other physiological parameters to correlate twin-REG anomalies with these. More advanced REG designs might also detect the phenomenon causing these effects more sensitively.

This kind of investigation can also be expanded to other unusual or anomalous phenomena linked to dying that medical research has documented. Near-death experiences (NDEs) often include elements that seem to transcend purely biological explanations. Terminal lucidity is another puzzle that challenges conventional understanding of brain-based consciousness. These two areas are the ones closest to further investigation like the one carried out by our team.

While these findings do not directly inform clinical practice, they may eventually contribute to improved end-of-life care by deepening our understanding of the dying process. Should consciousness extend beyond the brain in measurable ways, this could lend support to approaches to end-of-life care that take into account the physical and emotional needs of terminally ill patients, whilst also considering the possibility that consciousness itself undergoes a complex transition that merits respect and understanding. This perspective does not refute the importance of life-saving medical care when indicated; rather, it underscores the significance of transitioning to comfort care and compassionate end-of-life treatment when a cure is no longer feasible.

Ethical Considerations

The present study was conducted with meticulous consideration for ethical considerations, thereby ensuring that the dying process remained undisturbed and that patient privacy was fully protected. The REG devices operated in a passive manner, with no contact with patients or interference with medical care. All data were anonymised, and participation necessitated informed consent from patients, their doctors, and/or their designated carers or representatives.

Toward a New Understanding of Reality

It is strongly believed that this research makes a significant contribution to the emergence of a post-materialistic scientific paradigm. This emerging paradigm challenges the long-standing and dominant distinction between mind and matter that has characterised Western science for centuries. If consciousness can indeed influence quantum processes in the REGs—and if this influence becomes pronounced during the profound transition of death—it suggests that consciousness might be a more fundamental feature of reality than previously imagined.

This perspective is further substantiated by recent developments in quantum physics itself, where the role of context in observation and measurement has long been recognised as central to the description of nature

(D'Ariano & Faggin, 2022, Kauffman & Radin, 2023; Kauffman & Roli, 2023). It has been posited by numerous physicists and philosophers that consciousness may assume a fundamental role in the structure of reality. This role would not be limited to the observation of the physical world, but would also entail participation in its ongoing creation.

The implications of this phenomena extend beyond the scientific realm, encompassing philosophical, spiritual, and anthropological domains. Should these findings be corroborated and expanded upon by subsequent research, they have the potential to substantiate perspectives concerning consciousness and personal identity that persist beyond biological death, not as a matter of faith, but as empirical scientific observation.

Conclusion: Standing at the Threshold

The "coherence enigma" of non-local consciousness, as revealed by these novel research findings, opens new frontiers in our understanding of consciousness, death, and the nature of reality itself. This research has provided the first sound, empirical and statistically significant evidence that the dying process involves phenomena that extend beyond the current prevailing scientific paradigm, through the detection of measurable deviations from quantum randomness at the moment of death.

Although numerous questions have yet to be answered, the statistical rigour of the findings necessitates further scientific investigation. The fact that approximately one-quarter of death events produced effects so unlikely that they would occur by chance less than once in a hundred times suggests that something genuinely anomalous is happening at life's final edge — something that current science cannot yet fully explain.

As we stand at the threshold between the known and the unknown, this research invites us to consider possibilities that transcend our current understanding. It suggests that consciousness—the very essence of what makes us human—might be far more mysterious and far-reaching than we have dared to imagine. In the quantum realm where probability reigns and observation and context shapes reality, the moment of death appears to create ripples that extend beyond the boundaries of individual existence, thus hinting at connections that unite all Consciousness in ways we are only beginning to glimpse.

The journey to understand these phenomena has only just begun, but already it promises to transform our understanding of life, death, and the extraordinary mystery of human consciousness itself.

NB: This article is based on the collective efforts of our research team. The author presents his own interpretation of our common research results, and these may not necessarily reflect those of each individual. The oREGano team is to be commended for their efforts, while the responsibility for any shortcomings lies with the author.

Acknowledgments

This research was hosted and supported by "Fundacion Metta Hospice." It was also supported by Edi Bilimoria's private research funds and "The Linda G. O'Bryan Noetic Sciences Research Prize" of the year 2023. The members of the oREgano team also provided financial support.

A more detailed technical description of our report (Janu et al., 2023) can be found at https://noetic.org/prize-2023/

I dedicate this chapter to the fond memory of Peter Fenwick with my profound gratitude for his invaluable mentorship and his guidance that remains, even after this final project of his. And, for his dear wife Elisabeth with the utmost affection on the occasion of her 90th birthday.

References

D'Ariano, G, & Faggin, F. (2022). Hard problem and free will: An information-theoretical approach. In F. Scardigli (Ed.), *Artificial intelligence versus natural intelligence* (pp. 145–192). Springer.

Jahn, R. G., & Dunne, B. J. (1986). On the quantum mechanics of consciousness, with application to anomalous phenomena. *Foundations of Physics, 16,* 721–772.

Jahn, R. G., Dunne, B. J., Nelson, R. G., Dobyns, Y. H., & Bradish, G. J. (2007). Correlations of random binary sequences with pre-stated operator intention: A review of a 12-year program. *Explore, 3,* 244–253.

Janu, W., Basios, V., Moretti, P. F., Merry, P., Grathoff, A., & Arraez, V. (2023). *Detecting deviations from random activity as indications of consciousness beyond the brain.* Available at: https://noetic.org/prize-2023/

Kauffman, S. A., & Radin, D. (2023). Quantum aspects of the brain-mind relationship: A hypothesis with supporting evidence. *Biosystems, 223,* 104820.

Kauffman, S. A., & Roli, A. (2023). What is consciousness? Artificial intelligence, real intelligence, quantum mind and qualia. *Biological Journal of the Linnean Society, 139,* 530–538.

Nelson, R. D., Radin, D. I., Shoup, R., & Bancel, P. A. (2002). Correlations of continuous random data with major world events. *Foundations of Physics Letters, 15,* 537–550.

Nelson, R. (2006). The Global Consciousness Project. *Explore, 2,* 342–351.

Radin, D. I., & Nelson, R. D. (1989). Evidence for consciousness-related anomalies in random physical systems. *Foundations of Physics, 19,* 1499–1514.

Schwartz, S. A. (2015). Six Protocols, Neuroscience, and Near Death: An Emerging Paradigm Incorporating Nonlocal Consciousness. *Explore, 11,* 252–260.

Wahbeh, H., Radin, D., Cannard, C., & Delorme, A. (2022). What if consciousness is not an emergent property of the brain? Observational and empirical challenges to materialistic models. *Frontiers in Psychology, 13,* 955594.

Epilogue

The preceding chapters covered a wide variety of near-death phenomena and described research that has been performed during the past years. The more "classical" phenomena, namely near-death experiences (NDEs), end-of-life dreams and visions, (paradoxical) terminal lucidity, and after-death communications, have been reported for centuries. But they have been scientifically investigated only since the mid to late 1800s, and this largely outside of mainstream medical and academic settings.

Regarding NDEs, respective research began in the 1970s. But with the exception of a few studies, comparable investigations regarding the other phenomena only commenced after the turn of the millennium. Since then, the number of researchers and research groups concerned with near-death phenomena and end-of-life experiences is steadily increasing—a trend that is mirrored by the increasing amount of academic publications about these topics.

It is furthermore becoming increasingly apparent that some near-death phenomena have not yet been recognized as serious research topics warranting systematic investigations, although they clearly do. This concerns for example the variety of coma experiences, including alternate lives and locked-in experiences even in patients with supposedly nonfunctional brains. It also concerns paradigmatic shared death experiences in which healthy people at the bedsides of dying people seem to share their transition, and end-of-life phenomena occurring in dying animals.

We are confident that the interest in these phenomena will continue to rise, also among academic researchers. Perhaps, even more unusual phenomena in near-death states can be identified, classified, and researched. It is time to lift the taboo that surrounds death and dying further. As stated in the Introduction, we hope that our book contributes to this development.

We are furthermore confident that more and more research into these phenomena will result in the description of increasing numbers of cases studies that provide added evidence fostering the notion that states of minds and brains are not always exactly correlated but can be decoupled—a finding that bears enormous scientific and philosophical implications. The question of what happens to individual beings at death is one of the most important questions scientists can assess. We should no longer ignore such questions but face them with curiosity. And although some experiences occurring in near-death states can be quite horrifying, especially those occurring in medically induced comas, the overall conclusions deduced from the obtained research findings is that dying is not something that needs to be feared. It often comes as a relief to the terminally ill and implies a spiritual reconnection to one's essence of being.

Although it will very likely always remain difficult to uncover what precisely happens after we have definitively crossed the river Styx, the data overall point to the existence of experiences of a much more interesting, rewarding, and uplifting nature than the mere extinction of consciousness that, according to the physicalist paradigm, goes hand in hand with the extinction of brain functions. Rather, consciousness may emerge from the dying brain like a phoenix, spreading its wings towards new horizons. There can hardly be a more enthralling but also challenging field of research.

Michael Nahm,
Marjorie Woollacott,
Natasha Tassell-Matamua

Author Biographies

VASILEIOS BASIOS, PH.D., is a senior researcher in the Department of Physics of Complex Systems at the University of Brussels, specialising in self-organisation, emergence and the foundations of complex systems. He was tutored by the Nobel laureate Ilya Prigogine at the Solvay Institutes. Basios is passionate about advocating a transformative shift in science towards a post-materialistic paradigm. His aim is to encourage self-reflection within scientific practice and to support the development of resilient and flexible networks in order to advance this transformative vision. He is an adviser of the Galileo Commission and curates its working group, "oREGano."

KALI DAYTON, DNP, AGACNP, is a nurse practitioner, host of the *Walking Home From The ICU* and *Walking You Through The ICU* podcasts, and critical care outcomes consultant. She is dedicated to creating Awake and Walking ICUs by ensuring ICU sedation and mobility practices are aligned with current research. She works with ICU teams internationally to transform patient outcomes through early mobility and management of delirium in the ICU and the creation of Awake and Walking ICUs.

EVELYN ELSAESSER is an independent researcher and author in the field of death-related experiences, notably after-death communications and near-death experiences. She is a team member of the research project "Investigation of the Phenomenology and Impact of Spontaneous After-Death Communications (ADCs)", as well as a founding and current member of the Board of Swiss IANDS (International Association for Near-Death Studies). Her latest book *Spontaneous Contacts with the Deceased—A Large-Scale International Survey Reveals the Circumstances, Lived Experience and Beneficial Impact of After-Death Communications (ADCs)* (2023) has been awarded a 2023 Scientific and Medical Network Book Prize.

BRUCE GREYSON, M.D., is the Chester Carlson Professor Emeritus of Psychiatry & Neurobehavioral Sciences at the University of Virginia, and a Distinguished Life Fellow of the American Psychiatric Association. His research has focused on the phenomenology and aftereffects of near-death experiences. Dr. Greyson co-founded the International Association for Near-Death Studies, edited the *Journal of Near-Death Studies* for 26 years, and has more than 200 scholarly publications on near-death experiences. He is co-editor of *The Handbook of Near-Death Experiences: Thirty Years of Investigation* (2009), and author of the recent book *After: A Doctor Explores What Near-Death Experiences Reveal about Life and Beyond* (2021).

CHRISTOPHER KERR, PH.D., is the Chief Medical Officer and Chief Executive Officer at Hospice & Palliative Care Buffalo. Born and raised in Toronto, Canada, Chris earned his M.D. as well as a Ph.D. in Neurobiology. Outside of direct patient care, Chris' focus is in the area of patient advocacy. He also has a wide range of research interests, including the experience of illness as witnessed from the bedside. His team's work on patient experiences at the end of life has been the subject of numerous reports in major media around the world, including several documentaries and the book *Death Is but a Dream* (2020) by Penguin Random House.

KARALEE KOTHE, M.A., is currently a Ph.D. student at the University of Colorado Denver, studying Clinical Health Psychology. Her research interests focus on end-of-life experiences, meaning in life, spirituality, understanding how our attitudes towards death affect our attitudes of life, and learning how to realize full human potential in clinical settings. She obtained her master's degree at the Spirituality Mind Body Institute at Teachers College, Columbia University, in 2021. In her future career, she hopes to work at the intersection of science and spirituality.

HANNAH MACIEJEWSKI, M.S., became a Research Coordinator at Hospice and Palliative Care Buffalo after obtaining an M.S. in Experimental Psychology. Throughout her time at Hospice and Palliative Care Buffalo, she has been afforded the opportunity and privilege to delve into many research interests including end-of-life experiences, the family caregiver experience, and the impact of medical systems and communications. Being able to honor the lives and legacies of patients and families continues to fuel her passion for hospice and palliative care research.

MARYNE MUTIS, PHD., is a psychologist and associate researcher at the University of Lorraine, France. Her research focuses on exceptional end-of-life experiences and the grieving process. She wrote the world's first thesis on the clinical aftereffects of terminal lucidity, which has led to numerous publications as well as national and international communications. She is currently engaged in post-doctoral research exploring the manifestations and boundaries of terminal lucidity.

MICHAEL NAHM, PH.D., is a biologist and research associate at the Institute for Frontier Areas of Psychology and Mental Health (IGPP) in Freiburg, Germany. His research interests focus on under-researched and unconventional phenomena in frontier areas of the sciences of life. These include various near-death phenomena, terminal lucidity, reincarnation cases, physical mediumship, hauntings and poltergeists, philosophical implications of such fringe phenomena, as well as theories and the history of psychical research. Nahm has published five monographs and more than 100 articles on these subjects.

ALAN PEARCE is a journalist, author, and former BBC foreign correspondent with extensive experience covering global conflicts and security issues. Pearce has also authored several books on topics ranging from the Deep Web and digital privacy to coma and near-death experiences, and consciousness studies. His works, including *Coma and Near-Death Experience* (2024) and *Deep Web for Journalists* (2017), aim to inform and equip readers with valuable insights into complex subjects, blending his journalistic expertise with a commitment to exploring hidden truths. His articles have appeared in prominent publications, including *The Sunday Times* and *Time Magazine*.

MARIETA PEHLIVANOVA, PH.D., is a Research Assistant Professor of Psychiatry and Neurobehavioral Sciences within the Division of Perceptual Studies at the University of Virginia School of Medicine. She holds a Ph.D. in Experimental and Cognitive Psychology from the University of Pennsylvania and a Bachelor's in Statistics from American University. Her research focuses on near-death experiences and children's reports of past-life memories. She is interested in various aspects of these experiences, including cognitive, personality, and genetic factors contributing to their occurrence, veridical perceptions reported by experiencers, their impact, cross-cultural comparisons, and the development of supportive resources for experiencers within healthcare settings.

Author Biographies

WILLIAM PETERS, M.A., M.ED., is the founder of the Shared Crossing Project and director of its Research Initiative (SCRI). He presents on extraordinary end-of-life experiences (shared crossings) and the benefits of conscious dying. William teaches methods designed to enable shared crossings for the dying and those who attend to them. He is a psychotherapist at the Family Therapy Institute in Santa Barbara. His two near-death experiences and various shared death experiences (SDEs) inform his work. William is the author of *At Heaven's Door: What Shared Journeys to the Afterlife Teach about Dying Well and Living Better* (2022), the first research based general public book on the SDE.

NANCY PHILPOTT, R.N., M.S., is the Research Manager for the Shared Crossing Research Initiative. A licensed Registered Nurse and Vocational Nurse, Nancy holds a B.S. in Nursing from West Texas A&M University and an M.S. in Health Administration from Southwest Texas State University. Nancy specializes in assisting healthcare professionals and caregivers in preventing and recovering from compassion fatigue and burnout. While practicing as a health professional, Nancy experienced multiple shared death experiences (SDEs) with patients and family members. She is passionate about assisting health professionals in understanding, applying, and integrating knowledge of SDEs to enhance their end-of-life care.

CHRIS A. ROE, PH.D., holds a Chair in Psychology at the University of Northampton, UK. He is the International Affiliate for England of the Parapsychology Foundation and is a Vice-President of the Society for Psychical Research. His research interests are around the phenomenology of paranormal experience, particularly as it affects wellbeing, as well as experimental approaches to test claims for extrasensory perception and psychokinesis, particularly where they involve psychological factors. Recent research has been concerned with the relationship between altered states of consciousness and psychic experience, and phenomena associated with survival of bodily death, including near-death experiences, terminal lucidity episodes, after-death communications, and mediumship.

RUPERT SHELDRAKE, PH.D., is a biologist and author of more than 100 technical papers and nine books, including *The Presence of the Past*. He studied at Cambridge and Harvard Universities and was a fellow of Clare College, Cambridge and a research fellow of the Royal Society. From 2005–2010, he was Director of the Perrott-Warrick Project for the study of unexplained human and animal abilities, funded from Trinity College, Cambridge. He is currently a fellow of the Institute of Noetic Sciences in California and of the Temenos Academy in London. He lives in London. His web site is www.sheldrake.org.

PAM SMART worked as a school secretary before working with Rupert Sheldrake as a research assistant since 1994. She has taken part in research on the return-anticipating behaviour of dogs, including her own dog Jaytee, and on other unexplained powers of animals, as well as on scopaesthesia in people and non-human animals and on telecommunication telepathy. She helps compile and maintain Rupert Sheldrake's databases which now contain more than 12,000 accounts of human and animal behaviour and has co-authored 13 papers in peer-reviewed journals. She lives in Ramsbottom, Lancashire, England.

NATASHA TASSELL-MATAMUA, PH.D., has researched in the very specialised area of near-death and other exceptional experiences of consciousness for over 15 years. She investigates and writes about the implications of such experiences for enhancing understandings about the nature of consciousness, as well as their interface with spirituality, the environment, and Indigenous knowledges. She has published and presented extensively in the area. She is currently involved in research on terminal lucidity in children and adults, alongside an international team of experts.

MONICA WILLIAMS, M.D., is an award-winning writer, international author, speaker and board-certified Emergency Physician. She has lectured and written extensively on transforming death and dying in Modern America, based on precepts from her book *It's Ok to Die* (2011). Considered an expert on medical decision-making at the end of life, she has been featured in multiple media sources including the Emmy Award winning TV show, "The Doctors", the Washington Post and Forbes. Her end-of-life preparation checklists have been adopted by the UCLA Healthcare System and the UK's National Health System. She presently serves as the Medical Director for the Shared Crossing Research Initiative.

Author Biographies

MARJORIE WOOLLACOTT, PH.D., is a professor and member of the Institute of Neuroscience at the University of Oregon. Her published research spans inquiry into the nature of consciousness, meditation, and end-of-life experiences. She has published over 200 scientific articles and written or edited nine books, including *Infinite Awareness: The Awakening of a Scientific Mind* (2018) (receiving eight book awards). She is past chair of the Department of Human Physiology of the University of Oregon, President of the Academy for the Advancement of Post-Materialist Sciences, Co-Director of the Galileo Commission and Research Director for the International Association of Near-Death Studies.

Academy for the Advancement of Postmaterialist Sciences

AAPS
ACADEMY FOR THE ADVANCEMENT
OF POSTMATERIALIST SCIENCES

The Academy for the Advancement of Postmaterialist Sciences (www.AAPS global.com) is a non-profit membership and education organization whose mission is to promote open-minded, rigorous and evidence-based enquiry into postmaterialist consciousness research. Our vision is to inspire scientists to investigate mind and consciousness as core elements of reality.

To achieve this paradigm changing mission, AAPS embraces the following values:

- Support rigorous applications of the scientific method
- Nurture curiosity and creativity in research
- Encourage open-minded exploratory and confirmatory investigations
- Model integrity and honesty in communication and education
- Value experimental and empirical data over dogma
- Create safe settings for sharing theories, evidence, and experiences
- Promote evidence-based innovation and positive societal change
- Expand awareness of the interconnectedness of all things
- Share postmaterialist evidence and understanding with the public

With these values in mind, AAPS is publishing an *Advances in Postmaterialist Sciences* book series to educate scientists, students, and science-minded readers about postmaterialist consciousness research and its applications. Our intent is that each volume combines rigor and creativity, expresses first person (inner experiences) as well as third person (external observations), and facilitates the bet-terment of humanity and the planet. Some volumes will address specific topics or themes, others will be wide ranging and diverse collections of research topics. Collectively they will help define and advance the evolution of postmaterialist theory, research and applications. The AAPS has collaborated with the Galileo Commission of the Scientific and Medical Network to produce this volume.

The Scientific and Medical Network

The Scientific and Medical Network (https://scientificandmedical.net) was founded in 1973. It is working with full awareness and appreciation of scientific method, but exploring and expanding, in a spirit of open and critical enquiry, frontier issues at the interfaces between science, health, consciousness, wellbeing, love and spirituality, to explore how to rediscover a meaningful spirituality to help rebalance our lives.

The Network is part of a worldwide contemporary movement for education, personal development, and compatible "spiritual emergence", networking: scientists, doctors, psychologists, educators, engineers, philosophers, complementary practitioners and other professionals, for mutual and societal benefit.

Galileo Commission

The Galileo Commission (https://galileocommission.org) is a project of the Scientific and Medical Network. It cosponsors the publication of the present book series and seeks to expand science beyond a materialistic worldview.

The world today is dominated by science and by its underlying assumptions, which are seldom explicitly articulated. The Galileo Commission's remit is to open public discourse and to find ways to expand science so that it can accommodate and explore important human experiences and questions that science, in its present form, is unable to integrate.

On the Banks of the River Styx

Index

A

ABCDEF Bundle 106, 110–111
after-death communications (ADCs) 1–3, 135, 141, 156, 162–171, 184
Alzheimer's disease 7, 25, 48–49, 67, 69, 108
Atwater, Phyllis 135
Avni, Gil 69
awareness during anesthesia 62, 65, 70–72, 84

B

Bacque, Marie Frédérique 36
Bailey, Polly 110–111
Barrett, William 120, 134, 141
Basios, Vasileios 3, 174
Becker, Ernest 20
Boehm, Leanne 99
Bourke, Daniel 162, 166–167, 171
Bozzano, Ernesto 134, 141, 156
brain
    death 69
    tumor 29, 52, 154
Brayne, Sue 8, 20, 31, 33, 41, 120, 148, 155

C

caregivers 7, 10, 14, 22, 24, 29, 33, 35, 38, 42–44, 47, 52–58, 107, 128–129, 133
Carruthers, Emma 101, 103
Chia, Mantak 101
coma
    medically induced comas 2, 69, 7–72, 83, 95–97, 100–104, 106–113, 178
    aftereffects of medically induced comas 73, 98–99, 103, 107–109
    coma experiences 2, 11–13, 16, 38–40, 47, 53, 62, 65, 68–70, 73, 95, 97–99, 100–102, 108, 154, 155, 167, 184
    alternate lives, experienced in comas 97, 100–101, 184
Cooper, Callum C. 85, 164, 165
crisis telepathy 140, 156–157, 168, 172
crisis apparitions 140, 156–157, 166, 168, 172

D

dark retreats 101, 103
Dayton, Kali 2, 106, 108, 110
dementia 23, 25, 26, 47–55, 57, 64–65, 67, 151
DMT visions 95, 103–104

E

EEG scans 68, 83–85, 95, 96, 104, 179
Eldadah, Basil 49
Elsaesser, Evelyn 3, 162–165, 171
Ely, Wesley 96, 108
end-of-life
    care 28, 43, 48, 53, 54–56, 120, 180
    dreams 1, 3, 21, 22, 100, 119, 120–125, 129, 184
    experiences (ELEs) 1, 3, 6–7, 15, 19–22, 29, 31, 35, 37, 42, 44, 50, 55, 56, 77, 87, 106, 119, 121, 122, 133, 134, 147–148, 154–157, 184, 191
        in animals 147–148, 154, 184
    visions 1, 2, 3, 19, 22, 87, 125, 134, 135, 147–148, 155, 156, 178, 184

Évrard, Renaud 10, 36
extrasensory perception 2
  veridical perception in compromised brain states 1, 70, 81, 82, 84–85, 87

F

Fenwick, Peter 8, 10, 20–21, 23, 31, 33, 41, 120, 156, 157, 182
fMRI scans 68

G

Global Consciousness Project 175
Greyson, Bruce 2, 7, 8, 10, 23, 33, 36, 64, 67, 77–87, 156

H

hallucination 20–21, 67, 86, 95, 96, 104–105, 107–108, 144, 167
Haraldsson, Erlendur 21, 22, 135, 166
Heim, Albert 78
hemihydranencephaly 64
hemispherectomy 64
Hull, Kathy 56
hydrocephalus 64

I

idealism 50
intensive care units (ICU) 2, 57, 79, 95, 100, 106–113, 174–179,
  ICU delirium 96, 108, 110
  ICU-acquired weakness 106–107, 109–110
  Awake and Walking ICU 106, 110–113

J

James, William 50

K

Kason, Yvonne 135
Kerr, Christopher 3, 87, 119, 122–123, 126, 128
Kripal, Jeffrey 167
Kothe, Karalee 2, 6, 10, 23
Kübler-Ross, Elisabeth 14

L

last rally 147–148, 150–151, 153, 155
locked-in experiences 2–3, 62, 67–69, 72, 184
locked-in syndrome 68
Lorimer, David 165

M

Maciejewski, Hannah 3, 119
Martial, Charlotte 78, 81–83, 85, 87
Moody, Raymond 77–80, 135–136, 140
Morrison, Sophie 165
Mutis, Maryne 2, 10, 35–36
Myers, Frederic W. H. 134, 140

N

Nahm, Michael 2–3, 7–8, 10, 23, 33, 36, 43, 50–51, 53, 62–65, 67, 69–72, 79, 85, 87, 147–148, 156–157
near-death experiences 1, 62–63, 77, 133, 183, 184
neurophysiological models 67
  distressing NDEs 67, 71, 78, 97
near-death visions (*See also* end-of-life visions)
non-local consciousness 50–51, 57, 174–175, 178, 181

O

O'Mahony, Seamus 119–120
organ donation 69–70
Osis, Karlis 21–22, 135
out-of-body experiences (OBEs) 1, 66–67, 69–71, 82, 84
   as "time anchors" for near-death experiences 85
Owen, Adrian 68

P

paradoxical
   awareness 62, 65–68, 70–72
   cognitive functioning 64
   consciousness 63–65
   lucidity 63–65, 67, 69
   improvement 63
Pearce, Alan 2, 71, 95, 104, 108
Pehlivanova, Marieta 2, 77, 80
Penfield, Wilder 63
Peters, William J. 3, 8, 133, 135–142, 144
Philpott, Nancy 3, 133
psi trailing 149–150

R

random event generators (REGs)
Radin, Dean
reincarnation cases
REM sleep 95, 96, 103, 104
Roe, Chris A. 2, 10, 19, 20, 23

S

Schwartz, Gary 175
shared death experiences 3, 42, 88, 133–144, 184
shared dreams 72

Sheldrake, Rupert 3, 147–149, 155, 156, 158
Smart, Pam 3, 147
spikes of brain activity near death 83
spirituality 54–55, 57, 80, 120
Strassman, Rick 103
stroke 23, 25, 47, 48, 53, 57, 64, 69, 107, 149
Styx, river 1–3, 77–78, 185

T

Tassell-Matamua, Natasha 2, 6, 10, 23, 56–58, 79, 164
terminal lucidity 1–3, 6–7, 47–48, 50–58, 154–156, 178, 180, 184
   in adults 19–30, 32–33, 53
   in children 2, 8, 53, 56
   in animals 153–154
   as experienced by witnesses 2, 35–45
   paradoxical terminal lucidity 2, 7, 64, 67, 72, 184
transplant cases 14, 31, 72
trauma, coping with 69, 81, 95, 99, 101, 124

V

van Lommel, Pim 50, 77–80, 83, 85, 135
Vicente, Raul 83–84, 87

W

Welch, Keasley 63
Wells, Isobel 97, 100
Williams, Monica 3, 133
Woollacott, Marjorie 2–3, 10, 23, 47, 50–51, 56–58, 80, 84, 141

Made in the USA
Middletown, DE
01 November 2025